"To read well, we have to listen well. ⌐   d for the ear, not primarily for the eye. Realizing tl   ;htly handle the Word of life."

Jeffrey D. Arthurs, Robinson Chair of Preaching and Communication at Gordon-Conwell Theological Seminary and author of *Devote Yourself to the Public Reading of Scripture*

"Long overdue, Sandy's latest contribution reminds digital natives around the globe of the 'big forgot' in relation to canon construction, interpretation, and communication—its original oral nature. The Bible's relational, experiential-based text, Sandy correctly concludes, requires an oral hermeneutic. Such will offer 'hearers' a richer, more robust understanding of Scripture without devaluing the inspired text. Timely, thorough, trustworthy."

Tom Steffen, professor emeritus of intercultural studies at Cook School of Intercultural Studies, Biola University, and coauthor of *The Return of Oral Hermeneutics: As Good Today as It Was for the Hebrew Bible and First-Century Christianity*

"Brent Sandy's work on the orality of the gospel for the first two centuries has tremendous implications for the relation between church and Bible, and even the relationship between salvation and justification. I recommend this book for all those interested in these profound subjects."

Gerald McDermott, author of *A New History of Redemption: The Work of Jesus the Messiah Through the Millennia*

"What would happen if we reminded ourselves every time we encountered the Bible that most all of its original audiences were listeners rather than readers? What would happen if we tried to read it not in a monotone but in a way intended to animate people with tone of voice and cadence, or if we retold biblical stories true to their historical contexts in first-person narrative? Brent Sandy challenges us to better understand the Bible's orality and reawakens our interest in its content. Thanks, Brent!"

Craig L. Blomberg, distinguished professor emeritus of New Testament, Denver Seminary

"In the way of Tertullian, What hath textuality to do with orality? Brent Sandy dispels and distills several misunderstandings for modern readers and interpreters of the Bible who regularly forget that people living in biblical times didn't enjoy individual, leather-bound copies of God's Word. Rather, living in oral cultures, they heard the Scriptures read aloud. Sandy takes us on an important journey to appreciate how understanding orality and oral cultures informs our interpretation of Scripture beyond what the world of the written text imparts to us in isolation. This book is a godsend for preachers and teachers who must grapple with both the textuality and orality of Scripture."

Matthew D. Kim, Raborn Chair of Pastoral Leadership at Baylor University's Truett Theological Seminary and author of *Preaching with Cultural Intelligence*

"Brent Sandy wakes up readers to the fact that while reading seems natural to us, it was not natural to ancient people, people who first experienced the events of the Bible. With conversational prose arranged in digestible sections, *Hear Ye the Word of the Lord* offers a fresh approach to this vital aspect of ancient cultures, so that those who hear it walk away not only much better informed concerning orality, but also inspired to engage with Scripture more holistically, creatively, and therefore, more faithfully. Sandy's contribution will tune our ears to listen better to the One speaking to us through Scripture."

Amy Peeler, Kenneth T. Wessner Chair of Biblical Studies at Wheaton College

"Because the Bible is written Scripture, it is only natural that we read and interpret it as literature. What is often lost is appreciation for the Bible's orality. In this concise and insightful book, Brent Sandy shows how modern readers can recognize Scripture's oral dimension and reach a whole new level of insight. *Hear Ye the Word of the Lord* will serve both church and academy well."

Craig A. Evans, John Bisagno Distinguished Professor of Christian Origins at Houston Christian University

"God's Word moved from being spoken and heard to being written and read. As Christianity moved westward, hearing as a community changed to reading as an individual. We now prefer written to oral. Brent Sandy urges us to allow a reader to *perform* Scripture. When, in a booming voice, the reader exclaims, 'The voice of the Lord twists the oaks,' we feel God's majesty. When the reader shouts 'Hosanna!' the electric energy of the triumphal entry courses in our veins. Sandy reminds us as a group: hear the Word of the Lord."

E. Randolph Richards, research professor of New Testament at Palm Beach Atlantic University

"In this volume, Brent Sandy not only provokes the academic to consider the impact of orality on the transmission and interpretation of Scripture but also provides creative and workable applications for the local church practitioner who wants to elevate the public reading (and therefore hearing) of Scripture in the gathered community of believers."

Kip Cone, lead pastor of Winona Lake Grace Church

HEAR YE

D. BRENT SANDY

FOREWORD BY JOHN H. WALTON

WHAT
WE MISS
IF WE
ONLY
READ

THE
BIBLE

THE WORD

OF THE

LORD

ivp
Academic
An imprint of InterVarsity Press
Downers Grove, Illinois

InterVarsity Press
P.O. Box 1400 | Downers Grove, IL 60515-1426
ivpress.com | email@ivpress.com

InterVarsity Press® is the publishing division of InterVarsity Christian Fellowship/USA®. For more information, visit intervarsity.org.

All Scripture quotations, unless otherwise indicated, are translated by the author.

The publisher cannot verify the accuracy or functionality of website URLs used in this book beyond the date of publication.

Cover design: David Fassett
Interior design: Daniel van Loon
Images: Sermon on the Mount (1877) by Carl Bloch / Wikimedia Commons

ISBN 978-1-5140-0298-8 (print) | ISBN 978-1-5140-0299-5 (digital)

Printed in the United States of America ∞

Library of Congress Cataloging-in-Publication Data
A catalog record for this book is available from the Library of Congress.

31   30   29   28   27   26   25   24 | 13   12   11   10   9   8   7   6   5   4   3   2   1

To all those who have been empowered to speak on God's behalf—

who faithfully heard, understood, remembered, lived,

and passed on the divinely spoken words—without you

the words of the Lord would have returned void.

CONTENTS

Foreword by John H. Walton | ix

PART ONE
SETTING THE STAGE

PROPOSITION 1 | 3
Oral Culture Can Be a Lost World

PROPOSITION 2 | 12
God Reached Across Great Distances—So Must We

PROPOSITION 3 | 18
Divine Revelation Was Intended for Hearers

PROPOSITION 4 | 23
Research Provides Important Insights into Ancient Oral Culture

PROPOSITION 5 | 31
The Goal Is to Include Their Hearing in Our Reading

PART TWO
GOD AND HIS AGENTS OF ORAL COMMUNICATION

PROPOSITION 6 | 39
Scripture Presents God as the Ultimate Oral Communicator

PROPOSITION 7 | 46
God Spoke Divine Truth to and Through Moses

PROPOSITION 8 | 58
God Spoke Divine Truth to and Through the Prophets

PROPOSITION 9 | 65
God Spoke Divine Truth to and Through Jesus

PROPOSITION 10 | 78
Jesus Empowered His Followers to Proclaim the Gospel as He Did

PROPOSITION 11 | 87
Jesus' Followers Faithfully Remembered and Communicated the Oral Gospel

PART THREE
IMPLICATIONS OF ORAL SCRIPTURE

PROPOSITION 12 | 99
Stories Were Performed and Heard in Ancient Oral Culture

PROPOSITION 13 | 108
We Can Become Better Hearers and Speakers of Scripture

PROPOSITION 14 | 120
We Can Restore Oral Scripture to Its Rightful Place

PART FOUR
EXPERIMENTS IN ORAL INTERPRETATION

PROPOSITION 15 | 133
Hearing Is More Than Reading: Understanding Scripture Holistically

PROPOSITION 16 | 145
Hearing Is More Than Reading: Imagining Creation and Incarnation

PROPOSITION 17 | 153
Hearing Is More Than Reading: Experiencing Jesus' Return to Nazareth

PROPOSITION 18 | 168
Hearing Is More Than Reading: Rethinking the Vine and the Branches

Conclusion | 183   Acknowledgments | 193   General Index | 195

Scripture Index | 203

FOREWORD

JOHN H. WALTON

INTERPRETING THE BIBLE well requires more than being spiritually sensitive to the truths of God. If we want to receive the message of God, we need to be on the same wavelength with it—like tuning into the right frequency on a radio. In today's world we have experienced a major shift in education from the person-to-person modality to the growing trend for remote platforms. And we have learned that the medium matters. We have recognized the challenges and benefits of this new form of communication in education. As Brent Sandy explains in this book, our current paradigm shift, perhaps even designated a quantum leap, is not the first in the history of communication. We have long recognized that the Bible was written for us, but not to us, and therefore requires us to make efforts to bridge the cultural gap between ourselves as readers and the writers of the ancient world. In this book, we become aware of yet another gap that we must recognize and factor into our reading: we must bridge the modality gap between the written word and the oral word.

The significance of this gap can be realized the moment we note that the default form of communication in the biblical world was oral, whereas the form to which we attach authority is written. We speak of inspired texts. We often study the Bible with an assumption that its books are the result of someone sitting down with blank parchment and scrawling out inspired thoughts. Perhaps a few of the books of the Bible could have come about in such a way, but generally the books of the

Bible are the end result of a long process in which the written form, the book, is the last step rather than the first. As Sandy points out, "Authors were fewer than the speakers. And the hearers were more than the readers."

Brent Sandy is an informed and capable guide as he leads us through the maze of implications that emerge from the basic reality that he unpacks. That is, the fact that most communication in the biblical world was oral makes a difference in how we read Scripture. We need such expert guidance to help us make necessary adjustments in our interpretation. After taking us on a grand tour revealing the essential orality of Scripture's origins, he contends that "we need to give more attention to the oral interpretation of Scripture." He then explains what that can look like. In the process we learn more about the importance of community as groups hear the word of God. Relationships mattered more; body language, inflection, and intonation supply the emotional setting; context provided guides to relevance that drew meaning into the minds of the hearers. Community hearing was experiential.

For example, though many today benefit from reading some of the famous sermons of Martin Luther King Jr., someone who was there, hearing them preached, could reflect further on the power of the moment, the electricity in the air, the sense that together, the audience was stirred in ways that can never be repeated even when people today might listen to a recording. This is the sort of visceral response that is reported by those who encountered Jesus on the road to Emmaus: "Were not our hearts burning within us while he talked with us on the road and opened the Scriptures to us?" (Lk 24:32). As Sandy makes us aware, an oral performance is an event, while a literary text is an artifact. Participation in an oral performance can be transformative in ways that reading a text can never achieve.

While Sandy does not discount the importance of rigorous and robust exegesis, he coaxes us to see a bigger picture—one that will allow us to seek to be transformed by Scripture as we find our place in an audience of "hearers" who experience the text, not just analyze it or excerpt from it. May we all become better interpreters by seeking to be better hearers.

PART ONE

SETTING THE STAGE

PROPOSITION 1

ORAL CULTURE CAN BE
A LOST WORLD

We were never born to read.

Maryanne Wolf

IMAGINE A WORLD WITHOUT WORDS. In place of babies' first words, endless gurgling. In place of people conversing, a few hand signals. In place of broadcasts and podcasts, silence. Actually, according to Genesis 1, in place of us, a blank canvas—a world without form, and void (Gen 1:2). We wonder, would even God be the same without words (Jn 1:1)?

The reality is, words are part and parcel of who we are. But what if words are only oral? Nothing inscribed on rock, potsherds, or page. Imagine trying to get along in today's world without reading and writing—and texting!

The French have a common expression, "Je n'ai qu'une parole," which literally translated is "I have only one word." It's not that they know only one word. The point is the same as when we say in English, "I give you my word." Or we can also say, "I'll take your word for it." In either case, the spoken word is enough, writing unnecessary. (Note that different words can convey the same idea, and they can point to a function beyond what appears on the surface.)[1]

---

[1] For example, most of us would understand, "The store is closing in five minutes" to be more than a statement of fact. We've been around stores enough to know that for shoppers and probably store

Jesus declared that "yes" or "no" is all that's needed in certain situations (Mt 5:37). More than that, he considered the words he spoke—inspired by no less than the Father himself, and backed by his actions—to be adequate for the most important exchange of information of all time: his own divine revelation (Jn 8:28; 12:50).

For most of us, that doesn't compute. If we didn't have the truth in written form, especially the words of Jesus, which we can scrutinize, memorize, plaster on the wall—we'd feel slighted, shortchanged, even unsure about what the revelation was all about. After all, aren't reading and writing an obvious advancement over the oral alternative?

But not so fast. Plato (fourth century BC) and other ancient philosophers questioned the value of written words in place of oral ones, especially for communicating important ideas. Socrates (fifth century BC) and the Stoic philosopher Epictetus (second century AD) are examples of Greco-Roman philosophers who wrote nothing when they surely could have. We only know about their philosophies through what their students recorded. Why? Because they considered teaching via written words inadequate.

In what ways? We won't understand all the reasoning, since most of us are deeply immersed in the culture of reading and writing. But for them, personal interaction and give-and-take with students was essential for communicating profound concepts. And since reading skills and backgrounds varied, teachers could not count on the ideas expressed in writing to be adequately understood by all readers. Even more, if students had written versions of a philosopher's thinking, they might not read carefully and think through the concepts sufficiently, missing important parts. Students might also neglect the necessary step

---

employees as well, the words would summon the hearers to do something. But if we were not familiar with the culture of stores, we may entirely miss the function of the statement. Thus, to understand what people say—or even to understand what we read in the Bible—it's essential to see that the words in a sentence (the locution) are likely to have an intent (an illocution) and a preferred response (the perlocution). For discussion, see John H. Walton and D. Brent Sandy, *The Lost World of Scripture: Ancient Literary Culture and Biblical Authority* (Downers Grove, IL: IVP Academic, 2013), 41-42; for more thorough treatment see Richard S. Briggs, "The Uses of Speech-Act Theory in Biblical Interpretation," *Currents in Research: Biblical Studies* 9 (2001): 229-76.

of applying philosophy to their life situations, something philosophers could better encourage in face-to-face discussions.[2]

Nonetheless, some philosophers did write (Aristotle and Epictetus) and sought to recreate in written form ways they would orally lead students into deep discussions. The result was the dialogue and symposium forms of philosophical essays. Plato is a case in point. All but two of his twenty-seven writings were dialogues. The essays featured dramatic argumentation with hypothetical participants discussing philosophical issues.[3]

For examples of an oral preference in more recent times, we could explore numerous cultures around the world.[4] In the case of early Americans in our country, "To native people, oral speech was more trustworthy than written words. . . . Writing could not make language more truthful or promises more binding."[5]

Or as reported by one of my former students ministering in Cameroon:

> During something like a boundary dispute, though the traditional council of the village has long since begun writing court verdicts in a log, often they will still bring all the concerned parties and any available elders out to the site of the dispute, regardless that the issue had previously been settled and recorded. Then, on location, a heated discussion will commence, concluding in a consensus which becomes the verdict. Quite interesting considering boundary disputes in America are settled by data in filing cabinets at city hall.[6]

---

[2]From a modern perspective, when we think about email and other digital communications increasingly replacing personal conversations, we can see a tie-in with ancient philosophers' reservations about written words. Face-to-face communication can be more effective with facial expression, tone of voice, body language, clarification, and feedback. Written and digital communications may have advantages in some respects, but they have limitations.

[3]For Plato's contribution to understanding oral culture and the changes writing introduced, see especially Eric Havelock, *Preface to Plato* (Cambridge, MA: Harvard University Press, 1963).

[4]See, e.g., Tom Steffen and William Bjoraker, *The Return of Oral Hermeneutics: As Good Today as It Was for the Hebrew Bible and First-Century Christianity* (Eugene, OR: Wipf and Stock, 2020).

[5]This statement appears on a placard at the Native American Museum in Washington, DC.

[6]For studies of oral culture in Africa, see Jan Vansina, *Oral Tradition as History* (Madison, WI: University of Wisconsin Press, 1985); Isadore Okpewho, *African Oral Literature: Backgrounds, Character and Continuity* (Bloomington, IN: Indiana University Press, 1992).

For an example of the preference for oral accounts of what Jesus said and did, note what an early Christian said a century after the time of Jesus, even though by then there were written accounts of Jesus and his disciples' lives. Papias preferred hearing over reading: "I do not believe that things out of books are as beneficial to me as things from a living and enduring voice."[7]

In other words, literacy isn't the panacea of perfect communication; never was, never will be, certainly not across all time, in all situations, for everyone. Humanity from the beginning was a society of social interaction with orality as the bedrock of interpersonal relations; thus textuality was unnecessary. (*Orality* refers to anything pertaining to spoken communication; *textuality* refers to written communication.) It was a collectivist culture in which speaking and hearing were the norm. The human brain was prewired for it; children growing up today still catch on fast. As research demonstrates, "we were never born to read."[8]

Reading and writing, on the other hand, took centuries to develop . . . and takes years to acquire; some of us are still learning the art of writing. The brain actually had to rewire itself for the advanced technology. "More than any other single invention, writing has transformed human consciousness."[9] But once it did, it's difficult to retrace the steps back into oral ways of thinking. The Western paradigm of textuality—the "default setting"—stands in the way.[10] Most of us are

---

[7]Eusebius, *Hist. Eccl.* 3.39.4.

[8]"Human beings invented reading only a few thousand years ago. And with this invention, we rearranged the very organization of our brains, which in turn expanded the ways we were able to think." Maryanne Wolf, *Proust and the Squid: The Story and Science of the Reading Brain* (New York: Harper, 2007), 3; regarding reading not being a naturally occurring human instinct, see also Steven Pinker, *How the Mind Works* (New York: Norton, 1997), 342.

[9]Walter J. Ong, *Orality and Literacy: The Technologizing of the Word* (London: Methuen, 1982), 78. Various scholars agree on this point: "the natural human being is not a writer or a reader but a speaker and a listener." See Eric Havelock, "The Oral-Literate Equation: A Formula for the Modern Mind," in *Literacy and Orality*, ed. D. R. Olson and N. Torrance (Cambridge: Cambridge University Press, 1991), 20. "Reading can only be learned because of the brain's plastic design, and when reading takes place, that individual brain is forever changed, both physiologically and intellectually." See Wolf, *Proust and the Squid*, 5.

[10]"The literary mindset ('default setting') of modern Western culture prevents those trained in that culture from recognizing that oral cultures operate differently." James D. G. Dunn, "Altering the Default Setting: Re-envisioning the Early Transmission of the Jesus Tradition," *New Testament Studies* 49 (2003): 139.

very comfortable in our textual skin and the culture of individualism.[11] We write alone, we read alone—typically.

ADJUSTING THE DEFAULT SETTING

It comes down to this. What we do with words—whether oral, written, printed, or digital—affects how we use our faculties, how we relate to people, how we spend our time, and most important, how we think.[12] The cultures of hearing and reading are not the same; there can be different ways of being and doing, calling on distinct functions of our brains. Which means, to understand Scripture correctly, it's essential to recognize how reading differs from hearing.

The farther apart, then, the worlds of hearing and reading are, the less those in one world will understand the other. And particularly, the less they will understand the communications of the other. "In antiquity, the most literate cultures remained committed to the spoken word to a degree which appears to our more visually organized sensibilities somewhat incredible or even perverse."[13]

This brings us to the challenge we face in this book. Not orality versus literacy, as if one is better than the other; but there are differences. Not hearing versus reading; there is room for both. Not that oral and written communication are opposites—as if there's a "great divide"; there is interface between them.[14] But being twenty-first century

---

[11]The weight holding us back is "a merciless captivity to an unrelenting master—the individualism of our culture and its expectations." Thomas M. Stallter, *The Gap Between God and Christianity: The Turbulence of Western Culture* (Eugene, OR: Resource, 2022), 3.

[12]Regarding the megatrend of the digital revolution rewiring our brains, see the comments in Walton and Sandy, *The Lost World of Scripture*, 11; See also John Dyer, "The New Gutenberg: Bible Apps Could Be as Formative to Christian History as the Printing Press," *Christianity Today* 66.9 (December 2022): 51-55; for a full treatment, see Maryanne Wolf, *Reader, Come Home: The Reading Brain in a Digital World* (New York: Harper, 2019).

[13]Walter J. Ong, *The Presence of the Word* (New Haven, CT: Yale University Press, 1967), 55; cited in Werner H. Kelber, *Oral and Written Gospel: The Hermeneutics of Speaking and Writing in the Synoptic Tradition, Mark, Paul, and Q* (Minneapolis: Fortress, 1983), 17.

[14]The "Great Divide" refers to the consensus today that earlier conclusions about the sharp differences between what is spoken versus written went too far; see Rafael Rodríguez, "Great Divide," in *The Dictionary of the Bible and Ancient Media* (London: T&T Clark, 2017), 163-64; and Raphael Rodríguez, *Oral Tradition and the New Testament: A Guide for the Perplexed* (London: Bloomsbury, 2014).

readers born and groomed in modern textual culture, can we suffi-ciently understand the meaning of documents originating in ancient oral culture simply by reading them?

More specifically, for biblical interpreters, if the culture was predom-inantly oral in which the supreme revelation of all time was birthed, formed, and transmitted—and it was—and if oral culture left an in-delible mark on written Scripture, including its words, forms, and structures—and it did—and if its authors were writing on the as-sumption that people would hear what they wrote—and they were—what might that mean for how we read and interpret the Bible in col-leges and seminaries, churches and Sunday school classes, and everywhere in between?

It can be a catch-22, seeking to understand a text—which was de-signed to be heard—without hearing it. Shouldn't we learn as much as possible about oral culture lest we misinterpret Scripture out of blindness to the very nature of Scripture? Isn't it our moral responsi-bility to do so?

> *It can be a catch-22,*
> *seeking to understand a text—*
> *which was designed to be heard—*
> *without hearing it.*

To be sure, the most important issue is not *how* God revealed, but *what.* The storehouse of eternal truths, whether preserved orally or in written form, is what matters most. But the *how* can influence the ways in which the *what* was presented and is properly understood. The medium and the message are inseparable.[15]

---

[15]"The medium is the message"; Marshall McLuhan, *Understanding Media: The Extensions of Man* (Cambridge, MA: MIT Press, 1994), 7.

CLARIFICATIONS

Now you may have doubts about some of what has been stated so far. Maybe you're not ready to rethink ways you have always understood the Bible. If so, no worries. Keep reading. What we've said up to this point is a preview of more to come and a simplified version of what's ahead. Hopefully, if you stay the course all the way to the end, you'll agree with the conclusions. Rome wasn't built in a day, you know.

There is something that needs to be set straight straightaway. The Bible in our hands certainly appears to be a fully textual product. The books were written; they were collected into a canon of sixty-six books; the Bible was printed; we can read it. What else do we need to know?

Well, divine revelation did eventually take on the form of textuality, but it wasn't that way at the outset. The initial culture into which God spoke was functionally oral. In those days, people knew of written documents, but only a limited number could read, and fewer still could write. As will become clearer as we proceed, it was a "text-possible-yet-hearing-prevalent society."[16]

The verses of Scripture quoted throughout this book are present for a reason. Readers may feel free to skip everything else, but don't ignore the word of the Lord. God has spoken and it's up to us to hear and heed him, otherwise—as in the days of the prophet Isaiah—he may judge us with deafness and blindness:

> *Keep on hearing; but may you not understand;*
> *keep on seeing; but may you not perceive.*

---

[16]Walton and Sandy, *The Lost World of Scripture*, 19-21, 85, 92, 136; it's also been called "a residually oral culture"; Walter J. Ong, "Foreword," in Werner H. Kelber, *The Oral and Written Gospel: The Hermeneutics of Speaking and Writing in the Synoptic Tradition, Mark, Paul, and Q* (Minneapolis: Fortress, 1983), xiv. Eric Eve comments that there is a "seeming paradox that the first-century Mediterranean world was both one in which texts proliferated and played a highly significant role, and also one in which oral habits still predominated." Eric Eve, *Behind the Gospels: Understanding the Oral Tradition* (Minneapolis: Fortress, 2014), 10; the community that preserved the Dead Sea Scrolls is an example of an oral-textual society (see Proposition 7 below for discussion).

Make the heart of these people hard—
    their ears closed,
    and their eyes shut. (Is 6:9-10)[17]

So here's the strategy for this book: (1) to explore what the Bible itself reveals about the culture in which it was formed, with textuality under the influence of orality; (2) to reckon with the oral impact on the composition and transmission of Scripture; (3) to learn from recent research about ancient oral culture; (4) to investigate the Gospels as testing ground for the impact of oral culture on divine revelation; and (5) to rethink our reading of Scripture so we can come closer to hearing it as the original audiences did.

The underlying question is, Is it time for a paradigm shift in the interpretation of Scripture? Are we missing something if we only read it? Is there a dynamic in hearing Scripture that's less present in reading it?

Sounds like we have our hands full. Actually, we'll be skipping some topics that are clearly pertinent. It would be useful to know how the brain functions differently when hearing and reading and what that means for different ways of thinking. But we'll leave that up to brain scientists.[18]

It would be helpful to live in an oral culture somewhere in the world in order to experience that unique way of life ourselves. But we'll have to depend on second-hand insights from people who have been immersed in oral cultures, as well as from social scientists who study such cultures.[19]

Clearly, we will not solve all the issues raised in this book. They are above my paygrade, and it will require a village to sort them all out

---

[17]The author's translations are italicized throughout this book; the translations are intended to convey the meaning of verses in light of the surrounding context.
[18]See, e.g., Iain McGilchrist, *The Master and His Emissary: The Divided Brain and the Making of the Western World*, 2nd ed. (New Haven, CT: Yale University Press, 2019); Stanislas Dehaene, *Reading in the Brain: The New Science of How We Read* (New York: Viking, 2009).
[19]For authors thoroughly acquainted with oral culture, see especially Steffen and Bjoraker, *The Return of Oral Hermeneutics*; in addition, note the International Orality Network, the Orality Institute, and the *Orality Journal*.

and construct a way forward. But failing to engage carefully with the evidence for biblical orality—or worse, mindlessly ignoring the evidence—could be like someone who plays tennis well thinking they can play the game of baseball with the same rules and objectives. A baseball coach might say to the tennis player, "Don't try to put spin on the ball; do your best to hit it straight, preferably through the gap, and as far as possible."

Likewise, a cultural intelligence coach might say to a textual interpreter, "Don't try to understand a statement simply as words printed on a page; do your best to understand it as it was originally heard."

But first things first.

PROPOSITION 2

GOD REACHED ACROSS
GREAT DISTANCES—SO MUST WE

To have great poets, there must be great audiences.

WALT WHITMAN

THE BIBLE. LITERARY MASTERPIECE, theological tour de force, consummate authority. Inspired truth from beyond the stars for those who can only look up to the stars. It's one of a kind.

The Bible is also our kind. It's God-talk in human-talk. After all, how else could God speak to us? With human forms the only option, accommodation was necessary. Otherwise we would never understand the most important communiqué of all time. When you have something significant to say and you want to make sure people get it, the message needs to be presented at a level listeners can relate to. "Every act of communication requires accommodation that will tailor the communication to the needs and circumstances of the audience."[1]

God's ministry of translating his lofty concepts into down-to-earth terms and forms stands out as the ultimate act of bridge-building. From his mind to ours is a very long span. *Even as the heavens are far above the earth, so my ways are far above yours, and my thoughts above your thoughts* (Is 55:9).

---

[1]John H. Walton and D. Brent Sandy, *The Lost World of Scripture: Ancient Literary Culture and Biblical Authority* (Downers Grove, IL: IVP Academic, 2013), 39; see also Kenton L. Sparks, *God's Word in Human Words: An Evangelical Appropriation of Critical Biblical Scholarship* (Grand Rapids, MI: Baker Academic, 2008), 230-59.

God chose a unique period in time, people group, messengers, and genres to accomplish his revelatory purposes.[2] And thus he built a unique bridge to people immersed in oral culture with their own ways of communicating, hearing, and understanding.

The most unique of the unique was God becoming incarnate: God the Father embodied himself in the Son, the personified Word, and the Holy Spirit continues to build a bridge between God and his people by guiding them into all truth (Jn 16:8-14). It is a trinitarian ministry of revelatory communication and transformation.[3]

Unfortunately, many fail to realize that we need to span a great distance as well. People today need to understand the people then. Two thousand years and more is a long way from the original days of biblical revelation to our own. It's thousands of miles, with millions of people of diverse cultures traversing the bridge, and untold changes occurring across the centuries.

There are two spans: from God to the original hearers, and from us back to the original hearers. Both spans are necessary to complete the bridge of communication between God and us.

If we're to understand the Bible, we need to understand the world of the Bible. There are two spans: from God to the original hearers, and from us back to the original hearers. Both spans are necessary to complete the bridge of communication between God and us. The star of communication shines brightest the closer we are to it. If there's a bridge out anywhere, we're in trouble. There are no detours.

---

[2]Paul's reference to the "fullness of time" (Gal 4:4) probably refers primarily to the strategic time in the history of the Jews. Regarding genres, see, e.g., D. Brent Sandy and Ronald L. Giese Jr., eds., *Cracking Old Testament Codes: A Guide to Interpreting the Literary Genres of the Old Testament* (Nashville: Broadman and Holman, 1995); regarding the unique genre of the Gospels, see Craig S. Keener, *Christobiography: Memory, History, and the Reliability of the Gospels* (Grand Rapids, MI: Eerdmans, 2019).
[3]See in particular Matthew Barrett, *Simply Trinity: The Unmanipulated Father, Son, and Spirit* (Grand Rapids, MI: Baker Books, 2021).

The biblical authors could not look into the future and anticipate the extent of the gap all the way to us. But we can and should build a bridge across the chasm back to them. It's divine truth, and we must go all in to understand it correctly. "A careful interpretation of Scripture is demanded by a commitment to its full authority. It is impossible to live under the authority of Scripture that is not properly understood."[4]

THE CHALLENGE

Bridging the gap can be more difficult than it may first appear. "We can easily forget that Scripture is a foreign land and reading the Bible is a cross-cultural experience. . . . No matter where on the planet or when in history we read it, we tend to read Scripture in our own *when* and *where*, in a way that makes sense on our terms."[5] Tragic and true, but there's more.

Cultural differences are like an iceberg. The part you recognize is dwarfed by what is hidden beneath the surface. Travelers today may quickly spot differences in other cultures, such as meanings of words, menu items, speed limits, and so forth. But deeper and more powerful cultural values are harder to detect and may catch us off guard, leading to culture shock.[6]

Attempting to understand an ancient text with our modern minds can be like having blinders on, keeping us from seeing what the cultures of biblical times were really like.

In *Misreading Scripture with Western Eyes*, Richards and O'Brien take up the problem of cultural blinders that Christians wear when they read the Bible. Nine differences between Western and

---

[4]Louis Igou Hodges, "New Dimensions in Scripture," in *New Dimensions in Evangelical Thought: Essays in Honor of Millard J. Erickson*, ed. David S. Dockery (Downers Grove, IL: IVP Academic, 1998), 223.
[5]E. Randolph Richards and Brandon J. O'Brien, *Misreading Scripture with Western Eyes: Removing Cultural Blinders to Better Understand the Bible* (Downers Grove, IL: IVP Academic, 2012), 11 (emphasis in original).
[6]See especially Colleen Ward, Stephen Bochner, and Adrian Furnham, *The Psychology of Culture Shock*, 2nd ed. (London: Routledge, 2001).

non-Western cultures are examined, some above and some below the surface, each applicable to understanding Scripture more in line with the original culture.[7]

A second book offers similar cautions about peering through the lens of Western individualism in contrast to the collectivism of the ancient Mediterranean world.[8] Both books are very helpful, but neither focuses on the issue before us in this book. So we're addressing yet another cultural blinder.

It would be a dream come true if we could understand Jesus and the Gospels the way first-century hearers did. Though often overlooked or downplayed, the axiom that the Bible was communicated to them, not us (credited in particular to John Walton), is the cornerstone of correct interpretation.[9] If Scripture was directed to them, yet for us, then we need to become them before we can be us. It calls us to think our way back into their world so we can be more than eavesdroppers.[10]

Applying Walt Whitman's analogy (see epigraph above), the Bible has one primary limitation. It's us. If we're not great audiences, the Bible's greatness is diminished. It's great because God inspired it, but its success in communicating divine truth depends on its hearers. If we shackle divine revelation in the chains of our own misunderstandings, reducing its value, hindering its impact, thwarting its author's intent, it's the universe's great loss, if not humanity's worst blunder.[11]

---

[7]Richards and O'Brien, *Misreading Scripture*, 16.

[8]E. Randolph Richards and Richard James, *Misreading Scripture with Individualist Eyes: Patronage, Honor, and Shame in the Biblical World* (Downers Grove, IL: IVP Academic, 2020).

[9]Adam E. Miglio, Caryn A. Reeder, Joshua T. Walton, and Kenneth C. Way, *For Us, but Not to Us: Essays on Creation, Covenant, and Context in Honor of John H. Walton* (Eugene, OR: Wipf and Stock, 2020); for a continuation of the concept, see Matthew S. Harmon, *Asking the Right Questions: A Practical Guide to Understanding and Applying the Bible* (Wheaton: Crossway, 2017), 55-61; see also John H. Walton, *Wisdom for Faithful Reading: Principles and Practices for Old Testament Interpretation* (Downers Grove, IL: IVP Academic, 2023), 25-30.

[10]For the "eavesdroppers" comment, see Craig L. Blomberg with Jennifer Foutz Markley, *A Handbook of New Testament Exegesis* (Grand Rapids, MI: Baker Academic, 2010), 92.

[11]I do not agree with everything in the article, but note the essay by Kurt Eichenwald, "The Bible: So Misunderstood It's a Sin," *Newsweek*, December 23, 2014.

AFFIRMATIONS

By now several things should be clear. The book you're reading is faith-based; we will take the full counsel of God seriously at the highest level we are enabled to understand it. But our goal goes beyond mental gymnastics; understanding Scripture has limited value if it doesn't result in exercising our faith and living increasingly transformatively (Rom 12:2).

Second, our firm commitment has always been and will always be that Scripture's meaning for us originates with its meaning for them, the original interlocutors.[12] This does not minimize the Holy Spirit ministering to people through the word of God, even if they have limited comprehension of the original meaning. Christians naturally want the Bible to speak to them today, and it does, but the Holy Spirit is not going to lead them to understand something outside the range of God's intent.[13] Devotional reflections on Scripture, ecclesiastical readings of Scripture, and scholarly probings into Scripture have their place, but only so long as they do not introduce humanly contrived ideas in conflict with what God was communicating. Stated succinctly, a text never means what it never meant.[14]

For the faithful proclamation of Scripture—whether in the church or academy—consistently "rightly dividing the word of truth" (2 Tim 2:15 KJV) is foundational. And that begins with the intended meaning for the original hearers and then moves carefully into recontextualization and application for today's hearers.[15]

---

[12]It's commonly agreed on by biblical scholars, such as stated by Paul Ray, "If we do not understand what the Bible meant in its original context . . . it is questionable whether we can accurately arrive at what it means today, at least on more than its most basic level." Paul Ray, "Some Hermeneutical Principles for the Biblical Historian," *Andrews University Seminary Studies* 58, no. 2 (2020): 185.

[13]Regarding God speaking through the Holy Spirit, see especially Myk Habets, "That Was Then, This Is Now: Reading Hebrews Retroactively," in *The Voice of God in the Text of Scripture: Explorations in Constructive Dogmatics*, ed. Oliver B. Crisp and Fred Sanders (Grand Rapids, MI: Zondervan, 2016), 108-11; also Ben Campbell Johnson, *The God Who Speaks: Learning the Language of God* (Grand Rapids, MI: Eerdmans, 2004); Ben Campbell Johnson, *GodSpeech: Putting Divine Disclosures into Human Words* (Grand Rapids, MI: Eerdmans, 2006); Nicholas Wolterstorff, *Divine Discourse: Philosophical Reflections on the Claim that God Speaks* (Cambridge: Cambridge University Press, 1995).

[14]See Walton, *Wisdom for Faithful Reading*, 19-25.

[15]Regarding contextualization, see two chapters in Jeannine K. Brown, *Scripture as Communication: Introducing Biblical Hermeneutics* (Grand Rapids, MI: Baker Academic, 2007), 232-73; other bibliography on contextualization includes David J. Hesselgrave and Edward Rommen,

Third, this book continues an exploration of a former book, but with a different purpose. In *The Lost World of Scripture*, coauthored with John Walton, we focused on the significance of the oral culture of Scripture for understanding biblical authority.[16] In this sequel, I am exploring what the orality of the written word means for how we should hear and interpret it.

In sum, this book seeks to span the distance between our modern Western culture under the influence of textuality and ancient culture under the influence of orality. People who only think in terms of the Gutenberg galaxy are near-sighted: for them the oral macrocosm of the biblical world is far away and fuzzy to see.[17] Hopefully, in the chapters ahead we will be able to provide corrective lenses in order to see distant things more clearly.

Contextualization: Meaning, Methods, and Models (Pasadena: William Carey Library, 2000); Bruce J. Nichols, *Contextualization: A Theology of Gospel and Culture* (Vancouver: Regent College Publishing, 2003); Dean E. Fleming, *Contextualization in the New Testament: Patterns for Theology and Mission* (Downers Grove, IL: IVP Academic, 2009); A. Scott Moreau, *Contextualization in World Missions: Mapping and Assessing Evangelical Models* (Grand Rapids, MI: Kregel, 2012); Jackson Wu, *One Gospel for All Nations: A Practical Approach to Biblical Contextualization* (Pasadena: William Carey Library, 2015); Ermias G. Mamo, *The Maturing Church: In Integrated Approach to Contextualization, Discipleship and Mission* (Carlisle: Langham, 2017); see also Justin Ariel Bailey, *Interpreting Your World: Five Lenses for Engaging Theology and Culture* (Grand Rapids, MI: Baker, 2020).

[16]Walton and Sandy, *The Lost World of Scripture*; for publications since then, I must recognize in particular Raphael Rodríguez, *Oral Tradition and the New Testament: A Guide for the Perplexed* (London: Bloomsbury, 2014); Eric Eve, *Behind the Gospels: Understanding the Oral Tradition* (Minneapolis: Fortress, 2014); Eric Eve, *Writing the Gospels: Composition and Memory* (London: SPCK, 2016); Kelly R. Iverson, *Performing Early Christian Literature: Audience Experience and the Interpretation of the Gospels* (Cambridge: Cambridge University Press, 2021).

[17]The "Gutenberg galaxy" refers to the whole new world in the West of printed texts after Gutenberg's invention; Marshall McLuhan, *The Gutenberg Galaxy: The Making of Typographic Man* (Toronto: University of Toronto Press, 1962).

PROPOSITION 3

DIVINE REVELATION
WAS INTENDED FOR HEARERS

*Be sure that you go to the author
to get his meaning, not to find yours.*

JOHN RUSKIN

FOR MOST CHRISTIANS the only form of divine revelation that we're accustomed to is the printed word. We assume the concept of inspiration applies to the final product as written. Thus we read the holy book confident that it is the direct revelation of almighty God.

However, on closer inspection, inspired truth was revealed orally. Starting with the book of Genesis, God's revelations were all by spoken word. In Exodus, even declarations as important as the Ten Commandments were first given orally (Ex 20:1, 22; Deut 4:12-13; 5:22), though subsequently Moses recorded in writing what God had said about the terms of the covenant relationship; and God himself etched the Ten Commandments in stone. Many of the psalms were likely birthed in oral performance.[1] Messages from God to and through the prophets

---

[1]Walter E. Brown and Jeffrey J. Rankin, "Oral Poetry," in *Dictionary of the Old Testament: Wisdom, Poetry, and Writing*, ed. Tremper Longman III and Peter Enns (Downers Grove, IL: IVP Academic, 2008), 497-501; D. Brent Sandy and Tiberius Rata, "Approaching the Psalms: Key Insights," in *Interpreting the Psalms for Teaching and Preaching*, ed. Herbert W. Bateman and D. Brent Sandy (St. Louis: Chalice, 2010), 4-5; John H. Walton and D. Brent Sandy, *The Lost World of Scripture: Ancient Literary Culture and Biblical Authority* (Downers Grove, IL: IVP Academic, 2013), 71.

were communicated orally (e.g., Jer 1:6-10). Summing up the process of inspiration, Peter declared, *Directed by the Holy Spirit, the prophets spoke from God* (2 Pet 1:21).

And then there's Jesus. Of course, he was a prophet as well: "That's all I have to say. What the Father told me, I tell you" (Jn 12:50 MSG). For centuries people as far back as Augustine (AD 354–430) have pondered Jesus' oral-only communication. Augustine wrote, "But we must first discuss a matter which is apt to present a difficulty in the minds of some. I refer to the question why the Lord has written nothing Himself."[2]

Augustine was correct. It is puzzling that the ultimate revelation of deity, the person who gave the extreme gift of himself for all humanity, didn't offer a single written form of what he wanted his audience to know. Wouldn't a firsthand record of his exact words be important for his followers in the years and centuries down the road? Why not a transcript of at least key portions of his teaching and sermons? If not that, Jesus certainly could have summoned a scribe to record word-for-word what he said.

Actually, it's unlikely these questions would have been asked two thousand years ago. We ask them because we're seduced by the necessity of written words. But divine revelation was first and foremost oral. Jesus showed no interest in having what he said written down. Nor is there any evidence that his immediate hearers thought to record anything, even though they recognized the importance of his words.[3]

Jesus simply yet boldly depended on others to tell others what he said. *Now go and proclaim what you've been hearing: "The Kingdom*

[2]Chris Keith, *Jesus' Literacy: Scribal Culture and the Teacher from Galilee*, Library of New Testament Studies 413 (London: T&T Clark, 2011), 2.

[3]We cannot rule out the possibility that stenographers could have been present to record Jesus' every word, but there's simply no evidence of it, contrary to some wishful thinking from a textuality mindset; Ben van Noort, *Jesus's Stenographers: The Story of the Red Letters* (Nashville: Westbow, 2018); Paul Rhodes Eddy and Gregory A. Boyd, *The Jesus Legend: A Case for the Historical Reliability of the Synoptic Jesus Tradition* (Grand Rapids, MI: Baker Academic, 2007), 249-52.

of heaven is at hand" (Mt 10:7). It wasn't long before *what he said circulated rapidly over the whole region of Galilee* (Mk 1:28).[4] Like seed blown in the wind looking for fertile soil to land in and take root, the gospel kept going, crossing into new regions and cultures: *What he said was reported all over Syria* (Mt 4:24). The gospel was reproducing itself.

The original language of Jesus' sermons was Aramaic, and initially that was the language of the good news. But Galilee and especially Syria included Greek-speaking Gentiles, so translation was soon necessary. And on the day of Pentecost, people who had assembled from all over the world heard the disciples speaking about what God had done— miraculously, in the visitors' home languages (Acts 2:6-12).

So, even as the number of people in the chain of transmission was increasing, the number of languages of the transmission was multiplying as well. Surprisingly, sharing only orally what Jesus had said was considered sufficient, both from his standpoint and that of his followers. And it continued throughout Jesus' lifetime and beyond. There's no evidence to the contrary.

What's more, even after the good news was encoded in written form, it retained its original oral intent to be heard, not read. Most people were not literate to the extent of reading literary documents, nor would they have had access to personal copies of written forms.[5] Thus, even when Jesus' life and teachings were eventually written down, most people continued to understand the Scriptures orally as the accounts were read aloud or recited from memory. Why then use only one of our five senses to understand Scripture?

---

[4]The Greek (*ē akoē autou*) could be translated "his message," "what was heard from him," "what he said," "the report about him," or even "news about him"; see Johannes P. Louw and Eugene A. Nida, eds., *Greek-English Lexicon of the New Testament: Based on Semantic Domains*, 2nd ed. (New York: United Bible Societies, 1989), 1.412; Frederick W. Danker et al., *Greek-English Lexicon of the New Testament and Other Early Christian Literature*, 3rd ed. (Chicago: University of Chicago, 2000), 36.
[5]See, e.g., Raphael Rodríguez, *Oral Tradition and the New Testament: A Guide for the Perplexed* (London: Bloomsbury, 2014), 2-10.

Thus, even when Jesus' life and teachings were eventually written down, most people continued to understand the Scriptures orally as the accounts were read aloud or recited from memory. Why then use only one of our five senses to understand Scripture?

RETHINKING ASSUMPTIONS

Admittedly, the prominence of orality in the whole process of revelation and transmission seems counterintuitive, at least to our intuition. What God said; what Moses said; what the prophets said; what Jesus said; what people heard—it was all fully authoritative. Could it be, then, that the speaking was inspired as much as the writing, that inspired speaking preceded inspired writing?

Consider also the apostles. Our default assumption is that their letters were inspired, which is true. But Paul, reflecting back on his time with the Thessalonians, declared his spoken words were authoritative as well: *When you received the message from God, which you heard from us, you didn't consider it of human origin, but just as it is, the word of God* (1 Thess 2:13).[6]

Nigel Cameron writes,

> The most common of all the acts of God in history is the use of quotation marks. . . . Certainly the prevalence of quoted divine speech, which peppers the canon, suggests a presumption in favor of speech as *the* category with which to understand God's communication with his creatures. . . . Yet not only *does* he speak, he surely *must*. For how else would we know of God?[7]

---

[6]For additional evidence, see Walton and Sandy, *The Lost World of Scripture*, 158-61.
[7]Nigel M. de S. Cameron, "Revelation, Idea of," in *Evangelical Dictionary of Biblical Theology*, ed. Walter A. Elwell (Grand Rapids, MI: Baker Books, 1996), 679, emphasis in original.

The extent of ancient oral culture's influence on Scripture can be mind-blowing to our modern-day sensibilities. The communication of divine truth was generally delivered orally and expected to be received aurally. God didn't write; he spoke, he breathed (2 Tim 3:16). And select people spoke for him. Yes, eventually they recorded in writing what they had heard or spoken themselves. But the authors were fewer than the speakers. And the hearers were more than the readers.

Alas! Was there never a form of divine revelation designed for people to read? Like us, for example? Was divine revelation really, originally, fully accommodated to a culture of orality? Would that make their hearing primary and our reading secondary?

If so, might our limited understanding of ancient oral culture be a speedbump, even a roadblock standing in the way of modern readers appreciating all that Scripture was intended to communicate? When we only read the Bible, if we're missing something, we have our work cut out for us.

PROPOSITION 4

RESEARCH PROVIDES IMPORTANT INSIGHTS INTO ANCIENT ORAL CULTURE

Whoever reads me will be in the thick of the scrimmage,
and if he doesn't like it—if he wants a safe seat in the audience
—let him read someone else.

D. H. LAWRENCE

READERS OF THE BIBLE may be unnerved by the growing number of discoveries coming to light revealing more and more differences between the cultures of the biblical world and our own. But we shouldn't be. It's a positive development when an insight helps us understand Scripture better. And there are many contributions to consider.

Earlier estimates about the number of people who were too poor to learn to read and write have been clarified in recent years.[1] Actually, to say "read and write" simplifies the situation too much: reading skills could vary widely, from recognizing a few words, such as the charges

---

[1]William V. Harris, *Ancient Literacy* (Cambridge, MA: Harvard University Press, 1989); for clarification see Ben Witherington III, "Education in the Greco-Roman World," in *The World of the New Testament: Cultural, Social, and Historical Contexts*, ed. Joel B. Green and Lee Martin McDonald (Grand Rapids, MI: Baker Academic, 2013), 188-94; E. Randolph Richards, "Reading, Writing, and Manuscripts," in *The World of the New Testament: Cultural, Social, and Historical Contexts*, ed. Joel B. Green and Lee Martin McDonald (Grand Rapids, MI: Baker Academic, 2013), 345-50; Larry W. Hurtado, "Oral Fixation and New Testament Studies? 'Orality,' 'Performance' and Reading Texts in Early Christianity," *New Testament Studies* 60 (2014): 330-34; Roger S. Bagnall, *Everyday Writing in the Graeco-Roman East*, Sather Classical Lectures 69 (Berkeley: University of California Press, 2012).

for which Jesus was crucified as posted by Pilate on the cross (Mk 15:26), to reading at a very advanced level, such as philosophical treatises.

Levels of literacy depended on several issues: social and economic status, the necessity of literacy for business purposes or government bureaucracy, and where people lived—with rural being the lowest level of literacy—encompassing as much as 85 percent of the population.[2] The majority of people (maybe as much 90 percent) would not have been skilled enough to fluently read one of the Gospels or Paul's letters.[3] Most heard; they didn't read.[4] Fewer still would have been able to compose a literary document themselves.

Adding to the complexity of reading, manuscripts were anything but user-friendly. Scribes of the early biblical manuscripts used only uppercase letters and did not put spaces between words, slowing down the act of reading. How readily can we read aloud something like this at first glance?

THEEMPHASISISTOUNDERSCORETHEIDEATHATIFICONTIN-
UECOMMUNICATINGBYTYPINGLIKETHISINONLYUPPER
CASELETTERSANDNOTINCLUDINGANYSPACINGSEPARAT-
INGWORDSIDOUBTYOUWILLBECAPABLEOFEASILYDECI-
PHERINGANDREADINGSMOOTHLYANDWITHOUTHALT-
INGWHATIWANTYOUTOTHOROUGHLYCOMPREHEND.

Not only did scribes write in all uppercase letters without spaces between words, they also did not regularly include punctuation or put breaks between paragraphs, leaving readers to figure out where a thought or section was supposed to end and a new one begin. Nor did

---

[2]For evidence of literacy in the Roman city of Pompeii, see Bruce W. Longenecker, *In Stone and Story: Early Christianity in the Roman World* (Grand Rapids, MI: Baker Academic, 2020), 143-53; for evidence in Judea, see Longenecker's bibliographical citations (276-77).

[3]For discussion, see Raphael Rodríguez, *Oral Tradition and the New Testament: A Guide for the Perplexed* (London: Bloomsbury, 2014), 2-5; John J. Pilch, *A Cultural Handbook to the Bible* (Grand Rapids, MI: Eerdmans, 2012), 147-51; Stanley E. Porter and Bryan R. Dyer, "Oral Texts? A Reassessment of the Oral and Rhetorical Nature of Paul's Letters in Light of Recent Studies," *JETS* 55, no. 2 (2012): 330-31.

[4]"Orality was a pervasive form of communication in ancient cultures, and written texts were orally communicated"; Shem Miller, *Dead Sea Media: Orality, Textuality, and Memory in the Scrolls from the Judean Desert*, Studies on the Texts of the Desert of Judah 129 (Leiden: Brill, 2019), 19.

they provide an indication that a word at the end of a line was being divided between that line and the next. Surprisingly, they made frequent use of abbreviations, particularly for divine names. With all of that, reading could be slow going, requiring considerable familiarity and practice in order to give a fluid oral presentation of a literary work.

The realization that the culture of the biblical world was a complex mix of orality and textuality dawned on specialists in biblical interpretation generally only in the last century.[5] But over the past several decades scholars have produced a cascade of studies, articles and books encompassing thousands of pages, too vast to synthesize and include in this brief book.[6] Such titles as *The Oral and the Written Gospel*; *Jesus in Memory: Traditions in Oral and Scribal Perspectives*; *Imprints, Voiceprints, and Footprints of Memory*; *Oral-Scribal Dimensions of Scripture, Piety, and Practice*—to mention just a few of the books by one author/editor—are an indication of the fountain of scholarship now available.[7]

QUESTIONS TO PONDER

If people were largely dependent on hearing instead of reading, what did that mean for how they learned what they came to know, how confident they were in that knowledge, and how they passed on what they knew?

Could an account be composed orally, which by repetition could reach a measure of standardization, and then could that oral text be encoded in an acceptable written form?[8]

---

[5]Remarkably, even to this day, the implications of oral culture have not been taken seriously by many members of the academy; Kelly R. Iverson, "Orality and the Gospels: A Survey of Current Research," *Currents in Biblical Research* 8 (2009): 99.
[6]See especially Iverson, "Orality and the Gospels," 71-106; and Nicholas A. Elder, "New Testament Media Criticism," *Currents in Biblical Research* 15 (2017): 315-37; already over 1,800 sources on oral poetry were included in a list compiled almost forty years ago: John M. Foley, *Oral-Formulaic Theory and Research: An Introduction and Annotated Bibliography* (New York: Garland, 1985).
[7]The works of Werner H. Kelber have propelled the study of oral culture and Scripture more than any other author, especially his seminal, *The Oral and the Written Gospel: The Hermeneutics of Speaking and Writing in the Synoptic Tradition, Mark, Paul, and Q* (Minneapolis: Fortress, 1983).
[8]"How can a text be 'oral'? An overly narrow definition of 'text' creates an apparent contradiction between orality and texts. . . . Whether oral or written, a text is a unit of speech that is designed to

To what extent did oral culture influence the ways that textual documents were written?

More specifically, in what ways may Jesus' orality have influenced the content and form of the Gospels?

Might Jesus and others have expressed things orally in ways that would be especially suited for future written accounts?

How accurate and reliable was an individual's memory over the span of several decades?

What was the relationship between an individual's memory and the group memory of the community in which the individual was a part?

Was ancient oral culture typically concerned with preserving fixed details, or was their focus more about the main concepts and storylines, with openness to minor variation in details?

Since people rarely read a story but heard someone else read it, what did that mean for the presenters' preparation and performance?

These questions are merely representative of the many generated by recent scholarship. Many other topics continue to simmer on the back burner, as scholars investigate increasingly complex issues.[9] The goal here is limited to what we can gather from an array of research to provide guidance for a broad range of modern readers and interpreters of Scripture that they will find useful and manageable.

KEY INSIGHTS

Here are some highlights from the scholarly research that are especially pertinent to this book.

First, a culture under the influence of orality tends to be "high context" (this refers to an elevated importance of context, whereas "low context" refers to a diminished importance of context). "Context is the information

---

be stored and transmitted." Shem Miller, *Dead Sea Media: Orality, Textuality, and Memory in the Scrolls from the Judean Desert*, Studies on the Texts of the Desert of Judah 129 (Leiden: Brill, 2019), 18-19.
[9]Remarkably, the implications of oral culture are neglected by the majority of the members of the academy; Kelly R. Iverson, "Orality and the Gospels: A Survey of Current Research," *Currents in Biblical Research* 8 (2009): 99.

that surrounds an event; it is inextricably bound up with the meaning of that event."[10] Actually, there are two senses that people of the biblical period lived in high-context cultures.

The first sense is that context can be determinative of meaning as much or more than the particular wording of a statement. Any text can be a pretext if it is not understood within its context. That is, someone may say or write something, which, when lifted out of the context, can be easily misconstrued. This can be true of any communication, but all the more so in the high-context assumptions of orality, especially given the "relatively flexible precision standards."[11] High-context speakers and authors do not seek an exactness with each statement. The context of the whole communication serves as a control on the meaning of its parts.

Jesus may seem to have made bizarre statements, such as, *Do not consider anyone on earth your father* (Mt 23:9), or *If anyone comes to me and does not hate father, mother, wife, children, brothers and sisters* (Lk 14:26), unless it's recognized that he was presuming his audience to be high-context hearers. Ultimately, the complexity of divine truth cannot be adequately expressed in a sentence or two in most instances (contrary to how some think about John 3:16 that it provides all one needs to know about salvation).

Especially for a communication originating in an oral culture, it must not be read or interpreted in piecemeal fashion; each part must be vetted against the larger context. What Jesus said about not taking the children's bread and tossing it to the dogs is an example of a statement that can easily be misconstrued apart from the context (Mt 15:26).

Possible evidence from the New Testament in support of the high-context culture is the absence of statements Jesus made quoted in the

---

[10]Edward T. Hall and Mildred Reed Hall, *Understanding Cultural Differences* (London: Intercultural Press, 1990), 6 (emphasis in original).

[11]Paul R. Eddy, "Orality and Oral Transmission," in *Dictionary of Jesus and the Gospels*, 2nd ed., ed. Joel B. Green, Jeannine K. Brown, and Nicholas Perrin (Downers Grove, IL: IVP Academic, 2013), 641.

rest of the New Testament, the well-known exception being the bread and the cup of the Lord's supper (1 Cor 11:5-26). Many have been puzzled that Jesus was not quoted more frequently in Acts and the epistles. But part of the issue may have been that the early Christians were more interested in the concepts Jesus had in mind than the exact words he used to convey those concepts. For them the conceptual communication mattered more than the propositional.

The second sense is that *high-context* can also refer to a speaker/author and the initial audience sharing common ideas and information that do not need to be expressed in what a speaker/author is communicating.[12] "Linguists have long been aware that most of what is communicated is not actually expressed in words but is assumed among those involved in the communicative act."[13] Not being privy to the shared assumptions unstated by a speaker/author can seriously impair understanding of what is stated.

High-context literature "leaves much to the imagination because the author assumes the hearers or listeners know the scenes described so well that they can supply the correct details."[14] This is especially true of ancient oral culture. Thus, audiences that do not share the same context need to reconstruct as much of the contextual information as possible by considering the life situation, experiences, culture, and history of the author and audience, including reading between the lines and using imagination as appropriate.

Second, encoding in written words a communication that was originally given orally shifts the understanding away from the experience of

---

[12]John H. Walton and D. Brent Sandy, *The Lost World of Scripture: Ancient Literary Culture and Biblical Authority* (Downers Grove, IL: IVP Academic, 2013), 43-44.

[13]Joel B. Green and Lee Martin McDonald, "Introduction," in *The World of the New Testament: Cultural, Social, and Historical Contexts*, ed. Joel B. Green and Lee Martin McDonald (Grand Rapids, MI: Baker Academic, 2013), 1; "The meeting of minds, the understanding, in a given situation involves not only words but also the nonverbal existential context"; Walter J. Ong, *Language as Hermeneutic: A Primer on the Word and Digitization*, ed. Thomas D. Zlatic and Sara van den Berg (Ithaca, NY: Cornell University Press, 2017), 16; for fuller discussion see Stephen A. Tyler, *The Said and the Unsaid: Mind, Meaning, and Culture* (Academic, 1978).

[14]John J. Pilch, *A Cultural Handbook to the Bible* (Grand Rapids, MI: Eerdmans, 2012), 46; see also Walton and Sandy, *The Lost World of Scripture*, 43-44.

communication between speaker and hearer into fractions of meaning that become fixed on pages (letters, words), which can only partly convey the fullness of the original communicative act.[15] Reducing spoken words to written or printed form is actually an act of decontextualization, resulting in a written account not containing a full sense of the original content, and therefore has inherent limitations.

To correctly interpret a written text, one that originated in an oral culture, the words on the page need to be resuscitated to the extent possible to appreciate the dynamic of the spoken word—counterfractioning the boundaries of the written word—so the communication can be understood in light of the original context and culture. Hence, again, the life situation, experiences, culture, and history of the author and audience are foundational for correctly experiencing their communications.

Third, meaning in an oral communication is constantly being negotiated between sender and recipient(s) as the speaker considers the best way to communicate the intended message in relation to the audience's situation and ongoing reception. At the same time, it's up to the hearers to engage with the speaker's train of thought, relating what they are hearing to their particular circumstances, and accepting or rejecting the communication. That kind of negotiation, of course, is less possible with fixed, written texts.

But there's hope. If rather than simply engaging with the words on a page, readers seek to put themselves in the shoes of both speaker and hearers, they can themselves become closer to active participation in the communication.[16] It entails interpreters discerning first

---

[15]Walter J. Ong, *Language as Hermeneutic: A Primer on the Word and Digitization*, ed. Thomas D. Zlatic and Sara van den Berg (Ithaca, NY: Cornell University Press, 2017), 18; regarding communication as a relational experience, see Jeannine K. Brown, *Scripture as Communication: Introducing Biblical Hermeneutics* (Grand Rapids, MI: Baker Academic, 2007), 15-16.

[16]"By comparison with readers of modern literature, the hearers of performances or 'readers' of oral traditional 'texts' must participate far more actively in realizing the work, and far more actively than scholars interested only in analysis of an artifact"; Richard A. Horsley and Jonathan A. Draper, *Whoever Hears You Hears Me: Prophets, Performance, and Tradition in Q* (Harrisburg, PA: Trinity Press International, 1999), 162.

the speaker's rationale, intent, and methods of persuasion, then possible ways the audience would have responded to the communication, given the experiences leading up to hearing what the speaker was saying, as well as what may lie ahead in their future.

Fourth, verbalizing a communication in oral culture is generally an act of performance. "A hermeneutic of speech in oral cultures demands that we do not assume total likeness between oral speech events in primary oral cultures and oral speech events of literates."[17] Oral cultures count on an oral presentation to be powerful and convincing, while the tendency in textual cultures, especially in churches, is for a reading of Scripture to be more of a lifeless recitation than a lively performance. Thus, in order to re-oralize written/printed words, a reader needs to approximate the consciousness of the original communicator, seeking to have an impact on the contemporary audience similar to the one the original speaker sought to have on the initial hearers.

The way we read Scripture is not the way they heard Scripture, making it vital that today's interpreters set aside their own culture of modernity and textuality and put the culture of ancient orality front and center.

In sum, we can see that the way we read Scripture is not the way they heard Scripture, making it vital that today's interpreters set aside their own culture of modernity and textuality and put the culture of ancient orality front and center. That's likely going to entail some culture shock, requiring altering our approach to Scripture. But the textual approach, in which most of us are schooled and which we innocently practice, can be a fault line in interpretation. We need to find a better way.

---

[17] Ong, *Language as Hermeneutic*, 61.

PROPOSITION 5

THE GOAL IS TO INCLUDE
THEIR HEARING IN OUR READING

There's truths you have to grow into.

H. G. WELLS

CONSIDER AN ANALOGY. The original audiences of God's revelation spoke Hebrew, Aramaic, and Greek, and God accommodated divine truth to those languages. Otherwise, "Hear ye the Word of the Lord" would have been in vain.

But God's revelation wasn't only for people long ago. Consequently, there have been thousands of translations into hundreds of languages completed across more than two thousand years, requiring enormous expenditures of time and resources. By accommodating biblical revelation to people who do not know the biblical languages, more and more people across the globe can have access to what God proclaimed.

Now compare culture. Language wasn't the only thing unique to the original audiences. Other aspects of their culture were unique too, including orality. But most people today seem unaware of how different we are from what they were. We read the very words of Scripture in our modern languages assuming that those words speak to us in the same way they did to people in the original cultures. But maybe not. We see the necessity of translating the original languages, but we

overlook the need to "translate" the cultural differences and understand the Bible accordingly.

It's a lack of cultural intelligence. It would be like traveling the world
today blind to all the differences in cultures we'd encounter. The people
of a given culture do not intuitively have the skills to relate to people
of other cultures. They may think they do, but many find out the hard
way they don't.

Studies in the field of cultural intelligence seek to raise awareness of
how to cue in on distinct features of various cultures and to provide
guidance in how to communicate and negotiate relationships within
different settings.[1] We need biblical cultural intelligence, but (to my
knowledge) no one has attempted to apply principles from the study
of cultural intelligence to better understand the ancient cultures of
the Bible.[2]

Thankfully, a variety of resources—dictionaries, commentaries,
study Bibles, and more—make available some aspects of the ancient
world that are typically off the radar.[3] "Backgrounds" is the common
term, in the sense of adding to what is known from Scripture. It can
be information about Herod the Great and his sons, about how taxes
were collected, about the production of olive oil and its uses, and
so forth.

---

[1]For cultural intelligence applied to business, see especially Geert Hofstede, Gert Jan Hofstede, and
Michael Minkov, *Cultures and Organizations: Software of the Mind: Intercultural Cooperation and Its
Importance for Survival*, 3rd ed. (New York: McGraw Hill, 2010); P. Christopher Early and Soon Ang,
Cultural Intelligence: Individual Interactions Across Cultures (Stanford: Stanford University Press,
2003); Brooks Peterson, *Cultural Intelligence: A Guide to Working with People from Other Cultures* (Lon-
don: Intercultural Press, 2004); David C. Thomas and Kerr Inkson, *Cultural Intelligence: Surviving
and Thriving in the Global Village*, 3rd ed. (Alameda, CA: Berrett-Koehler, 2017); for applications to
Christian ministry, see, e.g., Sherwood Lingenfelter, *Transforming Culture: A Challenge for Christian
Mission*, 2nd ed. (Grand Rapids, MI: Baker Books, 1998); Tina Stoltzfus Horst, *Dancing Between
Cultures: Culturally Intelligent Coaching for Missions and Ministry* (Life Development Publishing,
2017); Darrell L. Bock, *Cultural Intelligence: Living for God in a Diverse, Pluralistic World* (Nashville,
TN: B&H Academic, 2020).
[2]More specifically, this book is about oral/aural intelligence—the way truths were spoken, as
recorded in Scripture, and heard and understood. More research is needed into how the cultures
of speaking and hearing in the ancient world shaped the communication and reception of
divine revelation.
[3]For example, *Dictionary of New Testament Backgrounds*; *The IVP Bible Background Commentary: New
Testament*; *The IVP Bible Background Commentary: Old Testament*; *NIV Cultural Backgrounds Study
Bible: Bringing to Life the Ancient World of Scripture*.

"Foregrounds" are more important, not supplementary, but carefully grounded lenses through which we read Scripture.[4] This especially entails how people thought, communicated, and what their values were, for example, how people in an honor and shame culture related to one another.[5]

Admittedly, ancient oral culture isn't a barrier as high as the original languages. Nevertheless, it can be a roadblock to understanding Scripture. And with many people not even realizing the problem, it may be an even bigger barrier. Whatever the obstacles are, low or high, seen or unseen, we must not let them stand in the way of understanding Scripture. Using twenty-first century Western culture to interpret a document from a first-century Middle Eastern culture would be a disgrace to God's choice to reveal himself at that time and place (*in the fullness of time*; Gal 4:4).

Modern reading culture can be a roadblock to understanding Scripture.

Surprisingly, the orality of the biblical world has not been commonly recognized as important for understanding Scripture, even though research has been going on for decades.[6] Even practitioners of biblical interpretation seem to be unaware.[7] Of course, we will never

---

[4]See, e.g., James Barr, "Reading the Bible as Literature," *Bulletin of the John Rylands Library* 56, no. 1 (1973): 10-33.

[5]See, e.g., Jackson Wu and Ryan Jensen, *Seeking God's Face: Practical Reflections on Honor and Shame in Scripture* (Houston: Lucid Books, 2022); Jayson Georges and Mark D. Baker, *Ministering in Honor-Shame Cultures: Biblical Foundations and Practical Essentials* (Downers Grove, IL: IVP Academic, 2016).

[6]Most books on the world of the New Testament have little to say about oral culture as foreground for biblical interpretation; e.g., Bruce W. Longenecker, *In Stone and Story: Early Christianity in the Roman World* (Grand Rapids, MI: Baker Academic, 2020); Harry O. Maier, *New Testament Christianity in the Roman World* (Oxford: Oxford University Press, 2019); Moyer V. Hubbard, *Christianity in the Greco-Roman World: A Narrative Introduction* (Grand Rapids, MI: Baker Academic, 2010); *Dictionary of New Testament Background*, ed. Craig A. Evans and Stanley E. Porter (Downers Grove, IL: IVP Academic, 2000).

[7]Most hermeneutics textbooks, even recent ones, fail to emphasize the importance of oral culture for interpretation, including Jeannine K. Brown, *Scripture as Communication: Introducing Biblical Hermeneutics* (Grand Rapids, MI: Baker Academic, 2007); Graeme Goldsworthy, *Gospel-Centered*

completely understand ancient oral culture, but try we must. Understanding God's word is at stake, after all.

So where to begin? Can readers today understand the hearers then?
The first step is recognizing the extent of oral culture's influence on
Scripture. The second is grasping the differences between hearing and
reading Scripture. Third is figuring out how to get closer to hearing
Scripture as initial audiences did, even though we are primarily readers
of Scripture. Oral culture belongs in the foreground, not the background. As we will discover, it's more than supplementary information.

The goal of this book is to adapt our understanding of Scripture to
the original audience's ways of hearing with the goal of interpreting
God's speech-act as he intended. Along the way we will explore various
approaches to reading and interpreting Scripture orally—the Gospels
in particular—hopefully correcting our bias in favor of textual techniques of interpretation. If we fail in doing so, we could be limited to
seeing only "two-dimensional cardboard cutouts" rather than the fully
orbed events, people, and revelatory insights God intended.[8]

We're certainly not the first to go down this path.[9] But unfortunately,
previous proposals, while helpful, have had limited impact, both on
those who take reading the Bible seriously, and on those who seek to
faithfully proclaim the meaning of Scripture. People who read, interpret, and teach the Bible in churches, colleges, and seminaries are
the ones who especially need to recognize ways they can improve their
understanding of the most important communication of all time. Any

---

Hermeneutics: Foundations and Principles of Evangelical Biblical Interpretation (Downers Grove, IL:
IVP Academic, 2006); Stanley E. Porter and Beth M. Stovell, eds., *Biblical Hermeneutics: Five Views*
(Downers Grove, IL: IVP Academic, 2012). Regarding Joel B. Green, ed., *Hearing the New Testament:
Strategies for Interpretation*, 2nd ed. (Grand Rapids, MI: Eerdmans, 2010), we'd expect considerable
attention given to orality, but the focus is actually on reading (making the title a misnomer).
[8]For the two-dimensional cardboard cutout metaphor, see Stephen C. Barton, "Historical Criticism
and Social-Scientific Perspectives in New Testament Study," in *Hearing the New Testament: Strategies
for Interpretation*, 2nd ed., Joel B. Green, ed. (Grand Rapids, MI: Eerdmans, 2010), 38.
[9]For example, regarding residual effects of orality on written texts and how that helps to interpret
them, see Joanna Dewey, *The Oral Ethos of the Early Church: Speaking, Writing, and the Gospel of Mark*,
Biblical Performance Criticism 8 (Eugene, OR: Cascade, 2013); regarding performances of oral
texts and how that helps audiences to appreciate meanings in new ways, see Thomas Boomershine,
The Messiah of Peace, Biblical Performance Criticism 12 (Eugene, OR: Cascade, 2015).

obstacle standing in the way of understanding Scripture needs to be removed.

The logic of this book then is as follows. In part two we will track the evidence through Scripture for the oral communication of divine truth. There's more there than we often realize, and we need to be convinced of that before we'll be convinced of the need to interpret Scripture as oral communication. In part three we will examine how stories and literature were told and heard at the time of the New Testament and consider steps we can take toward becoming better hearers and performers of Scripture. In part four we will offer various attempts to hear and experience the revelation of divine truth, as hearers would have, vis-à-vis modern readers.[10]

Well, the stage is about set except for one final caveat: to accomplish what we're up to is going to be a big challenge. I'm going to have to call on all the musicians and instruments in the orchestra, from piccolo trumpet to tenor tuba, to make the point of this book heard loud and clear—and ideally as interesting to listen to as, for example, Stravinsky's "Rite of Spring."

Hopefully you're ready for the music to begin.

---

[10]For a helpful example, see *When God's Word Speaks: Stories of the Power of Scripture in the Lives of God's People Today* (Wycliffe Bible Translators, 2016).

PART TWO

GOD AND HIS AGENTS OF ORAL COMMUNICATION

PROPOSITION 6

SCRIPTURE PRESENTS GOD AS THE ULTIMATE ORAL COMMUNICATOR

Sing praises to the one who has soared through the skies
from the beginning; he speaks with the voice of thunder.

PSALM 68:33

WE MAY HAVE NEVER NOTICED THIS, but Scripture has an inherent paradox. It is spoken yet written revelation.

The Bible, being so widely available today—even now on our digital devices—is easily taken for granted. It's hard to imagine that for 1,500 years for the New Testament, and more for the Old Testament, individuals didn't have access to anything of the sort. It wasn't until a century after Gutenberg's invention of the printing press in the 1400s that the first complete Bible in English was available in printed form. Since then we've had the printed version of divine revelation in our hands and on our laps for almost five hundred years.

It seems perfectly natural. It's God's inspired book. Except that it wasn't a book.[1] "What we call the biblical 'books' represent, at least

---

[1] "The modern concept of 'book' shapes our perception of the Hebrew Bible and the textual world of ancient Jews"; Shem Miller, *Dead Sea Media: Orality, Textuality, and Memory in the Scrolls from the Judean Desert*, Studies on the Texts of the Desert of Judah 129 (Leiden: Brill, 2019), 2.

some of the time, the last step in the process of literary production rather than the first step."[2] Indeed, it was a process, and it began with God speaking. "God spoke" is where creation and revelation began.

"God spoke" is where creation and revelation began.

God didn't write. Yes, he handwrote the Ten Words on stone tablets (the Ten Commandments are referred to in Hebrew as the ten "words," or "sayings": Ex 34:28; Deut 4:13; 10:4). But remarkably, beyond that God chose to reveal an entire host of heavenly truths—what we read in our Bibles—by speaking them.[3]

> In that most readers of the Bible fail to recognize the implicit orality underlying Scripture, in this section of the book, we are rehearsing the extensive evidence for oral communication. What we read all across the pages of Scripture is what God spoke. We tend to see only the final written account, but there's much we miss getting to that point. Most important, the oral culture of the ancient world had a profound impact on the origin and nature of Scripture.

God's work creating a universe was framed by the repeated declaration, "And God said, 'Let there be . . . ,'" and there were: cosmic islands of stars (galaxies), nurseries for birthing new stars (nebulae), supermassive black holes (quasars), "mystical jewels of God" stretching across what is now estimated to be 93 billion light years of space and reportedly expanding every second.[4] Can we conceive of that? No, not at all. But that's the

---

[2]John H. Walton, "No Books, No Authors: Literary Production in a Hearing-Dominant Culture," in *Write That They May Read: Studies in Literacy and Textualization in the Ancient Near East and in the Hebrew Scriptures: Essays in Honour of Professor Alan R. Millard*, ed. Daniel I. Block, David C. Deuel, C. John Collins, Paul J. N. Lawrence (Eugene, OR: Pickwick, 2020), 263.
[3]"The Bible is profoundly unique among books because it is, *in its essence*, both divine and human discourse." Kenton L. Sparks, *God's Word in Human Words: An Evangelical Appropriation of Critical Biblical Scholarship* (Grand Rapids, MI: Baker Academic, 2008), 205 (emphasis in original).
[4]"The mystical jewels of God" was first penned by poet Robert Buchanan.

nature of God and anything he says. "The heavens declare the glory of God; the skies proclaim the work of his hands. Day after day they pour forth speech; night after night they reveal knowledge" (Ps 19:1-2 NIV).

> The voice of the Lord is powerful;
>   The voice of the Lord is majestic.
> The voice of the Lord breaks the cedars . . .
>   The voice of the Lord strikes with flashes of lightning.
> The voice of the Lord shakes the desert . . .
>   The voice of the Lord twists the oaks. (Ps 29:4-9 NIV)

God spoke directly with Adam and Eve: *Be fruitful . . . fill the earth . . . take control of it . . . rule over it* (Gen 1:28). And, *You dare not eat from the tree of the knowledge of good and evil.* But they failed to comply and suffered the consequences: curses on the serpent, on the ground, and on Adam and Eve (Gen 2:17; 3:6; 3:14-19)! And life has been out of sorts ever since; no eating from the tree of life, no longer enjoying the Garden and God's presence, endless natural disasters, pandemics, wars, and rumors of wars. Before long, people had become so irreparably sinful that God made another shocking declaration, *I will wipe humans, whom I have created, off the face of the earth* (Gen 6:7). He was going to uncreate much of what he had created. And he did, except for Noah and his family.

It was hundreds (maybe thousands) of years later when it was time for God to have a few words with Abraham: *I am God Almighty. You need to walk before me and be blameless, and I will confirm my covenant with you* (Gen 17:1-2). Hundreds of years after that he challenged Moses with unexpected words, *I am sending you to Pharaoh to bring my people out of Egypt* (Ex 3:10). Then to the Israelites he proclaimed, through Moses: *You have seen how I carried you on eagles' wings and brought you out of Egypt to myself. Now if you listen to my voice, and obey me fully, and keep my covenant, then you will be a treasure for me above all other nations* (Ex 19:4-5).

Probably as important as creation itself, God spoke the bedrock of law and order into existence.[5] *Listen, Israel, to the laws and decrees I am speaking in your ears today* (Deut 5:1; cf. Ex 20:1; Deut 5:22). He told the Israelites that to avoid suffering as the Egyptians did, they would need to listen carefully to his voice and to his commandments, to obey him faithfully, and to do what was right in his eyes (Ex 15:26). He advised Moses, "I am going to come to you in a dense cloud, so that the people will hear me speaking with you" (Ex 19:9 NIV; cf. Ex 20:22; Neh 9:13).

God spoke to Joshua, Gideon, Samuel, Saul, David, Solomon, Elijah, Elisha. The books of the prophets are especially full of the oracles of God. For the record, God affirmed the importance of everything he said: "So is my word that goes out of my mouth; it will not return to me empty, but will accomplish what I desire and achieve the purpose for which I sent it" (Is 55:11 NIV).

When God speaks, the cosmos obeys:

- *God said, "Let the waters under the sky come together in one place so that dry ground may appear." And it was so.* (Gen 1:9)

- *At the sound of your voice, the waters retreat; the thundering of your words hurries them along.* (Ps 104:7)

- *Jesus got up and rebuked the wind and said to the sea, "Hush! Be silent!" And the wind stopped blowing, and there was a great calm.* (Mk 4:39; cf. Mt 8:26; Lk 8:24)

People, unfortunately, can be guilty of selective hearing:[6]

- *Pay attention, you deaf. . . your ears are open but you hear nothing.* (Is 42:18-20)

- *Their ear is uncircumcised so they cannot hear.* (Jer 6:10)

---

[5]See, e.g., Peter J. Leithart, *The Ten Commandments: A Guide to the Perfect Law of Liberty* (Bellingham, WA: Lexham, 2020): "The Ten Words are a character portrait of Jesus the Son of God; and if we want to know how to follow Jesus, we should begin with the Ten Words" (6).

[6]There's a T-shirt on the market with big bold letters, "I have selective hearing," and in small letters underneath, "I'm sorry; you were not selected."

- *The heart of these people has become dull; they barely hear with their ears.* (Mt 13:15, quoting Is 6:10)

Turning to the New Testament, God continued speaking. With an audible voice at both Jesus' baptism and transfiguration, he verbally authorized his Son, the radiance of his glory and the representation of his essence (Mt 3:17; 17:5; Heb 1:3). According to the Gospel of John, when Jesus was facing the reality of his upcoming death, a voice reverberated from heaven assuring him that God would be glorified in what was going to happen (Jn 12:27-29). Actually, bystanders thought it had thundered or an angel had spoken. But more than during Jesus' time on earth, God's speaking never ends, even until the very climax of time: He who was seated on the throne said, *Watch! I am going to make everything new!* (Rev 21:5; see also 1:8).[7]

Nothing is more important than what God says and what we hear.

Spoken to an audience marked by weak praise and uncertain faith, the author of the book of Hebrews offers a theological primer on oral revelation. Verbs referring to speech and hearing underscore the point:

> *At many times and in many ways, God spoke to our fathers by the prophets, but in these last days he has spoken to us via his Son. . . . To which of the angels did God ever say . . . when he brings the firstborn into the world, he says . . . Of the angels he says . . . to which of the angels has he ever said . . . Therefore we must pay much closer attention to what we have heard.* (Heb 1:1-2, 5-7, 13; 2:1)

God speaking was the standard protocol of making himself known. God spoke profound thoughts in a form and manner of human speaking so that he could communicate divine truth to human hearers.

---

[7]For discussion, see Richard Bauckham, *The Theology of the Book of Revelation* (Cambridge: Cambridge University Press, 1993), 25-33.

It's incarnational communication: God-speech in human speech. Which means that fundamental to the historic faith of both Old and New Testaments are the twin notions that God speaks and we listen. Nothing is more important than what God says and what we hear.

Of course, like Father, like Son. God as a speaking God was intrinsically and equally true of Jesus. He didn't write, the only possible exception being some unknown words written in the dirt (Jn 8:6-8—if that passage should even be included in our Bibles). He had many important things to share, such as the Sermon on the Mount. Maybe there's a reason he didn't need to write; his speech and life said it all.

The Holy Spirit was also involved in oral communication:

- *David reported, "The Spirit of the Lord spoke through me; it was his word on my tongue."* (2 Sam 23:2)

- Jesus asked, "How is it then that David, speaking by the Spirit, calls him 'Lord'?" (Mt 22:43 NIV)

- *Previously the Holy Spirit spoke through the mouth of David.* (Acts 1:16)

- The Holy Spirit spoke the truth . . . through Isaiah the prophet. (Acts 28:25 NIV)

- We speak about these things, not with words taught us by human wisdom, but with those taught by the Spirit. (1 Cor 2:13 NET)

- *Directed by the Holy Spirit, the prophets spoke from God.* (2 Pet 1:21)[8]

The Holy Spirit's role continued in the early church, prompting and inspiring people to speak.

- *Peter, filled with the Holy Spirit, spoke up.* (Acts 4:8)

- *When they had prayed, the place where they were assembled together was shaken, and they were all filled with the Holy Spirit and began to speak the word of God courageously.* (Acts 4:31)

---

[8]See also Is 59:21; Jn 16:13; Acts 4:25; Heb 3:7; 10:15-16.

- *Some men . . . stood up and argued with Stephen. Yet they were not able to resist the wisdom and the Spirit with which he spoke.* (Acts 6:9-10)

- *Let the one who has an ear hear what the Spirit says to the churches.* (Rev 1:7)

That the Trinity did not write can certainly seem paradoxical, given that we have the word of the Lord in written and printed form.[9] If we ponder why God chose not to write, we won't get very far. What options did he have? Golden tablets that drop out of the sky? Buried treasure waiting to be discovered? A booming voice from beyond the universe?

One way for communicating divine truth is God's creative acts, which are a representation of how he thinks (see Ps 19:1-4; Rom 1:20). But while we can "read" his creation for insights into his character and intentions—and we probably don't do that enough—God intends to reveal deeper truths than what the architecture of his creation can.

God's other basic option is human agency. And that was his choice. In his eternal wisdom, he took steps to empower and inspire representatives to speak on his behalf. Moses is a good starting point. (Eventually we'll come to Jesus, the ultimate revelation of divine truth via the most unusual human agency ever.)

---

[9]Actually, there's another paradox. What sense does it make for the spoken words of the living God to be inscribed on dead material using lifeless ink? Originally, parchment made from animal skins, or papyrus sliced from a reed growing in the Nile River, were the writing materials for Scripture. More recently, paper made from cellulose fibers extracted from dead trees is used for printing Bibles. The question remains, Can the life-giving words of the living God effectively come to life out of such lifeless material?

PROPOSITION 7

GOD SPOKE DIVINE TRUTH TO
AND THROUGH MOSES

*The Lord spoke to Moses from the mountain
and declared, "This is what I want you to speak
to all the people of Jacob and Israel."*

Exodus 19:3

IT'S REMARKABLE. For the unseen, supreme, matchless God, who is beyond the universe, to communicate the most profound information of all time to and through imperfect humans, such as Moses, who are confined in the universe—it would entail a significant undertaking.[1] At least four things appear necessary: God's communication of heavenly truths in ways earthly hearers could understand; exceptionally reliable human hearers; highly dependable memories; and unfailing representatives.

For that strategy to work, the word from God needs to be faithfully heard, understood, remembered, lived, and shared. And God depends on humans to pull it off. Otherwise, what Jesus declared, if we fail to be the salt of the earth, would seem to apply if we mess up God's communications: it is "good for nothing but to be cast out and trodden under foot" (Mt 5:13 KJV).

---

[1]Regarding God being beyond the universe and time, see, e.g., Gregory Ganssle, ed., *God and Time: Four Views* (Downers Grove, IL: IVP Academic, 2001); Gregory Ganssle and David M. Woodruff, eds., *God and Time: Essays on the Divine Nature* (Oxford: Oxford University Press, 2002).

Adding to the challenge, there would need to be a way for God to authorize the messages he communicates via human speakers. Subsequent hearers would need assurance that the communication came from God and was not humanly contrived. Otherwise, who would listen? Who would be transformed? Here's a prime example of God's solution.

MOSES AS AGENT OF AUTHORITATIVE REVELATION

When God spoke to Moses out of a burning bush, which wouldn't quit burning, he was supernaturally commissioning and authorizing the uniquely placed Moses to be his representative and spokesperson. He had spoken to Abraham and others before, but this was different. The aura of God speaking out of the fire added to the transcendence of the moment. It was an ordination of the highest order.[2]

The need was great. Israel had been oppressed in ruthless slavery in Egypt for a long time, and in the midst of their groaning, God remembered his covenant and determined to do something about the situation (Ex 1:11-14; 2:23-25; 3:7-10). The solution was Moses to the rescue.

But Moses had reservations, and rightly so. "What if they won't believe me or listen to me? What if they say, 'The LORD never appeared to you'?" (Ex 4:1 NLT). God responded by empowering Moses with three miracles to verify his authority. He could throw his staff on the ground, and it would turn into a snake; put his hand inside his cloak, and it would become leprous; take some water from the Nile and pour it on the ground, and it would turn to blood. "'This,' said the LORD, 'is so that they may believe that the LORD, the God of their fathers—the God of Abraham, the God of Isaac and the God of Jacob—has appeared to you'" (Ex 4:5 NIV).

Another way God authorized Moses was giving him two forms of a unique name: God said to Moses, "I am who I am. This is what you

---

[2]God speaking at Jesus' baptism and transfiguration was a second ordination of the highest order (Mt 3:17; 17:5).

are to say to the Israelites: 'I am has sent me to you.'" God also said to Moses, "Say to the Israelites, 'The LORD, the God of your fathers— the God of Abraham, the God of Isaac and the God of Jacob—has sent me to you'" (Ex 3:14-15 NIV). The means of ordaining Moses were increasing.

But Moses had yet another reservation: he did not feel eloquent.[3] Consequently God offered two responses: he would guide Moses on what to say and provide an assistant: *Inform Aaron that you'll tell him what to say, and I will guide you both in what to say and do* (Ex 4:15). The plan was straightforward: God would speak to Moses, and Moses would speak to Aaron, making it possible for both to speak on God's behalf: simple human beings fully empowered and authorized to receive complex divine revelation and speak it to others.[4]

The most impressive declaration that Moses was divinely empowered was God's assurance to Moses about the role Aaron would have: *he will be your voice, and you will be God for him* (Ex 4:16).[5] "This striking phrase suggests not only Moses' authority over Aaron, but also the close identification between God and his messenger."[6] Equally significant, God declared to Moses, *Look, I have made you God to Pharaoh* (Ex 7:1).[7]

The good news is, the plan worked. Moses proved to be a reliable recipient and faithful representative. He was fully commissioned as God's emissary, agent, deputy, and courier, and most of all, God's voice:[8]

---

[3]Moses was "more human than heroic and often a reluctant though dedicated leader"; James E. Bowley, *An Introduction to Hebrew Bible: A Guided Tour of Israel's Sacred Library* (New York: Pearson, 2008), 139.

[4]The possibility that Moses could pass on the divine message to another person, as God said could happen through Aaron—"*as if he were your mouth*"—is suggestive; the mantle of communication from God was not restricted to Moses, but can be taken up by other qualified recipients.

[5]For another translation, see, e.g., the JPS version, "He will speak to the people for you, with you playing the role of God to him."

[6]Peter Enns, *Exodus*, NIV Application Commentary (Grand Rapids, MI: Zondervan, 2000), 113.

[7]For another translation, see, e.g., the JPS version, "See, I place you in the role of God to Pharaoh."

[8]"Moses . . . represented the possibilities and the limits of those who are fully human in the overwhelming face of divinity, no matter how transformative that encounter was thought to be."

- *Moses said, "This is exactly what Yahweh has declared."* (Ex 11:4)

- *Moses came down from Mt Sinai and told the leaders of the people everything Yahweh had told him.* (Ex 19:7)

- "These are the commandments and the decisions that the LORD commanded the Israelites through the authority of Moses." (Num 36:13 NET)[9]

So with the aid of Aaron, Moses was the ambassador to the Israelites, fully commissioned and authorized to communicate the very thoughts and words of God. What God said, Moses said (well, most of the time; see Ex 32:11-14). The book of Deuteronomy is the words Moses spoke to all Israel on the other side of the Jordan (Deut 1:1). It summarizes and supplements what God had said to Moses on mountains and in tents over the previous forty years. When Moses spoke for God, it was the oral text of divine revelation.

When Moses spoke for God, it was the oral text of divine revelation.

In declaring the provisions of the Torah, the statement "The Lord spoke to Moses" occurs thirty-three times in Leviticus, and eighteen times in Numbers, in addition to similar statements in Exodus and Deuteronomy. Similarly, God repeatedly instructed Moses to speak to the people; for example, "This is what you are to say to the descendants of Jacob and what you are to tell the people of Israel" (Ex 19:3 NIV).

The reverse is true, however, regarding Moses' writing. There are only a few specific occasions in which God instructed Moses to put something in writing: After Joshua's defeat of the Amalekites, which was

---

Jared C. Calaway, *The Christian Moses: Vision, Authority, and the Limits of Humanity in the New Testament and Early Christianity* (Montreal: McGill-Queen's University Press, 2019), 3.
[9]See also Ex 24:3-4; Lev 27:34; Deut 1:1, 3; 6:1; 29:1.

only accomplished as long as Moses held up his hands, God said to Moses, "Write this on a scroll as something to be remembered and make sure that Joshua hears it" (Ex 17:14 NIV); after summarizing the terms of the all-important covenant relationship, God told Moses: *Write down these words for they are part of the covenant I made with you and with Israel* (Ex 34:27); faced with a rebellion among the Israelites, God instructed Moses to write the name of the leader of each of the twelve tribes on a staff to see which staff would sprout (Num 17:1-11); in preparation for crossing the Jordan into the Promised Land, God commanded Moses and the leaders of the people of Israel to set up large stones, plaster them, and "write very clearly all the words of this law" on the stones (Deut 27:8 NIV); and at the conclusion of Moses' life, God gave Moses a song that he was to write down and sing to the Israelites (Deut 31:19-22).

It seems clear that God intended Moses' role to be first and foremost the agency of speaking. He spoke for God so people could hear from God. Most Israelites would not have been able to read what he wrote anyway. But when Moses spoke, voila! They could understand the ultimately important words of the Lord. (Ezra reading the law and the people understanding is a later example; Neh 8:2-12.) It didn't mean the people would necessarily heed what Moses said God said, but at least they had good intentions: Moses told the people all the Lord's words and regulations, and they responded unanimously, *Everything Yahweh said, which we're supposed to do, we will do!* (Ex 24:3).

Now for Westerners under the spell of textual authority, it's common to assume that a written form of communication is superior to and more authoritative than anything oral.[10] "Since the Christian depends on Scripture for the knowledge of God, the authority and

---

[10]"Ancient texts often seem to be something that they are not, primarily because we read them as if they were products of modern society rather than of an ancient and sometimes alien world." Kenton L. Sparks, *God's Word in Human Words: An Evangelical Appropriation of Critical Biblical Scholarship* (Grand Rapids, MI: Baker Academic, 2008), 213.

interpretation of God's written revelation are, practically speaking, as important to the individual believer as God is."[11]

But in the case of Moses (and as we'll see is true for others too), we need to disabuse ourselves of the notion that only a written version can be as important to us as God himself.[12] The words God spoke to and through his servant were not less than God's words when put in writing. If anything, the oral was primary and the written secondary (though not suggesting the written was second-class).

Moses certainly did write, and we can read and find out what Moses wrote that God spoke (Deut 31:9). But is a written record sufficiently authorized on its own? Would self-referential claims that it is inspired be believable? Actually, in and of itself a written statement may not be convincing of its authority, nor is a miraculous attestation of a document easily accomplished. Attestation from something outside itself helps.[13]

Here's where the oral authority God granted to Moses comes into play. People could have full confidence in what Moses spoke because he had been supernaturally endowed as God's surrogate at the burning bush. The voice out of the fire, the revelation of divine names, and Moses' striking encounters with God on Mount Sinai, backed it up.[14] As long as the divine communication was heard, understood, remembered, and spoken correctly, it was the word of the Lord.

The empowerment of Moses as God's voice had a lasting effect. With full authorization as God's oral spokesperson, and as the (usually)

---

[11]Louis Igou Hodges, "New Dimensions in Scripture," in *New Dimensions in Evangelical Thought: Essays in Honor of Millard J. Erickson*, ed. David S. Dockery (Downers Grove, IL: IVP Academic, 1998), 209 (emphasis added).

[12]We need to beware of bibliolatry; see Glenn Kreider, "Bibliolatry," in *The Encyclopedia of the Bible and Its Reception*, ed. Hans-Josef Klauck (Berlin: de Gruyter, 2009), 1184-90.

[13]The statements in the Pentateuch regarding the authority of the written versions of God's law pertain not to itself but to the Ten Commandments, which God himself wrote (Ex 24:12; 32:15-16; Deut 10:4-5; 31:24; 29:20-21, 27).

[14]"A transcendent source gives to the Bible a derived authority from God that is living, unchanging and demanding and possesses the power to relativize all other thought"; Louis Igou Hodges, "New Dimensions in Scripture," in Dockery, ed. *New Dimensions in Evangelical Thought*, 213.

fearless leader of the Israelites—Moses could be trusted as the authority figure for what he spoke and for what he wrote, as now recorded in the Pentateuch, whether or not he personally spoke every word (for Aaron could speak on his behalf) or inscribed every word.[15] The written version derived its authority from the oral version.

In addition to the oral word of God being inspired, the inscribed written word of God was as well—on God's stone tablets or on scribes' parchment, it didn't matter. What Moses said was just as much the word of the Lord as the text he wrote and vice versa. His orality became his textuality. It was an oral culture with a textual component. Our point is not to devalue the written word but to reorient our thinking to the original and proper place of oral revelation.[16]

MOSES IN THE REST OF THE BIBLE

The prominence of Moses' authority continued well beyond his lifetime.[17] Joshua told the people to remember what the Lord had promised Moses about rest in the land (Josh 1:13; cf. Ex 33:14). God reminded the people of what he declared through his servant Moses (2 Kings 21:8-9; 2 Chron 33:8). The Levites rehearsed what God had done: "You came down on Mount Sinai; you spoke to them from heaven; you gave them regulations and laws that are just and right, and decrees and commands . . . through your servant Moses" (Neh 9:13-14 NIV).

In the poetic books, the most significant observation comes from Psalm 119. With all the references to God's laws, decrees, and statutes

---

[15]In regard to the authorship of the Pentateuch, it's not likely Moses wrote the details of his death and burial or being considered the greatest prophet ever (Deut 34:5-12), nor statements such as in the verses listed above about his being a reliable recipient and faithful spokesperson. But that does not negate Moses' function as the "authority figure" associated with the Pentateuch; see John H. Walton and D. Brent Sandy, *The Lost World of Scripture: Ancient Literary Culture and Biblical Authority* (Downers Grove, IL: IVP Academic, 2013), e.g., 60-65, 70-73.

[16]For discussion of various aspects of biblical authority, see Vincent Bacote, Laura C. Miguelez, and Dennis L. Okholm, *Evangelicals and Scripture: Tradition, Authority, and Hermeneutics* (Downers Grove, IL: IVP Academic, 2004); and Walton and Sandy, *The Lost World of Scripture.*

[17]See the collections of essays in Axel Graupner and Michael Wolter, eds., *Moses in Biblical and Extra-Biblical Traditions*, Beihefte zur Zeitschrift fur die alttestamentliche Wissenschafte 372 (Berlin: de Gruyter, 2007).

throughout the 176 verses of the psalm, remarkably nothing is mentioned about Moses, nor about written forms of the divine declarations. God's law had been orally revealed, and hundreds of years later it was still being understood and passed along orally.

Though Moses was referred to only a few times by the prophets, the similarities between him and them are noteworthy, especially since Moses was a prophet as well: "No prophet ever again arose in Israel like Moses" (Deut 34:10 NET). He was the paradigmatic spokesperson for God.

Even though the New Testament is separated from the Old Testament by a dark period in the history of Israel, Moses' reputation remained unaltered.[18] His name is cited more than eighty times in the twenty-seven books of the New Testament, which is more often than he was mentioned in thirty-three of the books of the Old Testament, from Judges to Malachi.

As recipient and agent of oral communication—plus as authority figure for what was written in the law—Moses' dual role was affirmed repeatedly.

- Jesus credits Moses with communicating the commands of God (Mk 7:8-10).

- Jesus said regarding himself, *Everything written about me in the law of Moses, in the prophets, and in the psalms must be fulfilled* (Lk 24:44); and *If you believed Moses, you would believe me, since he wrote about me* (Jn 5:46).

- The Pharisees said, *We know God spoke to Moses* (Jn 9:29).

- Paul explained, "I am saying nothing beyond what the prophets and Moses said would happen" (Acts 26:22 NIV).[19]

---

[18]See, e.g., John Lierman, *The New Testament Moses: Christian Perceptions of Moses and Israel in the Setting of Jewish Religion*, Wissenschaftliche Untersuchungen zum Neuen Testament 2. Reihe (Tübingen: Mohr Siebeck, 2004).

[19]See also Mk 7:10; 12:26; Jn 1:45; Acts 3:22; Rom 10:5, 19; 1 Cor 9:9; Heb 7:14. Just as frequently, Moses was referenced without indication of oral or written communication: Mt 8:4; 19:7-8; Mk 1:44; 10:3-4; Lk 5:14; Jn 7:22; Acts 6:14.

Also, though the law was clearly from God, it was commonly identified as the law of Moses, as recorded in the Gospels and Acts and as stated by the apostle Paul.[20]

Moses' name could refer to more than just him as a person. What he said and what he wrote became intrinsically part of his identity: "Moses has been preached in every city" (Acts 15:21 NIV); "Whenever Moses is read, a veil covers their heart" (2 Cor 3:15 NIV; see also Lk 24:27; 16:29, 31; Acts 21:21).

Regarding the relationship between Moses and Jesus, Jesus clearly affirmed Moses' authorization as God's spokesperson. But Jesus was God's accredited representative as well. Hence, Jesus would say, as repeatedly stated in the Sermon on the Mount, "You have heard that it was said to those of old . . . But I say to you . . ." (e.g., Mt 5:21 ESV). It was an implicit acknowledgment of Jesus' privilege, as deity, to take what Moses said to another level.[21] But that must not hide the point that Jesus was following in the pattern established by God through Moses. In a sense, he was the new Moses.[22]

All of this confirms Moses' role as the supernaturally authorized representative of God. When he spoke, it was as if God were speaking. When Moses wrote, it was as if God had written.

MOSES IN THE DEAD SEA SCROLLS

The Dead Sea Scrolls agree with the significance of Moses' role as God's lawgiver but reveal an orality that's unexpected. The scrolls were discovered in 1946–1947, with additional ones coming to light in years since.[23] Stored in caves near the Dead Sea, they comprise more than

---

[20]See Lk 2:22; 24:44; Jn 7:23; Acts 13:39; 15:5; 28:23; 1 Cor 9:9.

[21]"In the NT the teachings of Moses were recontextualized within the teachings of Jesus. . . . For the early Christians, Jesus superseded Moses as the primary authoritative revealer, and Jesus' reinterpretation of Moses became Scripture"; Dorothy M. Peters, "Dead Sea Scrolls," in *Dictionary of Jesus and the Gospels*, 2nd ed., ed. Joel B. Green, Jeannine K. Brown, and Nicholas Perrin (Downers Grove, IL: IVP Academic, 2013), 170.

[22]It's likely that Matthew's Gospel in particular sought to show that Jesus fit the pattern of Moses; Dale C. Allison Jr., *The New Moses: A Matthean Typology* (Eugene, OR: Wipf and Stock, 2013).

[23]For the history of the Dead Sea Scrolls, see Weston W. Fields, *The Dead Sea Scrolls: A Full History*, vol. 1 (Leiden: Brill, 2009).

nine hundred scrolls, most dated to either the first century BC or first century AD, representing a wide range of genres and texts. Some of the scrolls are copies of the Old Testament Scriptures, primarily of the five books of Moses. A greater number of scrolls consist of writings related to the faith and practices of the community of Israelites living in the Dead Sea area. In either case, scholars have been carefully studying the scrolls for years, and the impact on many areas of biblical studies has been profound.[24]

Scribes made copy after copy of the documents they valued most, providing an important window into the transmission of books of the OT. In some cases, manuscripts give evidence of being copied very carefully. In others, the evidence points the opposite direction. The tedious work of copying a text letter by letter, hour by hour, meant that perfect copying was nearly impossible. Scribes inadvertently wrote the wrong word, omitted a word, inserted a word, or even skipped a line of text. They would also make intentional changes if they felt the wording in the text they were copying needed to be improved. This could be true of biblical texts, including the Pentateuch.[25] Some scribes apparently considered their duty to edit and update the material for the benefit of those who would hear the texts read.[26]

It might seem that the scribes failed to appreciate the importance of the law of Moses, failing to copy precisely the books of the Pentateuch. But not so. Moses as mediator and lawgiver was held in high regard, the towering figure in religion and literature.[27] A common formula used in

[24]For an overview of the scrolls and their significance, see, e.g., Bennie H. Reynolds III, "Dead Sea Scrolls and Other Judean Texts," in *The Dictionary of the Bible and Ancient Media* (London: T&T Clark, 2017), 74-80.

[25]Bruce K. Waltke, "How We Got the Hebrew Bible: The Text and Canon of the Old Testament," in *The Bible at Qumran: Text, Shape, and Interpretation*, ed. Peter W. Flint (Grand Rapids: Eerdmans, 2001), 38.

[26]See especially Emanuel Tov, *Textual Criticism of the Hebrew Bible*, 2nd rev. ed. (Minneapolis: Fortress, 2001).

[27]James E. Bowley, "Moses in the Dead Sea Scrolls: Living in the Shadow of God's Anointed," in Flint, ed., *The Bible at Qumran*, 159.

the Dead Sea community, "as God spoke through Moses," made it clear that Moses functioned as God's alter ego.[28] In some of the Dead Sea community's own writings, Moses was referred to as "the anointed one" and was recognized as having full authority as God's spokesperson with intimate knowledge of the divine. Scribes could even perceive "themselves as belonging to a prophetic succession beginning with Moses."[29]

Looking back on the Dead Sea community from a modern perspective, the most notable feature of the textual community is their scribal endeavors and unique efforts to generate and copy manuscripts. But for them, the primary focus, instead, was determining how best to interpret and follow the law of Moses as a community and individuals. The community was fully committed to the Ten Words to the extent that anyone who acted against the law of Moses could be expelled.[30]

Regarding orality, the scribes and their scrolls are only part of the picture. Scribes not only copied manuscripts but recorded in written form oral texts that had become established traditions in the community. There's evidence that they themselves would read to others the documents they inscribed, as well as be advocates for adhering to what the texts said. "The communities associated with the Scrolls were 'oral' communities—that is, oral performance, oral texts, oral tradition, and oral transmission played an integral role in the daily lives of all members and leaders of the sectarian movement . . . ancient Jews 'read' the written text aurally through the oral performance of the reader."[31]

Thus, the Dead Sea Scrolls are evidence of much more than groups of scribes painstakingly inscribing letters and words on parchment and papyrus. The scribal communities had a sacred commitment to the law

---

[28]Bowley, "Moses in the Dead Sea Scrolls," 169.

[29]Martti Nissinen, *Ancient Prophecy: Near Eastern, Biblical, and Greek Perspectives* (Oxford: Oxford University Press, 2017), 352.

[30]For discussion see Daniel K. Falk, "Moses," in *Encyclopedia of the Dead Sea Scrolls*, ed. Lawrence H. Schiffman and James C. Vanderkam (Oxford: Oxford University Press, 2000), 576-77.

[31]Shem Miller, *Dead Sea Media: Orality, Textuality, and Memory in the Scrolls from the Judean Desert*, Studies on the Texts of the Desert of Judah 129 (Leiden: Brill, 2019), 18, 20.

of Moses.[32] Especially noteworthy, it was an oral community with a textual focus.[33]

CONCLUSION

Moses encapsulated the foundational elements of the message from God in the Old Testament. And he became the formulative pathway of divine truth from deity to humanity. God called, authorized, and spoke. Moses heard, understood, remembered, acted responsibly, spoke, and wrote. It was divine revelation. *Hear, O Israel! The Lord our God, the Lord is one!* (Deut 6:4).

It made no difference whether the word of the Lord was spoken by God or by Moses, or inscribed on stone tablets by God, or inked on parchment under Moses' authority. It was as divinely authorized as anything could be. Thus saith the Lord. Oral or written, the words were sacrosanct, certified, and inspired.

Without Moses' steady hand of leadership, the Israelites may have remained enslaved in Egypt; the Red Sea may never have parted. Without his voice representing God's voice, the Israelites may have continued to worship the golden calf and never entered the Promised Land. Without his authority, God's laws and design for the covenant relationship and the unique customs and practices of the chosen people may have never accomplished what God intended. Moses, an imperfect human, faithfully fulfilled the mission the perfect God entrusted to him. He communicated the very thoughts and words of God. If Moses had not spoken for God, the people would not have heard from God.

We turn now to an example from the prophets, another one of God's representatives authorized to speak in his place.

---

[32]A similar thing can be said about the Rabbinic tradition: "Rabbis claimed that the traditional teachings under their guardianship originated in an oral revelation which had, ever since, been transmitted exclusively by word of mouth. The rabbis highlighted the oral aspect of their teachings by calling it 'Oral Torah'"; Elizabeth Shanks Alexander, "The Orality of Rabbinic Writing," in *The Cambridge Companion to the Talmudic and Rabbinic Literature*, ed. Charlotte Elisheva Fonrobert and Martin S. Jaffee (Cambridge: Cambridge University Press, 2007), 38.

[33]Miller, *Dead Sea Media*, 24-25.

PROPOSITION 8

GOD SPOKE DIVINE TRUTH TO AND THROUGH THE PROPHETS

Announce these words, Jeremiah, to the people of Jacob and Judah:
"Hear ye, you foolish, senseless people! You have eyes,
but do not see; ears, but do not hear."

JEREMIAH 5:20-21

ALL OF THE PROPHETS were God's spokespersons, but Jeremiah provides a particularly insightful example.[1] Like Moses, God endowed Jeremiah with supernatural authorization: "'You must go to everyone I send you to and say whatever I command you.'... Then the LORD reached out his hand and touched my mouth and said to me, 'I have put my words in your mouth'" (Jer 1:7, 9 NIV).[2]

Jeremiah had authority not only to boldly proclaim divine revelation, which was important in and of itself. But his words could be a powerful force as well, a fortress of truth: *This very day I have made you an impregnable city, an iron pillar, a bronze wall. It's you against everyone in the land of Judah: kings, officials, priests—the people too!* (Jer 1:18). Add to that, kingdoms of the world would need to be on alert: Jeremiah would be able *to root out, tear down, destroy and overthrow* (Jer 1:10).[3]

---

[1] For insightful discussion of the difference between God's "word" and the prophet's "words," see Andrew G. Shead, *A Mouth Full of Fire: The Word of God in the Words of Jeremiah* (Downers Grove, IL: IVP Academic, 2012).

[2] For God's remarkable call to Ezekiel, which included a supernatural revelation and symbolic eating, see especially Ezek 2:7–3:3.

[3] Regarding Jeremiah's call to be a prophet, see Shead, *A Mouth Full of Fire*, 119-24.

According to the Authorized Version, "Thus saith the Lord" appears 147 times in the book of Jeremiah, 126 times in Ezekiel, and 43 times in Isaiah.

Jumping ahead, after twenty-three years of faithfully preaching the word of the Lord (Jer 25:1-3), Jeremiah received some unexpected instructions: "Get a scroll. Write on it everything I have told you to say about Israel, Judah, and all the other nations since I began to speak to you in the reign of Josiah until now" (Jer 36:1-2 NET). Everything that Jeremiah had proclaimed orally he was now to inscribe in writing.

But why write it all down? God explained: "Perhaps the people of Judah will repent when they hear again all the terrible things I have planned for them. Then I will be able to forgive their sins and wrongdoings" (Jer 36:3 NLT). Jeremiah's preaching had clearly fallen on deaf ears, which was not unusual for prophets. The monarchy and the temple were often the prophets' targets, because of abuse of the covenant relationship. And that charge wasn't well received by the people or the leaders. It wasn't the prophets' ineptitude but the leaders' hardness of heart that led to the unending announcements of God's judgment.

Fortunately, God didn't give up easily in seeking to persuade the people to repent. As a wakeup call, he had previously sent the prophet Jonah off to Nineveh, a Gentile city, to preach the word of the Lord. The inhabitants surprised Jonah and repented, even though he was a foreigner preaching about an unfamiliar God.

The king of Nineveh announced, "Everyone must pray earnestly to God. They must turn from their evil ways and stop all their violence. Who can tell? Perhaps even yet God will change his mind and hold back his fierce anger from destroying us" (Jon 3:8-9 NLT). What an ironic turn of events: the chosen people wouldn't listen to God, but the Gentiles did! Not surprisingly, Jonah was distraught: *I am angry enough to die!* (Jon 4:9).

The point was that God would go to great ends to draw his people back to himself. And having Jeremiah provide a written version of his prophecies, which could be read aloud in Jeremiah's absence, was another example of that (Jer 36:6-7). So Jeremiah enlisted the services of a local scribe by the name of Baruch to write what the Lord had told Jeremiah over the years past.

The authority of the written version of Jeremiah's preaching was underscored by Baruch writing *all the words of the Lord spoken through Jeremiah* (Jer 36:4).[4] And as people came to Jerusalem from outlying regions for special occasions, Jeremiah told Baruch to read his written version to all the people of Judah.

But trouble was brewing. Anticipating a problem, some officials warned Jeremiah and Baruch to go into hiding, fearing what Jehoiakim, the king, might do. Sure enough, Jehoiakim wanted to have the scroll of Jeremiah's prophecies read to him. And as an official read through "three or four columns of the scroll, the king would cut them off with a penknife and throw them on the fire in the firepot. He kept doing so until the whole scroll was burned up in the fire" (Jer 36:23 NET). Astonishing! The original and only manuscript of twenty-three years of Jeremiah's proclaiming the word of the Lord was burned to ashes!

Included in Jeremiah's prophecies were announcements of God's judgment on Jerusalem, warning the people to flee the city for disaster was impending. Jeremiah had even raised the question whether the temple had become a den of robbers (Jer 7:1-11). This of course came across as subversive to the king. He had already killed another prophet, and he was now determined to destroy everything Jeremiah and Baruch had said. They were next on his hit-list (Jer 26:1-24; 36:22-26).

---

[4]It's common in English translations to use the word *dictate* for Jeremiah's telling Baruch what to write. But that may imply more than the Hebrew actually intends: *Baruch wrote down on a scroll from the mouth of Jeremiah all the words of the Lord that he had spoken to him.*

But thankfully, all was not lost. Jeremiah and Baruch were perfectly willing to repeat the process and record the words of the Lord again. Only for the second version, they added additional words, probably reinforcing and strengthening the very things the king had objected to (Jer 36:32). In other words, "Take that, Jehoiakim!" God's truth was going to prevail regardless of the king's intentions. (See Jeremiah 36–37 for more details about this drama, including Jeremiah subsequently being beaten and imprisoned.)

This extended process of the communication of the word of the Lord to and through Jeremiah is significant, both from the standpoint of God's spokespersons, and from the perspective of the hearers. God's word was spoken initially to Jeremiah; preached by Jeremiah to the people and heard by them; repeated by Jeremiah so Baruch could hear it and write it down; read aloud to the people by Baruch so they could hear it again; read aloud again by Baruch, this time so the officials could hear it; read aloud by one of the king's officials so the king could hear it; and after supplementary statements had been added to the original written version, then likely read aloud again. That's a lot of speaking aloud and hearing the word of the Lord.

After all that, we would hope the people would have gotten the message that God intended, recognized their evil ways, and repented. But it didn't happen. Consequently, what God had announced would happen, did happen: *So I brought on them every curse of the covenant, which I had commanded them to obey, but that they failed to do* (Jer 11:8; cf. Deut 28:15-68).

Comparing Jeremiah with Moses, the similarities are clear. Both were supernaturally empowered to be recipients of what God spoke, as well as authorized agents to speak on God's behalf. What God said, they said, faithfully proclaiming the word of the Lord. They both acted responsibly in accord with their commissioning.

The result initially was the oral text of divine revelation, not written but truly authorized as the word of the Lord. What they spoke was then subsequently inscribed in written form, which was equally authoritative.[5] Jeremiah had a scribe, and though not stated, it's likely one or more scribes were involved in recording what Moses spoke as well.[6] The outcome in both cases was two forms of divine revelation: the *oral* word of the Lord and the *written* word of the Lord.

Of course, in Jeremiah's case there was an oral form plus two written forms, the first what Jeremiah had proclaimed across twenty-three years of preaching, and the second an expanded version of the first. Jeremiah's spoken communication could be faithfully recorded in written form in more than one version.

Examining the Hebrew text of the book of Jeremiah today, scholars find evidence of oral features as well as indications that the book was a compilation of shorter collections of Jeremiah's prophecies.[7] Near the end of Jeremiah we read, *The words of the Lord via Jeremiah end here* (Jer 51:64). Thus a later hand, whether Baruch or another compiler, had a role in the final shaping of the book. Additionally, the translation of the Hebrew text of Jeremiah into Greek reflects a textual source significantly shorter than the Hebrew text, and maybe earlier.[8] These hints about how the book of Jeremiah came into existence are not surprising given what happened when Jehoiakim burned the first written copy of Jeremiah's prophecies and Baruch produced a second version.

CONCLUSION

Moses and Jeremiah are significant examples of oral revelation in the Old Testament. But there are others. "The three most common forms of literature in the Old Testament: prophetic oracles, narratives, and

---

[5]"Ancient Prophecy was not basically scribal but oral activity, and the scribal processes that led to written records of prophecy were always a secondary development with regard to the spoken 'original' prophecies." Martti Nissinen, *Ancient Prophecy: Near Eastern, Biblical, and Greek Perspectives*, (Oxford: Oxford University Press, 2017), 52.

[6]See John H. Walton and D. Brent Sandy, *The Lost World of Scripture: Ancient Literary Culture and Biblical Authority* (Downers Grove, IL: IVP Academic, 2013), 60-61.

[7]See, e.g., J. A. Thompson, *The Book of Jeremiah* (Grand Rapids, MI: Eerdmans, 1980), 27-49, 56-59.

[8]Emanuel Tov, *Textual Criticism of the Hebrew Bible*, 3rd ed. (Minneapolis: Fortress, 2012), 137.

wisdom sayings (whether legal as in the Torah or general, as in Proverbs) all comport well with oral forms and reflect oral characteristics."[9]

Against the grain of our textual paradigm, the living God chose—as his fundamental means of communication to humanity—living voices from within humanity. He revealed himself to them, empowered them, and supernaturally authorized them to speak for him. It was an amazing privilege and responsibility. The God of the universe was/is a speaking God, yet rather than speak by some means so that all could hear his voice, he granted select humans the right to speak divine truth voiced as he did and authoritative as his was.[10] Incredible!

All of this suggests that we may need to reconsider the assumption that the inscribed form of God's revelation was more authoritative than the orally proclaimed form of God's word. The evidence suggests that the written version came second and achieved its authority from the authoritative spokespersons responsible for the oral form.[11] The oral words of the living representatives, faithfully speaking on behalf of the living God, *are* the word of the Lord. God spoke; Jeremiah spoke; Baruch wrote; it was all the same.

> *The oral words of the living representatives, faithfully speaking on behalf of the living God, are the word of the Lord. God spoke; Jeremiah spoke; Baruch wrote; it was all the same.*

---

[9] John H. Walton, "No Books, No Authors: Literary Production in a Hearing-Dominant Culture," in *Write That They May Read: Studies in Literacy and Textualization in the Ancient Near East and in the Hebrew Scriptures: Essays in Honour of Professor Alan R. Millard*, ed. Daniel I. Block, David C. Deuel, C. John Collins, Paul J. N. Lawrence (Eugene, OR: Pickwick, 2020), 268.

[10] See the classic by Francis Schaeffer, *He Is There and He Is Not Silent*, rev. ed. (Wheaton: Tyndale, 2001).

[11] "The burden of proof would be on those who would contend that a written text must have, or even would have preceded an oral text, since the latter is the default in a hearing-dominant culture." John H. Walton, "No Books, No Authors: Literary Production in a Hearing-Dominant Culture," in Block et al., *Write That They May Read*, 267.

When God told Moses that he could speak to his brother and put the words of God in Aaron's mouth, he seems to have established a precedent that others could be qualified to be God's spokespersons as well. The prophets are prime examples. Like Moses, Jeremiah proclaimed the word of the Lord, and his sermons subsequently became the basis of the written form of "thus saith the Lord."

Next, we turn to the Christian community and the account of the life of Jesus. We will explore ways that the Old Testament pattern for the communication of divine truth continued.

PROPOSITION 9

GOD SPOKE DIVINE TRUTH TO
AND THROUGH JESUS

I don't do anything on my own;
the things I speak are just what the Father taught me.

LUKE 8:8

IN THE UPPER ROOM, on the eve of Jesus' crucifixion, Philip, one of the disciples, ventured to put Jesus on the spot: *Okay, show us the Father, and we'll be satisfied* (Jn 14:8). The disciples, Jewish to the core, were in a quandary over Jesus' claim, *No one can come to the Father except through me* (Jn 14:6).

Jesus replied, evidently with a measure of impatience: *I have been with all of you such a long time, and you still don't know me, Philip? The one who has seen me, has already seen the Father. So how dare you say, 'Show us the Father?' Don't you believe that I am in the Father and the Father is in me?* (Jn 14:8-10).

Not waiting for an answer, Jesus followed up with a point he made multiple times: *The things I've been telling you, I don't speak on my own. The Father who abides in me, he makes it happen* (Jn 14:10). Later that same evening he said, *What you hear me saying are not my words but from the Father who sent me* (Jn 14:24); and just before Judas betrayed him, he prayed to the Father, *what you gave me to say I have given to them* (Jn 17:8). Previously Jesus had said, "I did not speak on my own, but the Father who sent me commanded me to say all that I have spoken . . . whatever I say is just what the Father has told me to say" (Jn 12:49-50 NIV).

Now the intent certainly wasn't that Jesus was incapable or unqualified to say anything on his own. Instead, this was a teaching moment. First, the function of his statements was a declaration of his oneness with the Father. As God incarnate, everything he was thinking and saying was precisely his Father's thoughts and words. One and the same.

Second, Jesus was underscoring his role in speaking both from God and for God. There are many things on this planet that people need to know that are unknowable apart from being revealed by the God of the universe. What the Son was saying was no more or no less than what the Father intends everyone to know and understand. Jesus was and is the God of the universe.

Third, Jesus' mission on earth focused on showing the world the Father, who he was and what he was like. The God of heaven was not distant, aloof, unapproachable. He was loving, understanding, down-to-earth—as demonstrated by Jesus.

The Son not only spoke divine truth, but his life actualized it. His parables, his miracles, his suffering lived out the full character of the Godhead. He was the living representative of the living God. "In Christ all the fullness of the Deity lives in bodily form" (Col 2:9 NIV). One and the same.

Fourth, by repeatedly emphasizing that his words were not his own, but the Father's, Jesus was assuring hearers of his authority. His oral statements were as wholly endorsed and endowed as anything could be because they were the words of God himself. *I do nothing on my own, but just as the Father taught me, I speak these things* (Jn 8:28).

Fifth, the third person of the Trinity was also an integral part of Jesus' life on earth:

- *Then Jesus, in the power of the Spirit, returned to Galilee . . . he began to teach in their synagogues and was praised by all. . . . He unrolled the scroll and found the place where it was written, "The Spirit of the Lord is upon me, because he has anointed me to proclaim good news to the poor."* (Lk 4:14, 17-18)

- *The one whom God has sent speaks the words of God, for he does not give the Spirit with limitations.* (Jn 3:34)

- *The Spirit is the one who gives life . . . The words that I have spoken to you are spirit and are life.* (Jn 6:63)

As suggested above regarding Moses and Jeremiah, self-referential claims of authority have limited value. Jesus' own assertions of his authority as God's representative were helpful, but to be recognized as reliable, a supernatural authorization outside himself was essential. And Jesus met that prerequisite, from his miraculous birth, to God speaking from heaven at his baptism and transfiguration, to his victorious resurrection, plus all the miracles in between.

Statements attesting Jesus' authoritative voice are frequent in the Gospels: *This is my one dear Son, in whom I take great delight; listen to him* (Mt 17:5). John the Baptist declared, *The one whom God has sent speaks the words of God* (Jn 3:34). As Jesus taught in the temple courts, people were wondering how Jesus knew so much; to which he replied, *What I've been teaching is not mine, but from the one who sent me* (Jn 7:16). In a heated dialogue with the Pharisees, Jesus said, *The one who sent me always speaks the truth, and I tell the world what I heard from him* (Jn 8:26; cf. 8:40; 15:15).

Moses, Jeremiah, Jesus: God's agents of oral communication. Their authority, their modus operandi, were the same. What God spoke, they spoke. The sum of their spoken words created a storehouse of eternal truths, an inexhaustible treasure.

But there was one significant difference: Jesus did not write. He had important things to say, poignant stories to tell, but that was enough.

We wonder why, but we never hear. We can be sure of only four of Jesus' followers eventually writing accounts of his life. But there's no evidence that happened anytime soon after Jesus' ascension.[1]

> Jesus told a lot of stories . . . an artist when it came to telling a tale. With his artful stories, Jesus captivated many. Some laughed. Some cried. Some got angry. Some were confused. Some were challenged. Some were affirmed. Some were offended. Some were delighted. Some had their thinking changed. Some got it. Some didn't. But everyone was confronted with the artist's truth.[2]

THE GOSPELS IN ABSENTIA

For those of us immersed in modern Western textuality, it's puzzling enough that Jesus *himself* didn't encode in written form the amazing news that he came to earth to make known. But for his followers not to do it *for* him—on the spot, or at least soon afterward—is all the more mindboggling. Waiting a decade or two or three or four to preserve Jesus' presentation of divine truth in written form seems impossible, if not a case of negligence.

Maybe Jesus' hearers were convinced that they should simply do what Jesus had done and continue to proclaim the truth orally. No need to write. If Jesus didn't think a written form was necessary, why should they? He wanted them to be like him, right? The rabbis concluded, "Whatever God delivered in oral form must be preserved, taught, and studied in oral form."[3] Perhaps the early Christians thought the same.

Living in a hearing-prevalent culture, faithful followers of Jesus told people about the gospel and backed that up with transformed lives.

---

[1] Alan Millard entertains the possibility that there could have been written accounts of Jesus' words made during his lifetime, but a possibility without evidence doesn't get us very far. Alan R. Millard, *Reading and Writing in the Time of Jesus* (New York: New York University Press, 2000).

[2] Jeffrey L. Hawkins, "Jesus Christ, Superstar," *Times Union* 157 (July 5, 2023): 5A.

[3] Elizabeth Shanks Alexander, "The Orality of Rabbinic Writing," in *The Cambridge Companion to the Talmudic and Rabbinic Literature*, ed. Charlotte Elisheva Fonrobert and Martin S. Jaffee (Cambridge: Cambridge University Press, 2007), 48.

What else was necessary? Would handing someone a piece of papyrus and saying, "Here, read what this says about Jesus," really work? Maybe it's our fault for not recognizing that simply telling people the stories about Jesus makes the most sense after all.

But still. The Gospels are the opening salvo, the four-gun salute, the front-page news of the newer testament. They are the buttress for everything else in the New Testament. Without the Gospels, how could we possibly understand the gospel? But the early Christians knew the gospel even though they didn't know the Gospels.

In Jesus' day and the days of the early church, the stories about Jesus and things he said were likely told and retold so many times that the gospel was well-known and understood. It was a repository of gospel truth preserved in the hearts and minds of faithful followers. "I will put my law in their minds and write it on their hearts" (Jer 31:33 NIV). Maybe we put too much emphasis on scrutinizing the written Gospels, and not enough on embracing the imbibed gospel, sealing it deeply in hearts and minds. Maybe a catechism of the Gospels should be the core of every Christian's maturing process.

There are many matters to consider. How long was it until the Gospels were finally compiled? And how well could people remember what Jesus said and did in the meantime? And to what extent did the communities of believers recount the stories about Jesus for their own benefit and pass them along to other communities? And with the orality of divine revelation so deeply ingrained, what might that mean for how hearers in the early church understood the word of the Lord differently than we do as textual interpreters?

Appreciating the oral culture of the early Christians and all that entailed is a challenge. Thousands of pages have been written from different viewpoints on the issues involved. We will only scratch the surface, beginning with some basic chronology.[4]

---

[4]On dating events in the Gospels, see especially Harold W. Hoehner and Jeannine K. Brown, "Chronology," in *DJG*[2], 134-38.

The Missing Twenty-Five Years

Jesus was born sometime before 4 BC, based on Herod the Great dying that year, and Matthew recording that the baby Jesus and Herod were alive at the same time (Mt 2:1-16). Though we cannot pinpoint how long before Herod died Jesus might have been born, Herod decided to out-Herod himself and have all the boys in Bethlehem two years old and younger killed. If that happened maybe a year before Herod died, and if Jesus may have been one-year-old at that point, then Jesus could have been born around 6 BC.

John the Baptist began his ministry in the fifteenth year of the reign of Tiberius Caesar (Lk 3:1-2), which, as best we can tell, was AD 28–29. Sometime after that, John baptized Jesus. Doing the math, Jesus would have been about thirty-four years old when he left his home in Nazareth and went to the Jordan River to be baptized.

The best evidence for the death of Jesus points to AD 33, which, if he was born in about 6 BC, would mean he was about thirty-nine years old when he was crucified.[5] On this calculation, if there were three years between Jesus' baptism and ascension, he was likely about thirty-six years old at the start of his public ministry.

The more pressing issue, however, is how much time transpired after Jesus' resurrection before the Gospels came to light. For that, thankfully, we have the book of Acts and the rest of the books of the New Testament as evidence. Admittedly, it's an argument from silence, but the silence is significant.

The book of Acts covers the period from Jesus' ascension, just forty days after the crucifixion, until approximately AD 60. It's an important record of the early days of the church, including the celebration of Pentecost and the Holy Spirit's tongues of fire; three thousand new believers in one day; early examples of persecution by fellow Jews;

---

[5]For evidence that Jesus could have been crucified as early as AD 29 and as late as AD 34, see Helen K. Bond, "Dating the Death of Jesus: Memory and the Religious Imagination," *New Testament Studies* 59, no. 4 (2013): 461-75.

Stephen's speech to the Sanhedrin and consequent martyrdom; the church scattered throughout Judea and Samaria; Saul's Damascus Road conversion; Peter's rooftop vision of a sheet lowered to the earth full of reptiles and other animals and told to kill and eat; Paul's missionary journeys proclaiming the gospel in cities of the eastern Roman Empire; and the list goes on.

But one thing is conspicuously absent in the Acts of the Apostles: there's no reference to any form of written records of the life of Jesus. The book is all about the believers' oral witness, declaring the good news boldly everywhere they went with no indication they had or knew about a written copy of Jesus' life and words. One would think such a document would have been important to back up what they were proclaiming. But apparently not. The gospel was integral to the initial followers' witness; the Gospels were not.

Particularly, when Paul arrived in Rome and met with the leaders of the Jews (as recorded at the end of the book of Acts), he included nothing about a Gospel or written record of Jesus' life and words. He spent a long day explaining the gospel to them, "giving his account of the kingdom of God, trying to convince them about Jesus from the Law of Moses and the Prophets' writings" (Acts 28:23 Voice). But regarding anything in writing about Jesus, nothing.

There's a pertinent reference by the author of 2 Peter to what Paul had written in his letters: "Our dearly loved brother Paul, according to the wisdom given him, has written about this. He says *essentially* the same in all of his letters, although uneducated and unstable readers misinterpret the difficult passages, just as they always misread Scripture, to their *spiritual* ruin" (2 Pet 3:15-16 Voice, emphasis original). Thus, for one written document to refer to another document was not out of the question.

But there's no mention in any of Paul's letters, nor in those of James, Peter, John, and Jude (twenty letters in all, plus Hebrews), nor even in the book of Revelation, of a written record pertaining to Jesus. Yet there were occasions when such a reference would seem to have fit perfectly, for example, in the instructions Paul gave his protégé Timothy—likely writing sometime after AD 62—about handling the word of truth accurately (2 Tim 2:15).[6] But total silence about a Gospel.

For us, the Gospels are the necessary foundation for understanding the gospel, but we're surprised that the word *gospel* never appears anywhere in the New Testament in reference to one of the Gospels. It's not that the gospel wasn't important. It's written versions of the gospel that weren't, at least yet. The silence in Acts and the rest of the New Testament suggests no one had compiled a Gospel by the early 60s.

There is one more potential piece of evidence to consider. Statements in Paul's letters could have been tied to accounts in the Gospels. For instance, in writing to Timothy, Paul quoted an apparent proverbial statement, *A worker deserves to be paid* (1 Tim 5:18). Unexpectedly, that statement matches word-for-word what Luke records Jesus saying (Lk 10:7; cf. Mt 10:10).[7]

The options are, Paul was intentionally quoting Jesus, or Jesus and Paul simply quoted the same proverb. If we conclude that Paul was quoting Jesus, there are two possibilities. In oral cultures, oral accounts can achieve a standardization similar to written forms, which we refer to as "oral texts." In other words, Paul may have known that Jesus used the maxim based on the oral text being passed along in the frequent retellings of stories about Jesus. The other possibility is that Luke's Gospel was in Paul's possession, and he quoted from the written account of Jesus' words.

There's no way to know which is correct. We certainly cannot use this as evidence one way or another whether Luke's Gospel was available to Paul when he wrote to Timothy. Most scholars are inclined to date Luke's Gospel later anyway.[8]

---

[6]The Greek word *logos* almost always referred to spoken words, not written; see John H. Walton and D. Brent Sandy, *The Lost World of Scripture: Ancient Literary Culture and Biblical Authority* (Downers Grove, IL: IVP Academic, 2013), 122-27.

[7]For another passage in Paul's letters with similarity to the Gospel accounts, compare 1 Cor 11:23-26 and Lk 22:19-20.

[8]In the opinion of most scholars, Luke likely compiled his Gospel after AD 70; N. T. Wright and Michael F. Bird, *The New Testament in Its World: An Introduction to the History, Literature, and Theology of the First Christians* (Grand Rapids, MI: Zondervan, 2019), 612.

Other evidence for when the Gospels were written is internal, especially clues in relation to the destruction of Jerusalem by the Romans in AD 70. But these hints are not very convincing. The general thinking among scholars has been that the Gospel of Mark was the first written account of Jesus' life, possibly compiled in the '60s, Matthew second and Luke third, with John's Gospel the latest, perhaps as late as the end of the first century. But the most recent research on dating the Gospels argues for them being written earlier than most scholars have traditionally thought.[9]

In any event, if Jesus' crucifixion, resurrection, and ascension were in the early 30s and the first Gospel wasn't compiled until the 50s or even 60s, the gap between when Jesus spoke and the first written record of his words would still have been sizable. Twenty or thirty years can be a long time. But maybe that's not a problem. As we'll see in the next proposition, oral transmission was God's design in order for the good news to travel far and wide.

HEARING LUKE'S PROLOGUE

The most helpful information in the Gospels about their composition and transmission is what Luke included in his preface (Lk 1:1-4). The primary point was to certify that his Gospel, though he doesn't call it that, was accurate and in line with the reports about Jesus already in circulation.[10] Most people today read the prologue from a textual perspective. But hearing it from an oral framework clarifies what Luke intended to communicate.

Luke made the following things clear:

- various accounts of Jesus' deeds preceded the text he was writing;

- eyewitnesses and others were involved in the transmission process;

---

[9]For early dating of the Gospels, see Jonathan Bernier, *Rethinking the Dates of the New Testament: The Evidence for Early Composition* (Grand Rapids, MI: Baker Academic, 2022).

[10]Such statements of reliability were common in Greek and Roman historical writings; for example, Thucydides, *History of the Peloponnesian War* 1.20-22; for comparisons between Luke's prologue and other ancient prologues, see Wright and Bird, *The New Testament in Its World*, 618-19.

- what had been passed along was reliable information;

- his text was based on previous reports and on his own careful investigation;

- his text was not intended to replace previous accounts;

- the writing was of his own initiative; and

- the goal was to compose a version that would confirm what Theophilus had previously heard.

Luke emphasized the trustworthiness of what he wrote in two primary ways. Though he had no firsthand knowledge of Jesus, he based his Gospel on what had been passed down, both by the earliest eyewitnesses and by others who reported what Jesus had done. And he undertook his own investigation to make sure that what he was going to include in his account would be accurate.

Many modern scholars have analyzed Luke's prologue, with most assuming that the mention of accounts preceding Luke's Gospel referred to earlier written sources.[11] But is that adequately supported?[12] Two principal reasons have led scholars to that idea.

The assumption is that Luke based his Gospel on previously written accounts, particularly Mark's Gospel and another source.[13] Although that's currently the most popular theory for the writing of the Gospels, some scholars are not convinced.[14] Nevertheless, the theory influences

---

[11] For example, Joel B. Green, "The Problem of a Beginning: Israel's Scriptures in Luke 1-2," *Bulletin for Biblical Research* 4 (1994): 61-85; David Moessner, "The Triadic Synergy of Hellenistic Poetics in the Narrative Epistemology of Dionysius of Halicarnassus and the Authorial Intent of the Evangelist Luke" (Luke 1:1-4 Acts 1:1-8)," *Neotestamenica* 42 (2008): 289-303; Darrell L. Bock, "Understanding Luke's Task: Carefully Building on Precedent (Luke 1:1-4)," *Criswell Theological Review* 5 (1991): 183-202; Robert H. Stein, "Luke 1:1-4 and Traditiongeschichte," *JETS* 26 (1983): 421-30; Merrill C. Tenney, "Historical Verities in the Gospel of Luke," *Bibliotheca Sacra* 135 (1978): 126-38.

[12] "It is by no means certain that the work of others in 'compiling an account' . . . refers to written narratives"; John D. Harvey, "Orality and Its Implications for Biblical Studies: Recapturing and Ancient Paradigm," *JETS* 45 (2002): 107.

[13] For discussion, see Stanley E. Porter and Bryan R. Dyer, eds., *The Synoptic Problem: Four Views* (Grand Rapids, MI: Baker Academic, 2016).

[14] For example, William R. Farmer, "The Case for the Two-Gospel Hypothesis," in *Rethinking the Synoptic Problem*, ed. David Alan Black and David R. Beck (Grand Rapids, MI: Baker Academic, 2001), 97-135; see also Eric Eve, *Relating the Gospels: Memory, Imitation, and the Farrer Hypothesis*, Library of New Testament Studies (London: T&T Clark, 2022).

the understanding of the prologue with the result that the previous reports Luke mentioned are generally assumed to be written. But that's not at all certain.

Another reason many presume Luke was referring to written precedents is two words he used, which are often misunderstood. Twice the Greek word *logos* appears in the prologue, which is taken by many to refer to written words. But throughout the New Testament, ninety-nine times out of a hundred *logos* denotes words spoken, not written.[15] For example, *the crowd was pressing around Jesus to hear the* logos *of God* (Lk 5:1).[16] So when Luke referred to servants of the word and to what Theophilus had been taught, it's just as likely, if not more so, that he had oral reports in mind.

Another word is an even more serious misunderstanding. If the etymology of a word determines its meaning, then the Greek word translated "to undertake" or "to endeavor" (*epecheirēsan*) can actually denote "to put a hand to something," in other words, "to write something."[17] But etymologies can often result in exegetical fallacies: "All of this is linguistic nonsense."[18] Consider the word in English, *pineapple*; does what we denote by the word have anything to do with pine or apple?

Actually, this is old news, emphasized over sixty years ago.[19] Tracing a word back to its roots to determine its meaning should have been obliterated from the consciousness of all students of Scripture long ago. Unfortunately, many interpreters and teachers/preachers

---

[15]"'Word' (*logos*) here means the message of the Gospel, especially as embodied in the words and deeds of Jesus"; Walter L. Liefeld, *Luke*, Expositor's Bible Commentary (Grand Rapids, MI: Zondervan, 1984), 822.

[16]For additional examples and discussion, see Walton and Sandy, *Lost World of Scripture*, 121-27.

[17]The Authorized Version has "Forasmuch as many have taken in hand."

[18]Carson is responding to a variety of etymologies purportedly defining the meaning of words; D. A. Carson, *Exegetical Fallacies*, 2nd ed. (Grand Rapids, MI: Baker Books, 1996), 28; see also Richard L. Schultz, *Out of Context: How to Avoid Misinterpreting the Bible* (Grand Rapids, MI: Baker Books, 2012), 63-65.

[19]James Barr, *The Semantics of Biblical Language* (Oxford: Oxford University Press, 1961), 107-60; and more recently, Peter Cotterell and Max Turner, *Linguistics and Biblical Interpretation* (Downers Grove, IL: IVP Academic, 1989), 113-15, 132-33.

continue to fall into the etymological fault line, and Luke's prologue is a prime example.[20] The New Living Translation, for example, disseminates this exegetical fallacy widely: "Many people have set out to write accounts" (Lk 1:1 NLT).[21]

But for the original hearers, it's unlikely they would have stumbled over the wording in Luke's prologue. For them, the word *logos* would not have suggested something written. And it's unlikely an etymology of a word would have influenced their understanding of the word's meaning.

It's hard to imagine that early Christians hearing Luke's Gospel being read aloud would have thought he was referring to written accounts in circulation. Unless they knew of written precedents, and there's no evidence there were any, their natural thinking would have been that Luke was referring to oral reports that had faithfully been passed along by eyewitnesses and other reliable sources.[22]

They also would have recognized that when Luke said, *It seemed right also for me to compile a proper account*, that he was not seeking to upstage or replace the previous accounts.[23] Since he was not an eyewitness himself, and since he was engaged in an endeavor on behalf of Theophilus, he set out to review everything he had heard so that he could compose a fully accurate account of the life of Jesus. There's no

---

[20]I find Bock's explanation confusing: he says that "'Setting the hand' to tell a story might well suggest written accounts here, except that other terms in the context suggest organized oral reports. So Luke's remark suggests the presence of written materials, but need not be limited to such sources"; *Luke 1:1–9:50*, BECNT (Grand Rapids, MI: Baker Academic, 1994), 55; note also the claim that "Luke used both written and oral sources for his Gospel." Darrell L. Bock and Benjamin I. Simpson, *Jesus According to Scripture: Restoring the Portrait from the Gospels*, 2nd ed. (Grand Rapids, MI: Baker Academic, 2017), 14.

[21]There's a third word at issue, translated "to draw up," which only appears here in the Bible and is uncommon in literature outside Scripture. The range of meaning includes "to draw up, organize, arrange, put together, set in order, compile, rehearse." But there's no known use of the word in the context of writing a document. Thus, it cannot be used as evidence that Luke was dependent on written precedents in compiling his Gospel.

[22]Craig S. Keener, *Christobiography: Memory, History, and the Reliability of the Gospels* (Grand Rapids, MI: Eerdmans, 2019), 229.

[23]Luke saying *also me* (*kamoi*) indicates that he was not seeking to replace the good work of his predecessors; "Luke joins himself to those others who have catalogued Jesus' life. They drew from the apostolic tradition for these accounts. . . . Any interpretation that Luke is contrasting himself to his predecessors does not honor the presence of *kai*." Bock, *Luke 1:1–9:50*, 59.

indication that Luke was suggesting that by creating his written account it was time for oral transmission to stop.

If this understanding of Luke's prologue is correct, then it confirms what we find elsewhere in the New Testament. The oral gospel was the predominant means, and likely the only means, the truth about Jesus was being passed along for at least the first couple of decades after Pentecost. The Gospels were indeed in absentia. The orality of the gospel continued well beyond Jesus' time on earth.

CONCLUSION

Though there's no evidence the Gospels were compiled soon after Jesus' public ministry ended, eventually they were encoded in written form. At that point the gospel became the Gospels. And then the Gospels were the gospel.

We can be sure of this: Jesus' role in God's plan was to be the living expression of divine truth. The impact of his life and spoken words on hearers was profound, greater than any written expression could ever be. Jesus didn't compose a text. He spoke the text. He embodied the text.

Jesus didn't compose a text. He spoke the text. He embodied the text.

JESUS EMPOWERED HIS FOLLOWERS TO PROCLAIM THE GOSPEL AS HE DID

Father, the words to speak, which you gave me,
I have given them to pass on.

JOHN 17:8

IT'S REMARKABLE HOW MUCH CONFIDENCE the early church had in sharing the good news in oral form, with no thought, apparently—at least for a couple of decades—of compiling written forms. It was simply a matter of following Jesus' example, obeying what he said, and being filled with the Spirit. The good news was being disseminated widely without anything in writing.

What Jesus had said and done—including healing the blind and lepers, raising a ruler's daughter and a widow's son back to life, exorcising demons—led to news about him popping up everywhere:

- *What he said was reported all over Syria.* (Mt 4:24)
- *The news of what he had done spread throughout that whole region.* (Mt 9:26; cf. 9:31)
- *What he said was reported quickly and widely throughout the whole region around Galilee.* (Mk 1:28; cf. Mk 1:45; Lk 4:14, 37)
- "The report of his power spread even faster." (Lk 5:15 NLT)

- "And the news about Jesus spread throughout Judea and the surrounding countryside." (Lk 7:17 NLT)

Jesus followers were in awe. But they weren't prepared for his parting words minutes before disappearing into the clouds: *You shall be my messengers* (Acts 1:8; cf. Lk 24:48). Suddenly it was on their shoulders. But how? And why?

Shocked and certainly disheartened at Jesus' departure, they ambled back down from the Mount of Olives and across the valley into Jerusalem. They probably wondered how long Jesus would be gone this time. Three days while he was in the tomb was long enough. Maybe this time it would be a few days too. Or at most a week or two, hopefully.

Too bad the angels didn't give a hint how soon he'd come back; only that he would return the same way he departed. Certainly, his followers had no idea it could be as long as a year, a decade, a century, or a couple millennia! Why? We can imagine some reasons, but all we can really say is, "Even so come, Lord Jesus!"

Regarding being suddenly appointed as Jesus' messengers, if the disciples had given much thought to it, they would have recognized that Jesus had already nudged them toward this calling. Early in his ministry he sent the Twelve on mission telling them to announce the same thing he had been announcing: *Proclaim this message: 'The kingdom of heaven has come near'. . . actually it won't be you speaking, but the Spirit of your Father will speak through you* (Mt 10:7, 20; cf. Mk 13:11).

Toward the end of his ministry Jesus declared, *The good news about the kingdom, a message for all nations, will be proclaimed all around the world* (Mt 24:14). The last thing he did—before being betrayed by Judas—was to pray for his followers: *Father, the words, which you gave me to speak, I have given to them to pass on. . . just as you commissioned me to go into the world I have commissioned them* (Jn 17:8, 18). Jesus had two compelling commands for his followers: hear and tell. The divine mandate was clear.

In praying for the second and subsequent generations of believers, Jesus referred to the disciples' oral role: *I am praying not only for these, but also for the ones who will believe in me through their spoken words* (Jn 17:20). And after his resurrection, according to Luke's account, Jesus told the Eleven that in his name the repentance and forgiveness of sins would be proclaimed to all nations (Lk 24:47).

Matthew concludes his Gospel with a similar authorization, recording Jesus' charge to the apostles. They were to disciple people of all nations, *teaching them to obey everything that I commanded* (Mt 28:20). The verbs *to disciple* and *to teach* are consistently used in the New Testament for oral communication. His hearers probably didn't give second thought to what Jesus had in mind for them. The way he communicated was the way they were supposed to.

Jesus' short-term public ministry was deliberate. Ignite a fire, and let it start a conflagration. It would be up to his followers to pick up where he left off and fan the flames. His ascension wasn't an act of bailing out; it was an empowerment: *Whoever believes in me can do what I've been doing, even better!* (Jn 14:12). And Jesus' initial followers did the only thing they knew to do: proclaim the gospel orally as he had.

If Jesus' followers hadn't told people what they had observed about Jesus, if they hadn't passed along the good news about his life and words, the impact of his earthly ministry could have been little more than a waft of smoke. Jesus' ascension would have been the cessation of salvation for a lost world, the hot embers dying out.

Talk about a responsibility! Jesus' full dependence on his followers that they would be his messengers could seem to be going out on a thin limb. Fortunately, waiting in the wings was the help they would need. Supernatural assistance would come upon them, guiding their role as messengers of the divine truths revealed in the life of Jesus (Jn 16:15).

Jesus had anticipated this very moment: the Holy Spirit will *be with you forever—the Spirit of truth* (Jn 14:16-17); *he will teach you everything, and will cause you to remember everything I spoke* (Jn 14:26); *the*

Spirit whom I will send from the Father—the Spirit of truth who goes out from the Father—he will speak about me (Jn 15:26-27); *he will guide you into all truth* (Jn 16:13). The sudden arrival of the Holy Spirit changed everything (Acts 2:1-41).

MESSENGERS NOT WITNESSES

Admittedly, Jesus' challenge to his followers to be his messengers is generally translated "to be witnesses" (Acts 1:8). But "witness" in English has taken on a connotation beyond Jesus' original intent.[1] The Greek word in question (*martyreō*) has a wide range of meaning: "to speak about something, telling what you know, what you observed, what you heard; to testify, to witness to the accuracy of something."[2]

As is often true, translators have a choice to make. What best fits the context? What did Jesus say elsewhere that might inform what he meant here? (Reading through the Gospels reveals much of Jesus' strategy as God's spokesperson and his vision for others to take up the mantle of oral communication.)

Being a witness has become common Christian lingo for trying to persuade people to become believers, sometimes including hellfire and brimstone, altar calls down the sawdust trail, dragging people into the kingdom. But is that consistent with what Jesus repeatedly asked of his followers? If our calling is to be messengers instead, that is, spokespersons, primarily telling the stories of and about Jesus, anyone can do that, and should.

Maybe it's appropriate to leave witnessing to gifted evangelists (Eph 4:11). "Since the majority of evangelistic activities in the United States for the past fifty years (at least) have focused on sudden

---

[1] For translations of Acts 1:8 that more accurately convey Jesus' intent, see the New Life Version, "You will tell about Me"; the World English Version, "You will speak of me"; the Easy-to-Read Version, "You will be my witnesses. You will tell people everywhere about me"; the New Living Translation, "You will be my witnesses, telling people about me everywhere."

[2] A *martys* "is called upon to tell what he has seen and heard, to proclaim what he knows." Ceslas Spicq, *Theological Lexicon of the New Testament*, 3 vols., trans. and ed. James D. Ernest (Wheaton: Tyndale, 1994), 2:448.

conversion (and methods that arise from this viewpoint), the challenge
to the church is to develop more holistic ways of outreach that take into
account the fact that the majority of people come to faith slowly,
not suddenly."[3]

Jesus had evidently been preparing his followers to be his messengers
all along:

- *Very truly I tell you, whoever believes in me can do what I've been doing, even better, since I am going to the Father.* (Jn 14:12)

- *Everything I heard from my Father I have revealed to you.* (Jn 15:15)

- "As the Father has sent me, I am sending you." (Jn 20:21 NIV)

That's a greater responsibility than most of us feel confident undertaking. Can we really have access to everything Jesus knew and understood? Can we do things even greater than he did? Maybe the function
of those statements is to energize us to take on the challenge he's calling
us to.

The apostle Paul is a good example of fulfilling Jesus' calling. Even before
writing letters, he was a messenger speaking with divine authority:

- "I proclaimed to you the testimony about God . . . my message and my preaching were not with wise and persuasive words, but with a demonstration of the Spirit's power." (1 Cor 2:1, 4 NIV)

- "We speak, not in words taught us by human wisdom but in words taught by the Spirit." (1 Cor 2:13 NIV)

- *The gospel I preached . . . I received by revelation from Jesus Christ.* (Gal 1:11-12)

- "When you received [God's] message from us . . . you accepted what we said as the very word of God—which, of course, it is." (1 Thess 2:13 NLT)

---

[3]Richard V. Peace, *Conversion in the New Testament: Paul and the Twelve* (Grand Rapids, MI: Eerd-mans, 1999), 286.

- "You know what instructions we gave you by the authority of the Lord Jesus." (1 Thess 4:2 NIV)[4]

The authority of Paul's spoken words is probably unexpected. But as far as he was concerned, what he proclaimed orally was fully inspired and authoritative. Interestingly, he did not make the same claim for what he wrote in his letters. But being derivative of what he taught and preached, it's a legitimate deduction that the written versions were equally authoritative.[5]

Paul, like Moses, Jeremiah, and Jesus, had been supernaturally authorized as God's messenger. His experience on the road to Damascus with a voice from heaven speaking to him, who was Jesus himself—as witnessed by his companions—confirmed that (Acts 9:3-7; 22:6-9; 26:12-16). His authority as apostle was undeniable.

But was there supernatural authorization for other Christ-followers? Yes, on Pentecost, when the filling of the Holy Spirit—accompanied by supernatural wind and fire—catapulted the disciples into the limelight. They were suddenly communicating in many foreign languages, *speaking the wonders of God* (Acts 2:11). God-fearing Jews from every nation under heaven were present to witness the event (Acts 2:5-13), providing corroboration of the miracle that occurred. Peter's sermon on that day was only the beginning of the disciples powerfully speaking of God and for God.

Multiple Stages of Messaging

Many people were privileged to hear Jesus in person: twelve disciples, seventy-two others whom Jesus sent on a mission (Lk 10:1), plus Pharisees and Sadducees, crowds, Gentiles, and so forth. Most of these almost certainly told others about their experiences listening to this unique person speaking with unusual authority.

---

[4]See also Acts 20:27; Cor 2:17; 5:20; 13:3, 10; Gal 1:10-11; 1 Thess 4:2; Tit 1:3.
[5]For fuller discussion, see John H. Walton and D. Brent Sandy, *The Lost World of Scripture: Ancient Literary Culture and Biblical Authority* (Downers Grove, IL: IVP Academic, 2013), 158-62.

Over time, many came to true faith in the person and work of Jesus and recognized the importance of proclaiming what they had heard and experienced in Jesus' presence. Like Andrew telling his brother Peter, *We have found the Messiah!* (Jn 1:41), the eyewitnesses as faithful hearers, were involved in oral transmission of the good news, passing it along far and wide.

(Unfortunately, there's not a convenient word in English to designate people that pass along oral information. "Informer, reporter, courier" have the wrong connotation. Maybe "oral communicator" or "messenger" is most appropriate, unless we use "tradent"—associated with the word "tradition"—which is what scholars typically use.)

On the heels of the eyewitnesses, people like Luke and Paul came along, and they learned about Jesus from the eyewitnesses. As noted above, Paul in particular had a divine encounter on the Damascus Road, and he subsequently referred to his privilege to have seen Jesus in person (1 Cor 9:1; 15:8). Not long after his conversion Paul went to Jerusalem and stayed with the disciples, enabling him to gain insight into the life of Jesus. It was foundational for his passing along the gospel to many people in many places in the years ahead.

In Acts we find messengers telling ever larger audiences across the eastern Roman Empire about the gospel. Messaging became more than person-to-person communication but involved community reenactments of stories about Jesus, which became a primary means for the oral transmission of divine revelation. There were likely hundreds of communities in which the stories were recounted over and over again.

An example is the occasion when Paul was speaking about the gospel in a crowded room late into the night, and a young man sitting on a windowsill nodded off and fell three stories to his death. Thankfully, Paul went down and was able to revive the youth, and then returned to the room upstairs and continued talking until daylight the next day (Acts 20:7-12).

At an early stage of messaging, oral translators became necessary. It was not translating written documents, but a messenger who was bilingual giving an account in another language. Even within Palestine, multiple languages were spoken, and beyond the borders more people would have benefited by hearing the gospel in their native tongues. On the day of Pentecost, the gospel was proclaimed in many languages (Acts 2:6-12).

With messengers repeatedly telling stories about Jesus, the accounts gradually moved toward achieving a level of standardization, resulting in oral texts.[6] An oral account, which had been recounted often enough, could take on a textual quality. The essence of the story, characters, terminology, and quotations became fixed, though not necessarily details impertinent to the point of the story. It would have been inexcusable for a messenger to alter an established portion of an account, though some leeway with minor matters was likely unavoidable and culturally acceptable.[7]

We might also imagine that oral texts could reach a stage of being documented, as scribes began to record portions of oral texts in written form. Then in a further development, the accounts could be textualized into a full written composition. Finally, they could become scripturalized when recognized as an essential portion of the canon of Scripture.[8] But the full details of the transition from oral gospel to written Gospels will likely never be completely known.

Conclusion

Summing up, these deductions seem valid:

- Moses, Jeremiah, Jesus, Paul, Christ-followers: commissioned as authorized messengers, called to proclaim divine truth orally.

---

[6]Rodríguez contends that "performances of the tradition accrued a sense of stability and repetition by way of multiple performances through time . . . performances of the Jesus tradition [that] neither depended upon *script* nor left behind *transcript*." Rafael Rodríguez, *Structuring Early Christian Memory: Jesus in Tradition, Performance*, Library of New Testament Studies (London: T&T Clark, 2010), 4 (emphasis original).

[7]See the discussion in Proposition 11, "Variants were common in the oral texts of Jesus' words and deeds." Walton and Sandy, *The Lost World of Scripture*, 143-51.

[8]The progression from documentized to textualized to scripturalized is proposed by John H. Walton, "No Books, No Authors: Literary Production in a Hearing-Dominant Culture," in *Write That They May Read: Studies in Literacy and Textualization in the Ancient Near East and in the Hebrew Scriptures: Essays in Honour of Professor Alan R. Millard*, ed. Daniel I. Block, David C. Deuel, C. John Collins, Paul J. N. Lawrence (Eugene, OR: Pickwick, 2020), 265-66.

- The sum and substance of the gospel: an oral storehouse of recollections of Jesus' words and deeds, held in memory, not initially on page or book.

- Messengers speaking the gospel so that others could hear: no one writing, no one reading.

The oral gospel. Remarkable. In due time it would become the written repository we know as the Gospels. But Jesus said nothing about that, and apparently no one knew it was coming. The word *write* was not in Jesus' lexicon of instructions. The gospel simply continued to be passed along orally. In God's providence the news of the good news encoded in written form would come later.

The word write *was not in Jesus' lexicon of instructions.*

PROPOSITION 11

JESUS' FOLLOWERS FAITHFULLY REMEMBERED AND COMMUNICATED THE ORAL GOSPEL

Every day in the temple and house to house
the apostles did not stop teaching and telling
the good news about the Messiah, Jesus.

ACTS 5:42

IF JESUS' FOLLOWERS were to be good messengers, they needed to have good memories. By definition, the gospel cannot be inert and at the same time be good news. News this good calls for faithful remembering and frequent recounting. If more than a few people in the world were going to learn about the marvelous Messiah from Nazareth, Jesus' followers needed to take their responsibilities seriously.

Remembering is inherent in being human. Otherwise we'd go through life not knowing anything that happened the previous moment. We'd have to relearn to walk with every step, relearn to eat with every bite, relearn everything we know in a split second, or we wouldn't know anything, because a second later, we wouldn't know what we knew the second before! Thank God for creating us in his image, including the aptitude for remembering.

Jesus' hearers remembering what he said is precisely what Jesus counted on. He said it should happen, and it would happen.

- *Place in your ears these words.* (Lk 9:44)

- *The Holy Spirit . . . will bring to your memory all that I said to you.* (Jn 14:26)

- *Remember the things I said to you.* (Jn 15:20)

- *I have spoken these things to you in order that when the time arrives you can remember them since I told you.* (Jn 16:4)[1]

It doesn't take rocket science to realize that if people who heard Jesus failed to remember what he said and then pass on the memories, the whole experiment would have disintegrated. Surprisingly, there's no evidence Jesus had a backup plan. It was either faithful followers retaining and sharing the good news, or everybody on the planet remaining as hopeless and hapless as ever.

Surprisingly, there's no evidence Jesus had a backup plan. It was either faithful followers retaining and sharing the good news, or everybody on the planet remaining as hopeless and hapless as ever.

Thankfully, for our sake, and for goodness' sake, Jesus' followers did as he said: they remembered and repeated the news about him. As recorded in the Gospels, the disciples did their fair share: *Peter remembered what Jesus said* (Mt 26:75; Mk 14:72; Lk 22:61). *Then they remembered what he had said* (Lk 24:8). *When he was raised from the dead, the disciples remembered that Jesus had spoken about this* (Jn 2:22). *After Jesus was glorified, then they remembered* (Jn 12:16; cf. 1 Jn 1:1-3).

The book of Acts records similar statements. Peter declared before the Sanhedrin, *It's impossible for us not to tell the things we have seen and heard* (Acts 4:20); *every day in the temple and house to house the apostles*

---

[1]See also Mt 16:9; 26:13; Mk 8:18; 14:9; Lk 22:19; 24:6; Jn 18:20-21.

did not stop teaching and telling the good news about the Messiah, Jesus
(Acts 5:42). Peter, upon seeing the Holy Spirit come on all those assembled
at the house of Cornelius, commented, "I remembered what the Lord had
said" (Acts 11:16). All those living in Asia heard what the Lord had said,
both Jews and Greeks (Acts 19:10).

Jesus knew that ideas are more readily embraced and remembered
when students are more than mere listeners. Hence his teaching style
encouraged deliberating and discussing. He dialogued with his interlocutors, drawing them into unexpected subject matters, challenging
what they thought they knew, opening himself to questions, and
prompting them to wrestle with his thought-provoking ideas. Jesus'
making what he said memorable was all the more important if there
would be no written records of his life anytime soon.

Is there any doubt what made it essential to remember what Jesus
said and to tell others? It was the explosive force of the bigger-than-life
character, deity in humanity, amazing deeds, powerful words, transforming effect. Jesus was the "big bang."[2] Everything he said and did
was earthshaking: people were amazed and in awe at his teachings
(Mt 7:28-29; 9:8; Mk 1:22; 10:24, 32; Lk 4:32; 5:9), at his miracles
(Mt 4:24-25; 15:31; Mk 2:12; 7:37; Lk 5:26; Jn 2:23; 6:2, 14), and at
his exorcisms (Mt 9:33; Mk 1:27-28).

But is it reasonable to think that the memories of Jesus' followers
were reliable for as many as twenty-five years or more until written records were compiled? The importance of remembering has led to
extensive research on the capabilities of human memory.

SOCIAL GROUPS AND MEMORY

Research has confirmed that personal memory is not the same as collective memory.[3] What an individual remembers does not have the

---

[2]So Michael F. Bird, *The Gospel of the Lord: How the Early Church Wrote the Story of Jesus* (Grand Rapids, MI: Eerdmans, 2014), 3.
[3]For overview, see Alan Kirk, "Collective Memory/Social Memory," in *The Dictionary of the Bible and Ancient Media* (London: T&T Clark, 2017), 59-63; Nicholas A. Elder, "New Testament Media

same credibility as what a group remembers. A sociologist, Maurice Halbwachs, who unfortunately died in a concentration camp just before the end of World War II, advanced the study of memory theory.[4] He was particularly interested in the relationship between memories of individuals and memories of the communities of which individuals are a part. (The term is *social memory*.)

Recollection of events by one individual may not match the recollection by another individual, and over time, even those memories can become increasingly vague. But when groups of people come together and recount events of the past, their memories coalesce into agreed-upon accounts of events. The vividness of things people experience as a group increases the likelihood of accurate remembering (experiences in concentration camps are an example). Research demonstrates that corporate memory is consistently more reliable than individual recollections.

Thus, memory in an oral and collective culture, such as in the world of the Bible, is generally more reliable than in a textual and individualist culture like ours today. The act of remembering and reporting entails a plurality of memories in oral cultures. Personal memory is the starting point, but in time the social memory of the group tends to take precedence as individuals come to agreement on what they remember. "Collective memory endures and draws strength from its base in a coherent body of people."[5]

The shaping and confirming of individual memories together into group memory—as recollections of individuals come into alignment

---

Criticism," *Currents in Biblical Research* 15 (2017): 321-23; Eric Eve, *Behind the Gospels: Understanding the Oral Tradition* (London: SPCK, 2013), 108-34; for thorough discussion, see Alan Kirk and Tom Thatcher, eds., *Memory Tradition and Text: Uses of the Past in Early Christianity*, Semeia Studies (Atlanta: SBL Press, 2005); Robert K. McIver, *Memory, Jesus, and the Synoptic Gospels*, SBLRBS (Atlanta: SBL Press, 2011); Anthony Le Donne, *The Historiographical Jesus: Memory, Typology, and the Son of David* (Waco, TX: Baylor University Press, 2009); Craig S. Keener, *Christobiography: Memory, History, and the Reliability of the Gospels* (Grand Rapids, MI: Eerdmans, 2019), 365-400.
[4]For an overview of his contributions, see Nicholas A. Elder, "New Testament Media Criticism," *Currents in Biblical Research* 15 (2017): 321-22.
[5]Maurice Halbwachs, *The Collective Memory, with an Introduction by Mary Douglas* (New York: Harper, 1950), 48.

with recollections of the whole—leads to confidence in the accuracy of the memory. When a group achieves agreement, remembrances become confirmed and stable, and the collective memory becomes dominant. Any irregularities are subject to correction within the community itself.[6]

The telephone game, with one person successively passing on to another person a story, is the wrong image for collective memory.[7] We need to conceive of the "transmission of memory and tradition not as links on a chain, where if one chain breaks the whole thing goes to hell in a hand basket . . . but as a social net, with mutually reinforcing links."[8]

Recollections about Jesus transitioned "from eyewitness memories into the collective memories of groups of early followers of Jesus and from thence into the written texts of the Gospels."[9] With that understanding of memory, it is reasonable to think that the collective memories of Jesus' followers could be reliable for decades.[10]

KEEPERS OF THE SPRING?

The memory of the initial hearers, the eyewitnesses, is sometimes thought to have a higher probability of guaranteeing the accuracy of the gospel records than group memory.[11] The number of eyewitnesses

---

[6]"When a memory is shared within a group it becomes in some sense a corporate memory, since others can now rehearse the same memory in new performances, and similarly the group can also regulate and correct the factuality of any new recital by common consent"; Bird, *Gospel of the Lord*, 96.

[7]Regarding the telephone game, see Keener, *Christobiography*, 411-12.

[8]Elder, "New Testament Media Criticism," 326, referencing Alan Kirk, "Memory, Theory, and Jesus Research," *Handbook for the Study of the Historical Jesus*, ed. Tom Holmén and Stanley Porter (Leiden: Brill, 2011), 824.

[9]Eric Eve contends that the compilers of the Gospels relied primarily on their memories in composing their accounts, though not to deny their use of previously written materials; Eric Eve, *Writing the Gospels: Composition and Memory* (London: SPCK, 2016); cf. Robert K. McIver, *Memory, Jesus, and the Synoptic Gospels*, SBLRBS (Atlanta: SBL Press, 2011), 123.

[10]In addition to the previous note, see Barry Schwartz, "Christian Origins: Historical Truth and Social Memory," in *Memory, Tradition and Text: Uses of the Past in Early Christianity*, ed. Alan Kirk and Tom Thatcher, SBL Semeia Studies 52 (Atlanta: SBL Press, 2005), 43-56.

[11]This is a major contention of Richard J. Bauckham, *Jesus and the Eyewitnesses* (Grand Rapids, MI: Eerdmans, 2006); for summaries, see Eve, *Behind the Gospels*, 135-58; Bird, *Gospel of the Lord*, 48-62; Darrell L. Bock and Benjamin I. Simpson, *Jesus According to Scripture: Restoring the Portrait from the Gospels*, 2nd ed. (Grand Rapids, MI: Baker Academic, 2017), 6-28; Keener, *Christobiography*, 402-9.

and servants of the word (Lk 1:2) is unknown. But there was an entourage of close associates who regularly traveled with Jesus: in addition to the twelve disciples, Mary Magdalene, Joanna, Susanna, *and many others who were ministering to them out of their means* (Lk 8:1-3). Luke also mentioned seventy-two whom Jesus sent on a mission (Lk 10:1).

One would think that the people who had been healed of various diseases would have been especially good candidates to be faithful witnesses. If anyone should have been convinced of Jesus' deity and be eager to pass along the good news, those who had been healed should have been.[12] But there's record only of a few of the people Jesus healed becoming true followers: for example, the formerly blind Bartimaeus (Mk 10:52). Further, there's no evidence that Jesus' miracles were designed to recruit followers. After healing someone he never hinted at becoming one of his disciples.

One day Jesus responded to a plea from ten lepers, and he healed all of them (one was a Samaritan and the rest presumably Jews). But only the Samaritan was noble and gracious enough to return and express his thanks for being healed (Lk 17:11-18). On occasion Jesus did say, *Your faith has saved you* (e.g., Lk 17:19). But we have to wonder whether that was saving faith or simply faith in Jesus' ability to heal.

The bigger question is whether the eyewitnesses might have functioned as keepers of the spring. Did they possess purer memories of Jesus' life and teachings and thus function as guarantors—before the Gospels were written—so that the oral gospel stayed true to the earliest memories of Jesus? The question presumes that during the decades between Jesus and the written accounts of his years of ministry, impurities may have entered into memories of his words and deeds, and the spring water needed to be tested. If so, who would be more qualified to do that than the eyewitnesses?

---

[12]See, e.g., Eric Eve, *The Healer from Nazareth: Jesus' Miracles in Historical Context* (London: SPCK, 2009).

Eyewitnesses as gatekeepers is a thought-provoking possibility. But the question is, Were they necessary? If this were the telephone game, then yes, keepers of the spring should go from the head of the line to the end and confirm that what was said at the beginning is what made it through all the way to the end. But that misses the point of corporate memories being capable of accurately preserving oral accounts.

It's true that Luke mentioned the eyewitnesses as valid sources for the record of Jesus' life he was compiling, but not as the quality control for the preservation of it. We can conclude that the eyewitnesses likely contributed to the collective memory of groups, but there's little reason to believe that they were the ranking authorities for the authenticity of the Jesus stories.

VIRTUOUS MEMORY

The biblical account makes clear that memories of the messengers were worthy of the truths Jesus had spoken. The preservation of the oral accounts of Jesus' life were in perfectly good hands among Jesus' faithful followers for however long was necessary.[13]

On trial in the middle of the night, the high priest challenged Jesus about things he had taught. To which Jesus replied, *Why do you question me? Ask those who heard what I spoke. They certainly know what I said* (Jn 18:21). In other words, Jesus may even have said something like, "I have no doubt that my followers will remember what they heard me say." To which the high priest had no rejoinder. But one of the officers standing nearby did; he shamelessly punched Jesus in the face. (See Jn 18:22-24 for more detail.)

Later when the early Christians were accused and persecuted, there was no attempt to cast doubt on the credibility of their memories. Their

---

[13]Regarding the term *virtuous*, see Richard S. Briggs, *The Virtuous Reader: Old Testament Narrative and Interpretive Virtue*, Studies in Theological Interpretation (Grand Rapids, MI: Baker Academic, 2010). His point is that the moral formation of the reader influences the quality and effect of the reading. My point is that the moral formation of Jesus' followers—shaped by the respect they had for him and his teachings—influenced the quality and reliability of their memories.

critics assumed the trustworthiness of the believers. One time, Peter and John were taken before the Sanhedrin because of what they were claiming about Jesus. The highest religious authorities were trying to determine how to stop the rapidly spreading movement (Acts 4:13-21). But recognizing that the two Christ-followers had personally been with Jesus, the only thing they did was to command them not to continue teaching about Jesus. Trying to refute the apostles' memories apparently would have accomplished nothing. Of course, not surprisingly, the Sanhedrin's order of silence didn't stop anything anyway.

On another occasion Peter was called before the Sanhedrin—this time other apostles were with him—and the authorities once again insisted they stop speaking about Jesus (Acts 5:17-41). However, even flogging them to get the point across was of no use: *Every day, both in the temple and house to house, they did not stop teaching and declaring the news about the Messiah, Jesus* (Acts 5:42).

Similarly, as the Christian movement spread farther and wider around the Mediterranean world, energized by the evangelists' memories of Jesus, there's no suggestion anyone questioned the reliability of the memories. Though this is admittedly an argument from silence, it is noteworthy that none of the philosophers in Athens, nor a theater full of rioting Gentiles in Ephesus, nor the two Roman governors, Felix and Festus, nor king Agrippa, nor the leaders of the Jewish community in Rome, doubted Paul's recollections. Though these listeners were not persuaded by the gospel that he preached, they didn't challenge the foundational memories essential to that gospel.

The biblical record is not in doubt: the memories of Jesus' followers were not in question. It's a given: people heard Jesus, observed him, remembered him, and told others about the amazing things he said and did. Maybe the most important factor is what Jesus promised: *The Holy Spirit . . . will bring to your memory all that I said to you* (Jn 14:26). It's no wonder that the memory of the messengers was sufficient.

CONCLUSION

By now it should be self-evident. Despite the irony of it all—with the repository of divine truth in written form in our laps, on our desks, and installed on our devices, plus thousands of printed books about Scripture filling whole libraries—the Bible originally wasn't a book or an inscribed text.[14] It was the word of God revealed orally, remembered faithfully, proclaimed verbally. The oral dimension may seem to be tucked discreetly inside the covers of our Bibles, but the reality is, it was ever present in the communication of God's divine revelation.

By analogy, Scripture is the air we take into our souls. What we inhale into our lungs, a mix of primarily oxygen and nitrogen, we take for granted. And unless we undertake a scientific analysis, we're likely unaware that the lesser component of the air we breathe is oxygen (about 20 percent); the larger is nitrogen (close to 80 percent). Similarly, what Scripture consists of, unless we analyze it, surprises us. The lesser component is textuality; the larger is orality.

God spoke holy words at the beginning of time and will continue speaking them until the end of time. But he also depends on faithful representatives to speak holy words on his behalf in the meantime. *Otherwise, how can they believe in whom they have not heard of? And how can they hear without someone speaking to them?* (Rom 10:14).

The story we have recounted, however, is unfinished. Eventually God's oral word became the written word. That's part two of the story, but it will have to wait for another time. Now we turn to what the oft-neglected oral culture of Scripture means for our understanding and interpretation of God's oral word and God's written word.

---

[14]For example, the Lanier Theological Library in Houston, Texas: www.laniertheologicallibrary.org/.

PART THREE

IMPLICATIONS OF ORAL SCRIPTURE

PROPOSITION 12

STORIES WERE PERFORMED AND
HEARD IN ANCIENT ORAL CULTURE

Jesus always used stories and illustrations
when speaking to the crowds.

Matthew 13:34 (NLT)

If it's true that God and his agents of communication spoke divine truth intended for people to hear; that Jesus in particular spoke to be heard, not read, nor gave any indication he expected what he said to be written; that his initial followers proclaimed the gospel orally as he did; that even when the Gospels were written it was with hearing in mind; then how seriously should we take all this orality?

Is it possible that the entire New Testament was written primarily to be heard, not read? Unexpectedly, yes, that seems to be correct.

In addition to the Gospels, Paul and other authors assumed their letters would be read aloud in the hearing of various audiences. "After this letter has been read to you, see that it is also read in the church of the Laodiceans and that you in turn read the letter from Laodicea" (Col 4:16 NIV). "I charge you before the Lord to have this letter read to all the brothers and sisters" (1 Thess 5:27 NIV).[1]

---

[1]See especially Ben Witherington III, *What's in the Word: Rethinking the Socio-Rhetorical Character of the New Testament* (Waco, TX: Baylor University Press, 2009); also Ben Witherington III, *New Testament Rhetoric: An Introductory Guide to the Art of Persuasion in and of the New Testament* (Eugene, OR: Cascade, 2009); for critique, see Stanley E. Porter and Bryan R. Dyer, "Oral Texts? A Reassessment

Equally true, the book of Revelation was written to be heard: *Blessed is the one who reads aloud and those who hear the message of this prophecy* (Rev 1:3). *The Spirit and the bride are saying, 'Come!' And let the one who hears say it also, 'Come!'* (Rev 22:17). The narrator goes on to warn everyone who hears the words of the prophecy not to add anything (Rev 22:17-18).[2]

Isn't that enough evidence? Whether we're ready for the verdict or not, the court rules in favor of biblical orality. The writing of the Bible was intended for people's hearing. Speaking and hearing were predominant from beginning to end of divine revelation. Case closed.

But there's a problem. For most of us the case isn't closed. Swayed by the culture of modernity, we presume a totality of Scripture's textuality. Focusing on the writtenness we overlook the spokenness. But what other option is there?

Well, that's where we're headed now. Spokenness was not only true of the Bible. In those days, "the vast majority of people were habituated to the spoken word, [consequently] much of what was written was meant to be recited and listened to."[3] And though the books come to us in written form, they are "oral to the core both in their creation and in their performance . . . [authors] deliberately incorporated [oral] elements into their writings in order to assist a listening audience."[4]

In response, the following is a proposal for the oral interpretation of Scripture.[5] The goal is to incorporate oral elements into our reading

---

of the Oral and Rhetorical Nature of Paul's Letters in Light of Recent Studies," *Journal of the Evangelical Theological Society* 55 (2012): 323-41.

[2]As we'll see below, authors knowing that their written forms would be heard convinced them to style their writing with hearers in mind. It's referred to as an "oral register"; Paul R. Eddy, "Orality and Oral Transmission," in *Dictionary of Jesus and the Gospels*, 2nd ed., ed. Joel B. Green, Jeannine K. Brown, and Nicholas Perrin (Downers Grove, IL: IVP Academic, 2013), 641.

[3]Werner H. Kelber, *The Oral and Written Gospel: The Hermeneutics of Speaking and Writing in the Synoptic Tradition, Mark, Paul, and Q* (Minneapolis: Fortress, 1983), 17.

[4]Paul J. Achtemeier, "*Omne verbum sonat*: The New Testament and the Oral Environment of Later Western Antiquity," *Journal of Biblical Literature* 109 (1990): 19.

[5]Citing Walter Ong, "an oral hermeneutic is needed to interpret language in its fulness, beyond what can be captured in text"; see introduction to Walter J. Ong, *Language as Hermeneutic: A Primer on the Word and Digitization*, ed. Thomas D. Zlatic and Sara van den Berg (Cornell University Press, 2017), 3.

and speaking of Scripture in order to get closer to how it was originally spoken, heard, and experienced. It's a three-legged stool of interpretation. God intends his words to be heard and to be understood at the highest level we're enabled to understand them, which means we need to think our way back into the culture of ancient orality since the Bible was designed specifically with that culture in mind.

The point is not that Christians should stop reading and studying the Bible, but to read it with our minds tuned into hearing it and to speak it with our voices shaped by how it was originally proclaimed. The orality of the biblical world is not our reality; we do not live and breathe oral culture; it is not possible to turn back the hands of time; so it makes sense to investigate possibilities to make up for the limitations inherent in our modern reading of Scripture. Thankfully, there's an abundance of evidence to draw on about ancient hearers and performers.

A Culture of Hearing

In oral cultures worldwide, storytelling has probably always been the norm.[6] Certainly in the world of the Bible, it was customary to listen rather than to read. Few people were capable of reading literary works, and fewer still had access to copies of literature.

Even so, Greek and Roman authors were busy producing poetry, history, dramas, comedies, oratory, philosophy, and so forth. And several libraries were collecting scrolls of literary works, such as in Alexandria, Egypt. It was assumed that enough people would be able to read the literature on behalf of those who couldn't.

---

[6]Sources for this discussion of the features of oral communication include Elizabeth Minchin, ed., *Orality, Literacy and Performance in the Ancient World*, Orality and Literacy in the Ancient World 9 (Leiden: Brill, 2012); Kelly R. Iverson, "Orality and the Gospels: A Survey of Current Research," *Currents in Biblical Research* 8 (2009): 71-106; Nicholas A. Elder, "New Testament Media Criticism," *Currents in Biblical Research* 15 (2017): 315-37; Joanna Dewey, "Oral Methods of Structuring Narrative in Mark," *Interpretation* 43 (1989): 32-44; Paul J. Achtemeier, "*Omne verbum sonat*: The New Testament and the Oral Environment of Later Western Antiquity," *Journal of Biblical Literature* 109 (1990): 3-27; Larry W. Hurtado, "Oral Fixation and New Testament Studies? 'Orality,' 'Performance' and Reading Texts in Early Christianity," *New Testament Studies* 60 (2014): 321-40; John H. Walton and D. Brent Sandy, *The Lost World of Scripture: Ancient Literary Culture and Biblical Authority* (Downers Grove, IL: IVP Academic, 2013), 77-110.

Examples from the Bible include Moses reading the "Book of the Covenant" to the people (Ex 24:7); Joshua reading all the commands of Moses to the people—men, women, children, and foreigners (Josh 8:34-35); Josiah reading the Book of the Covenant to all the people of Judah and Jerusalem, and Ezra reading the law of Moses to the exiles who had returned to Jerusalem (2 Kings 23:1-3; 2 Chron 34:29-32; Neh 8:1-18; 13:1). Hearing the words of the Lord was transforming: "As God's law was read, the people began to weep . . . they had heard God's words and understood them" (Neh 8:9, 12 Voice).

Hearing accounts spoken generally occurred in groups of people. Only in rare instances would a text be read aloud for one person alone (see, e.g., Jer 36:21). Group readings had their own set of dynamics.

People listening to presentations would corporately respond to what they were hearing, with the result that the reactions and perceptions of some would influence the responses of others (cf. Acts 4:13-17). In contrast to reading privately, in which a reader tends to derive independent conclusions, hearing in a group typically leads to more unified conclusions.[7] As noted previously, an oral culture is likely to be more community-oriented than a textual one.

In most cases, literary readings were before small groups, not like plays performed in amphitheaters seating thousands. A reader was a real, live person, not an author far removed; the reader was personally present before an audience, possibly with relationships to members of the audience (cf. Acts 10:25-33). The speaker would naturally function as a surrogate for the author.

When a reader read or recited a piece of literature before an audience, the hearers' attention was primarily focused on the content being presented. The document itself and the words an author or scribe had written on the manuscript were secondary. The authority of what was

---

[7]"Unlike the private act of reading, which accentuates individualistic thought, the communal context of performance exerts forces that have a homogenizing influence over the interpretive process"; Kelly R. Iverson, *Performing Early Christian Literature: Audience Experience and the Interpretation of the Gospels* (Cambridge: Cambridge University Press, 2021), 30-31.

being presented depended more on the audience's perception of the author and/or reader, and less on the written form to which hearers did not have access (cf. 1 Cor 2:1-14).

When authors wrote knowing that the majority of their audiences would be hearers, and that someone would read aloud to others what they were writing, they would compose their texts with both the future reader and hearers in mind. The goal was to write in ways that would help the presentation to be effective and the message to be understood correctly.

Techniques to accomplish that could include short versions of narratives occurring rapid-fire one after another (such as in Mark's Gospel); evocative language (cf. Acts 2:23-24); unusual wording to ring in listeners' ears (cf. Acts 2:36-37); visual imagery designed to stimulate audiences' imagination (cf. Acts 4:11); graphic descriptions designed to stir hearers' emotions (cf. Acts 5:39); and so forth.[8]

An audience had the advantage of being able to detect differences in inflection and volume of the presenter's voice, as well as changes in facial expressions and body language. That could add a lifelike dimension to the audiences' perception of what they were hearing. As will be seen below, presenters could be performers of texts more than simply readers.

For readers preparing to present a written document, given the standard lack of spaces between words, little punctuation, and other factors (see Proposition 4), they would need to become thoroughly familiar with the content of what the author wrote. Hence, they would be in a position to assist an audience by explaining what an author meant.

With a speaker present before an audience and recounting a narrative, it was an experiential event. That is, live audiences experienced a much more dynamic interaction with the story in contrast to reading

---

[8]See Joanna Dewey, "Oral Methods of Structuring Narrative in Mark," *Interpretation* 43 (1989): 32-44.

privately or even someone reading aloud and with little expression.[9] Hearers could be drawn into accounts and experience them almost like they were present at the events and even participants in the action.

Since speech is continuous and linear, taking in the whole of a presentation comes more naturally by hearing rather than when reading a document. Hearers tend to follow a flow of thought better and not be concerned with individual parts.

> In reading a text it is possible to look back a few pages to check what had been written earlier. Having read the text, you can take it with you and read it again later. . . . But with an oral tradition none of that is possible. An oral performance is evanescent. It is an event. It happens and then is gone. . . . It is not a thing, an artefact like a literary text.[10]

As explained above in Proposition 4, in oral cultures there is an elevated importance of context. The larger setting of a statement can be essential to understand what the words in a sentence intend. What someone says at one point may not mean what it seems to at face value. As an audience heard an account, they more readily grasped the overall message.

In a second sense, the elevated importance of context refers to the life situation, experiences, culture, and history of the author and audience. What speakers and hearers knew in common is often not included in what was written. Thus, the more that can be uncovered about the life-context, the more likely the interpretation will be correct and robust.

A Culture of Performing

The *Iliad* and *Odyssey,* attributed to Homer, are examples of literature that was widely performed in the Greek world. There's evidence to suggest the epics actually could have been composed in the act of

---

[9]See Alberto J. Quiroga Puertas, *The Dynamics of Rhetorical Performances in Late Antiquity* (London: Routledge, 2019).
[10]James D. G. Dunn, "Altering the Default Setting: Re-envisioning the Early Transmission of the Jesus Tradition," *New Testament Studies* 49 (2003): 150.

performance. It would have meant a bard taking traditional stories, such as about the Trojan War and the travels of Odysseus, and crafting poetry in hexameter verse, apparently even without previously writing down the poetic lines. Then by performing the poetry over and over, the wording became standardized and was passed along as oral literature, which was then written down at a later time.[11]

As Greek literature and then Latin literature continued to develop over the centuries, guilds of public reciters made it their profession to read (maybe memorize) and reenact stories of the past. Some were itinerant performers traveling from city to city to the delight of all who would listen.

Presentations of stories before an audience were generally dramatic performances designed for entertainment. Men in particular often gathered for an evening of pleasures (known as a symposium), which included professional recitations of various forms of poetry. A performance was an opportunity to imagine how an account could best be understood. Even if the performer were to read or quote a text word-for-word, it could be interpreted in various ways by emphasizing specific words and portions of the text, by employing emotional cues, by varying vocal effects and body language, including gestures and facial expressions, thereby bringing a text to life.

Speechmaking was a highly developed art in the Greco-Roman world. Quintilian, a master of ancient rhetoric—born approximately the year Jesus was crucified and lived to about AD 100—wrote a twelve-volume treatise on the best ways to make oral presentations effective. One of his statements was, "The power of eloquence lies not only in the nature of facts, but in arousing emotion, which is not there,

---

[11]Ian Worthington, ed., *Voice into Text: Orality and Literacy in Ancient Greece,* Mnemosyne, Bibliotheca Classica Batava Supplementum 157 (Leiden: Brill, 1997); E. Anne Mackay, ed., *Signs of Orality: The Oral Tradition and Its Influence in the Greek and Roman World*, Mnemosyne, Bibliotheca Classica Batava Supplementum 188 (Leiden: Brill, 1998); Elizabeth Minchin, ed., *Orality, Literacy and Performance in the Ancient World,* Orality and Literacy in the Ancient World 9 (Leiden: Brill, 2012); for summary, see John H. Walton and D. Brent Sandy, *The Lost World of Scripture: Ancient Literary Culture and Biblical Authority* (Downers Grove, IL: IVP Academic, 2013), 79-83.

or in making an existing emotion more intense. This is adding force to facts."[12]

For Quintilian, emotions were considered of particular value in getting a point across.[13] Rational persuasion alone was considered insufficient. In modern performances, "meaning is more directly connected with the emotional impact of the events and characters involved . . . [while] reading activates different sensory registers in the brain."[14] This is not to say that intellect is less important than the emotional side of our being. Valid insights and understanding depend on both. As Quintilian noted, force complements fact.

It was common in the ancient world for oral performances to focus on creating dynamic experiences for hearers. It was the performers' responsibility to bring stories to life. As groups listened, they were drawn into the action; they became emotionally involved and responded corporately. Persuasive performances were the lifeblood of the culture at the time of the Bible.

Persuasive performances were the lifeblood of the culture at the time of the Bible.

Similar to oral performances at the time of the New Testament, Jesus delivered his sermons and stories for maximum impact. When he said, *If you tell this mountain to get up and throw yourself into the sea, I assure it will happen* (Mk 11:23), were the listeners shell-shocked? When he said, *If you're going to do an act of charity, don't let your left hand know*

---

[12]I've provided a simplified version of Quintilian's statement; here's the full statement from his *Institutio Oratoria* (6.2.23-24): "The power of eloquence lies not only in driving the judge to the conclusion towards which he will be led by the nature of the facts, but either in arousing emotion, which is not there, or in making an existing emotion more intense. This is called *deinosis*, that is to say language that adds force to facts."

[13]Kelly R. Iverson, *Performing Early Christian Literature: Audience Experience and the Interpretation of the Gospels* (Cambridge: Cambridge University Press, 2021), 183-84.

[14]Thomas Boomershine, *The Messiah of Peace*, Biblical Performance Criticism Series 12 (Eugene, OR: Cascade, 2015), 11.

what your right hand is doing (Matt 6:3), did his audience gasp, and then chuckle at the incredulity of the statement? When he said, *Let the dead corpses take care of the burials of the other corpses; your priority is to go, proclaim the kingdom of God* (Lk 9:60), did a hush fall over the audience with no one daring to breathe?

It's likely that the accounts of Jesus' life would have been similarly performed by Christians. With the desire and eagerness of the early Christians to share the good news about Jesus in convincing ways, they would have taken advantage of the best ways to do it.[15] The book of Acts suggests ways that was beginning to happen.

For example, when Peter went to the home of the Gentile Cornelius and stood before a crowd of people assembled there, he recounted major events in the life of Jesus in such a convincing way that they all received the Holy Spirit and were baptized (Act 10:27-48). In a synagogue in Antioch of Pisidia, Paul declared, "All you Israelites and God-fearing Gentiles, pay attention" (Acts 13:16). And then Paul went on to tell about John the Baptist's preaching and Jesus' rejection, execution, and resurrection, with the result that on the following Sabbath almost the whole city came together to hear more (Acts 13:16-44).

The question is, With the influence of oral culture on Scripture and on the life of the early Christians, are there ways we can do more than just read the Bible in our modern ways? Can we understand the good news closer to ways the initial hearers apparently did?

---

[15]See George A. Kennedy, *New Testament Interpretation Through Rhetorical Criticism* (Charlotte, NC: University of North Carolina Press, 1984); George A. Kennedy, *Classical Rhetoric and Its Christian and Secular Tradition from Ancient to Modern Times*, 2nd ed. (Charlotte, NC: University of North Carolina, 1999); James Fredal, *Rhetorical Action in Ancient Athens: Persuasive Artistry from Solon to Demosthenes* (Carbondale, IL: Southern Illinois University Press, 2006); Ben Witherington III and Jason A. Myers, *New Testament Rhetoric: An Introductory Guide to the Art of Persuasion in and of the New Testament*, 2nd ed. (Eugene, OR: Cascade, 2022); Timothy A. Brookins, *Ancient Rhetoric and the Style of Paul's Letters: A Reference Book* (Eugene, OR: Cascade, 2022).

PROPOSITION 13

WE CAN BECOME BETTER HEARERS AND SPEAKERS OF SCRIPTURE

Jesus would repeatedly call out,
"Those who have ears to hear; let them hear!"

LUKE 8:8

THE ORALITY OF DIVINE REVELATION was profound in every way: (1) the voice of God in the person of the Father, the Son, and the Holy Spirit speaking eternal truths in human words; (2) humans hearing and understanding the majestic words of the Lord; (3) the empowerment of authorized humans to speak God's words, yet in their own words; and (4) the words transmitted by millions of humans across thousands of years and miles, initially orally, eventually in writing. Remarkably, it was the only means by which the people of this earth would have opportunity to hear the words of the Lord.

Except there's a slight problem. God revealed himself to specific people in a specific window of time, and he accommodated his revelation to those unique cultures and languages. Since the people of ancient oral culture heard in the ways suggested in Proposition 12, for us to grasp what God revealed to them, we need to adapt our reading and hearing to ways that they heard and understood. God spoke *to* them, and if what he said is to be *for* us, translating both language and culture is necessary.

With the long history of our culture of textuality—and much of it now transitioning to digital—there's much to do if we're to get the full benefit of God's original revelation in oral culture.[1] Our modern Western culture—and specifically our ways of reading—can get in the way.

In a chapter by Robert Mulholland titled "How to 'Read' without 'Reading,'" he observes that when we read Scripture, "the rational, cognitive, intellectual dynamics of our being go into full operation to analyze, critique, dissect, reorganize, synthesize, and digest the material we find appropriate to our agenda."[2] That's bad news, but it's not too surprising in that we're products of the Enlightenment. Rationalism and scientific thinking have pulled us into its wake. Readers tend "to be thinking about [the story] rather than participating in the story. Often they are thinking so hard they can't feel anything."[3] If the assessments are accurate—especially when it comes to reading Scripture—we may be missing something.

Many of us come to the Bible about the same way we read an issue of *National Geographic* or an online news source. It's mostly intellectual engagement. We find information that's interesting, but it's easily water off a duck's back. Information alone does not usually lead to transformation.

The strategy for understanding Scripture, then, must be more than our typical reading, especially if we're going to feel anything. We need to have open minds *and* open hearts to hear Scripture in all its richness and to be moved by it. Perhaps we can learn to read better with open minds, but we're more likely to hear better with open hearts. God

---

[1]"As a new generation encounters the Bible for the first time, they will not experience it exclusively orally as in the days before the printing press, or primarily in print as was the case for the past several centuries. Instead, for them, 'the Bible' will always be a multimedia category." See John Dyer, "The New Gutenberg: Bible Apps Could Be as Formative to Christian History as the Printing Press," *Christianity Today* 66.9 (Dec 2022): 51-55.

[2]M. Robert Mulholland, *Shaped by the Word: The Power of Scripture in Spiritual Formation*, rev. ed. (Nashville: Upper Room, 2000), 19.

[3]Thomas Boomershine, *The Messiah of Peace*, Biblical Performance Criticism Series 12 (Eugene, OR: Cascade, 2015), 11.

incarnated himself in Scripture; he speaks through Scripture; and it's in hearing his words where we're more likely to meet him.

HEARING THE WORDS OF THE LORD

The book of Hebrews provides a model for hearing God speak.[4] The author wanted hearers to understand that the words of the Old Testament were more than written words; they should be heard as if God himself were speaking. From the first verse—*God spoke through the prophets* (Heb 1:1)—to the last chapter—*God said, "I will never leave you nor forsake you"* (Heb 13:5, quoting Deut 31:6), it was an unfolding drama of God's authoritative speech acts. Shocking consequences were announced if senses were dulled to hearing God's voice.

- To not listen well could result in falling from grace: "That is why we ought to pay even closer attention to the voice that has been speaking so that we will never drift away from it . . . where sin and disobedience receive their just rewards" (Heb 2:1-2 Voice).

- Not hearing God speaking, hearts may become hardened, as happened during the Exodus: "Today, if you listen to his voice, don't harden your hearts the way they did in the bitter uprising at Meribah" (Heb 3:15 Voice, quoting Ps 95:7-8).

- Hearers were warned: "See that you don't turn away from the One who is speaking; for if the ones who heard and refused the One who spoke on earth faced punishment, then how much more will we suffer if we turn away from the One speaking from heaven" (Heb 12:25 Voice).

---

[4]For discussion see especially Daniel J. Treier, "Speech Acts, Hearing Hearts, and Other Senses: The Doctrine of Scripture Practiced in Hebrews," in *The Epistle to the Hebrews and Christian Theology*, eds. Richard Bauckham, Daniel R. Driver, Trevor A. Hart, and Nathan McDonald (Grand Rapids, MI: Eerdmans, 2009); Stephen E. Fowl, "'In Many and Various Ways': Hearing the Voice of God in the Text of Scripture," in *The Voice of God in the Text of Scripture: Explorations in Constructive Dogmatics*, ed. Oliver D. Crisp and Fred Sanders (Grand Rapids, MI: Zondervan, 2016); Myk Habets, "That Was Then, This Is Now: Reading Hebrews Retroactively," in *The Voice of God in the Text of Scripture: Explorations in Constructive Dogmatics*, ed. Oliver D. Crisp and Fred Sanders (Grand Rapids, MI: Zondervan, 2016).

God can speak and discipline like a Father, and errant children had better listen up (Heb 12:9-11)! *To fall into the hands of the living God is terrifying!* (Heb 10:31). *There is no doubt: our God is consuming fire!* (Heb 12:29). Yes, there is good reason to fear the wrath of the Almighty God.

Of all the quotations from the Old Testament in Hebrews, and there are many, they are presented as God speaking, not as citations from a written document. "Hebrews treats biblical quotations not as the Word written but as the spoken Word of the tripersonal God."[5] Though God's words were preserved in written form, the oral nature of God's spoken words mattered most.

God speaks and summons all to be good listeners.[6] "We too can hear the Word of God in the present tense and experience the event of God's self-revelation. . . . Hebrews cuts behind the human speaker or author of a text, to God, the real speaker."[7] Hearing God speak, even though it's through the written words of Scripture, allows us to grasp the presence of God and his powerful voice more personally. It's a conversation.[8] He spoke and speaks. We listen and respond. What he says is living and active, piercing and poignant. "Scripture is the optimum record of the intrusion of the Word of God into human history."[9]

Similar to Hebrews, Jesus' quotations as recorded in the Gospels emphasize the spokenness of God's words as well. "Have you not read what God said to you, 'I am the God of Abraham, the God of Isaac, and the God of Jacob'"? (Mt 22:31-32 NIV).[10] Jesus frequently introduced the words of God in the Law as "You have heard that it was said." And he made clear that his words were not really his own: "the one whom God has sent speaks the words of God" (Jn 3:34 NIV).

---

[5]Habets, "That Was Then, This Is Now," 97.
[6]"Believers engage God's word, we listen to God's voice, to direct our love and longing towards reaching our true home in God." Stephen E. Fowl, "'In Many and Various Ways': Hearing the Voice of God in the Text of Scripture," in Crisp and Sanders, *The Voice of God in the Text of Scripture*, 46.
[7]Habets, "That Was Then, This Is Now," 97-98.
[8]See, e.g., Brother Lawrence, *The Practice of the Presence of God in Modern English* (Marshall Davis, 2013).
[9]Mulholland, *Shaped by the Word*, 42.
[10]Jesus also referred to what was written in the law; see Mk 10:5; Lk 10:26; 24:44; Jn 5:46-47.

For readers, the words on a page can be far removed from the God who spoke them. He can seem to be light years away. We may take less seriously words inscribed in a book, on whatever size sheets of paper or size font. But if the words are spoken to us by God himself, that's different. The reality of God's presence, the potential for divine and human intimacy, is enacted by his speaking and our hearing.[11]

To hear God speak is more than reading about his speaking. It's the indirectness of written words replaced by the directness of what God says through those words. The former pales in comparison to the latter. Our focus should be listening for the voice of God, rather than only analyzing the printed words on a page.[12] "Our passion should not be for Scripture per se but for the one who reveals himself in Scripture. The Christian life is a relationship with a person, not with a book."[13]

Hearing God speak invites us to draw near, to listen to his heartbeat, to pay attention to what he cares about, how he loves, what makes him angry. It's interpersonal communication.[14] The closer our relationship with him, the more likely our transformation into the likeness of his Son, to think like he does, to speak like he does, to act like he does, to pray that his name would be honored, that his will would be done, that his kingdom of love and grace would come. Nothing is more important than learning about God, hearing from him, and responding in worship and action.

Consider what Scripture records that God said to the Israelites during the wilderness experience: "Be holy as I am holy." On one hand, we could intellectually analyze the statement, seeking a clear definition of what the word *holy* meant in that context—particularly in light of

---

[11]See, e.g., Greg Paul, *Close Enough to Hear God Breathe: The Great Story of Divine Intimacy* (Nashville: Thomas Nelson, 2011).

[12]I am not entering into the complex theological discussion of what it means or doesn't mean to say that God speaks to us, but I am definitely not affirming that God speaks outside the intended meaning of biblical revelation; for an overview of the issues, see Kevin J. Vanhoozer, "Word of God," in *Dictionary for Theological Interpretation of Scripture*, ed. Kevin J. Vanhoozer (Grand Rapids, MI: Baker Academic, 2005), 850-54.

[13]Mark L. Strauss, *How to Read the Bible in Changing Times: Understanding and Applying God's Word Today* (Grand Rapids, MI: Baker Books, 2011), 71.

[14]Jeannine K. Brown, *Scripture as Communication: Introducing Biblical Hermeneutics* (Grand Rapids, MI: Baker Academic, 2007), 13-16.

the purity regulations in the Law—and the extent to which a person can actually be holy.[15] We could compare the circumstances of the same statements in Jesus' Sermon on the Mount and Peter's letter (Mt 5:48; 1 Pet 1:15-16). Our interpretation could end up being an interesting way to understand God's command to be holy. But we may not feel anything.

But what if we imagine God speaking those words directly to us in a very compassionate way? Maybe we're struggling, wondering how best to deal with a difficult situation or an impending confrontation. God draws near and says, "Remember, you're my representative: 'Be holy as I am.'"

Or maybe it's a moment when we recognize that we have done wrong. Jesus stands alongside us, maybe with his arm around our shoulders, and says in a quiet, loving way, "Okay, I understand. I've been tempted too. But you can do better next time. Do your best to be holy as I am."

The point is, Scripture is a record of God speaking. It's up to us to be sensitive hearers of those spoken words. It's in hearing God's words where we're more likely to meet him.

HEARING THE WORDS OF SCRIPTURE

Not everything in the Bible comes to us as "Thus saith the Lord." Much about God is revealed through his interactions with people across the metanarrative of Scripture. We learn about Job's experiences and God permitting him to suffer unimaginable losses; about David's experiences, being relentlessly hunted down by Saul in order to kill him, yet under God's hand of protection; about the devastating death of Lazarus—and even after being entombed for four days, Jesus saying to roll the stone away and calling out, "Lazarus, come forth!"; about Peter's quandary, announcing he didn't want Jesus to ever wash his feet,

---

[15]John H. Walton, *Wisdom for Faithful Reading: Principles and Practices for Old Testament Interpretation* (Downers Grove, IL: IVP Academic, 2023), 202-3.

even though Jesus had stooped far lower than expected and was washing the other disciples' feet.

In all of that and more, we need to listen closely to what God is communicating even as we do when God is speaking directly. There may be differences in form, but it's all divine revelation intended for us to hear.

On the sobering night of Jesus' betrayal, arrest, denial, and trial, about to be bound, mocked, spit on, punched, slapped, lashed, and more, he sought a quiet place in the Garden of Gethsemane to pray. With his body sensing what lay ahead, his soul gripped by grief, his despair so deep, the Father sent an angel from heaven to minister to him.

Even so, falling flat on the ground, probably with his face in the dirt, he prayed fervently and repeatedly, *Abba Father, you can do all things. Remove this cup of suffering from me. But not what I wish, it's up to you* (Mk 14:36).

It was a cry of horror, of loneliness, of hopelessness, yet of yieldingness. Sweating profusely, it was as if globules of blood were falling on the ground. Unfortunately, Jesus sensed that his "anxious prayers had met a stone wall of no response."[16] The cup of crucifixion was going to be his to drink, bitter potion though it be.

The Son of God, the prince, the priest, the prophet, the king who was supposed to be on his throne, was at that moment precisely where he didn't belong—yet where he did belong. He was there willingly, yet anxiously, on behalf of the whole human race.

The stories of Scripture are powerful, and we must go all in to hear and feel their power, as if we were present for the events themselves. If we're just casually reading interesting stories from the distant past, they will not have the effect on readers as the accounts did for the original audiences, and that's a great loss. "The hearing of the story is an experience more analogous to watching a great film, and it differs remarkably

---

[16]Philip Yancey, *The Jesus I Never Knew* (Grand Rapids, MI: Zondervan, 1995), 195.

from reading it from a critical perspective in a book. Indeed, it is an experience of suspense and anticipation of events, of hope and disbelief, of closeness to or alienation from the characters."[17]

Imagine being present to hear Patrick Henry's rallying-cry, "Give me liberty or give me death"; or Virginia Wolff's lecture, "A Room of One's Own"; or Martin Luther King Jr.'s oration, "I Have a Dream"; or Vince Lombardi's pep talk, "Gentlemen, this is a football." We'd have to have been there to appreciate the full effect—the drama of the moment— and to be moved by it as the original hearers were.

Equally electrifying, what would it have been like to be present on these occasions? At Jesus' baptism, a voice suddenly boomed from beyond the universe, splitting the sound waves, *This is my son!* (Mt 3:17); or John the Baptist, upon recognizing Jesus, uttered one of the most unexpected declarations in human history, *Behold the lamb of God!* (Jn 1:29); or Jesus—instantly stopping the howling winds and foaming waves—interrupted the forces of nature, *Peace be still!* (Mk 4:39); or Jesus, in the middle of the darkest night in divine and human history, crying out from the cross, *My God, my God, why have you forsaken me?!* (Mt 27:46; Mk 15:34). We'd have to have been more than bystanders to appreciate all that was going on.

> *We'd have to have been more than bystanders*
> *to appreciate all that was going on.*

But we can do more than read the famous words of the likes of Jesus, Patrick Henry, Martin Luther King Jr., and others. The events can be recreated, at least in part, via movies, stage productions, or even, on a smaller scale, in school classrooms or in churches. The drama of the moments can even be recreated in our minds if we explore the

---

[17]Thomas Boomershine, *The Messiah of Peace*, Biblical Performance Criticism Series 12 (Eugene, OR: Cascade, 2015), 12.

circumstances leading up to what was stated, the emotions inherent in the audience and the speaker, and the effect of the presentations. Movies such as the *Passion of the Christ* may not perfectly reflect the biblical text, but for discerning viewers, they can bring to life biblical events like no other form can. *The Chosen* is another example. The more of the original setting and drama that can be included, the more meaningful and moving the recreated experience will be.

To the extent that we can retrieve the emotions of the original accounts in Scripture, people today may become better "doers" of the word, not just hearers. "Be ye doers of the word, and not hearers only" (James 1:22 KJV).

SPEAKING THE WORDS OF SCRIPTURE

As recounted in Proposition 10, Jesus appointed his followers to be his messengers. He prayed to his Father, *The words you gave me, I give to them . . . just as you sent me into the world, I am sending them* (Jn 17:8, 18). The same way Jesus had communicated, his followers were supposed to continue communicating. They were fully commissioned as his authorized representatives to function in his absence.

It was a divine mandate. The disciples probably didn't give second thought to what Jesus had in mind: it would mean telling and retelling the stories of and about Jesus. They would take the things he said and the accounts of what had been done and pass them along to others. No script, just their memories, plus their best efforts to convince others of what they had become convinced of.

If Jesus' followers hadn't told people what they had observed about him, if they hadn't passed along the good news about his life and words, Jesus' selfless incarnation and horrible crucifixion could have been vain. Jesus' full dependence on his followers is almost inconceivable.

It's a challenge and responsibility that continues to this very day. And the risk is just as great. Now it's up to us to be Jesus' messengers, to speak his words, to tell his stories. It's our calling to be his representatives, spokespersons, telling the stories of and about Jesus. Anyone can do that and should.

> How are they to believe in one they have not heard of? And how are they to hear without someone preaching to them? . . . Faith comes from what is heard, and what is heard comes through the preached word of Christ. (Rom 10:14, 17 NET)

Consider this: professors give lectures, preachers give sermons, prosecutors give their closing arguments—differences in form, but all important. But what if, in place of speaking, any of those only handed out scripts of what they wanted to say and then walked out in silence? We'd be shocked. We might consider them negligent.

Why? It would be a lost opportunity. The presence of speaker and audience to each other with the advantage of verbal emphasis and nonverbal language is an opportunity for a more convincing presentation. The spoken word has potential for impact that the written word is less likely to have. Even in our textual day and age, we recognize that oral presentations can be more effective than written explanations.

God is the originator and the master of oral presentation. He voiced his thoughts in our words. He told Moses and the prophets to do likewise. Jesus did the same and told his followers to do what he did. Nothing was said about a script to pass out or to read from.

God valued speaking for good reason. It's what he did and what he calls us to do. It's not that he devalued written communication. That would have its place in due time; Jesus referred to what was written in the law (Lk 24:44). But orality was the priority for revealing divine truth, and still is.

Can orality become our priority too? Even though we only have a written document, can we recover the power of the spoken word? Can we hear as the original audiences did when they experienced what Jesus said and did? And then in turn, can we tell others what he said and did in power and effectiveness?

The Dynamism of Scripture

The Bible is full of drama: from Herod the king trying to get the wise men to reveal where the real king of the Jews was born, resulting in Joseph and Mary escaping Palestine under the cover of darkness; to a Pharisee, a ruler of the Jews, approaching Jesus under the cover of darkness, trying to determine whether Jesus was truly God; to Mary Magdalene going to the tomb while it was still dark, and finding it empty, concluding that someone had stolen Jesus' body. "The Bible is replete with dramatic elements: action, suspense, romance, intrigue, strong characters, conflict between good and evil."[18]

Jesus' interactions with the Pharisees and Sadducees seemed to be always full of drama. Jesus minced no words.

> Woe to you, experts in the law and you Pharisees, hypocrites! You cross land and sea to make one convert, and when you get one, you make him twice as much a child of hell as yourselves! . . . Blind guides! You strain out a gnat yet swallow a camel! . . . You are like whitewashed tombs that look beautiful on the outside but inside are full of the bones of the dead and of everything unclean. (Mt 23:15, 24, 27 NET)

There's drama everywhere in Scripture, even in the letters. Paul unloaded on the Galatians: "Don't act like fools! Has someone cast a spell over you? Did you miss the crucifixion of Jesus the Anointed that was reenacted right in front of your eyes? . . . Are you so foolish? Do you think you can perfect something God's Spirit started with any human effort?" (Gal 3:1-3 Voice). Paul appealed to Philemon with every ounce of persuasion possible to take the runaway slave Onesimus back. Jude dramatically dressed down dreamers who had fallen into Balaam's error: mere clouds without rain, bare trees without fruit and uprooted, twice dead, wild waves of the sea, wandering stars! If any book of the Bible is full of drama, it's the book of Revelation.[19]

---

[18]R. Larry Overstreet, *Biographical Preaching: Bringing Bible Characters to Life* (Grand Rapids, MI: Kregel, 2001), 144.

[19]Justin Jeffcoat Schedtler, *A Heavenly Chorus: The Dramatic Function of Revelation's Hymns* (Tübingen: Mohr Siebeck, 2014).

There are two ways to think about Scripture. On the one hand, there is no such thing as drama. On the other, everything is drama. We can speak about what Jesus said and did with no expression, no passion, no amazement. Or we can throw ourselves into the situations and speak with a sense of being enthralled, awestruck, filled with breathless wonder. In the words of Quintilian, facts aren't enough; force is essential (see Proposition 12).

If we are to be Jesus' faithful representatives, speaking for him as he spoke, so that people who hear us will hear him as the initial hearers did, then two things are necessary. First, we need to become attentive hearers of what Jesus said and how he said it, as well as of what he did and why. We will have to give careful thought to the immediate circumstances, to the progressive revelation of his ideas, to his overall ministry, to his audience, and so forth.

Second, we will need to determine how best to present what Jesus said and did so our audiences hear and feel what the original hearers did. We want to maximize the passion and power of the spoken word, which printed words on a page do not have, especially when presented without expression.

PROPOSITION 14

WE CAN RESTORE ORAL SCRIPTURE
TO ITS RIGHTFUL PLACE

The good news about the kingdom, a message for all nations,
will be proclaimed all around the world.

MATTHEW 24:14

THE CHALLENGE FOR CHURCHES, classrooms, Bible studies—
essentially, any assemblies of people interested in the Bible—is to put
into practice the orality of Scripture. One of the church's highest pri-
orities, if not the highest, is to tell God's stories so people can hear them.
The life of the church—children, youth, and adults, worship services,
Sunday school classes, small groups—should be filled with the words
of Scripture enacted in interesting and arresting ways.

Church assemblies that primarily focus on worshiping, singing
hymns and/or praise music, listening to sermons—in the absence of
the word of the Lord presented powerfully—is a recipe for biblical
illiteracy and shallow Christianity. Rather than what humans say or
sing, what God says should be most prominent in worship services.
Unfortunately, in sermons, what the speaker has to say can seem more
important than what God has to say.

Worship is our response to who God is and what he says, but it's
hearing and meditating on the word of the Lord that induce worship.
Invite the fire of the Holy Spirit, and the worship experience can be

spiritually energizing and exhilarating. Worship leaders and the instruments of worship, however, are better off in the background. The word of the Lord is the focus of attention.

Church traditions are to be commended that regularly include an Old Testament and New Testament reading in Sunday services. But if those readings are not presented in ways to capture the attention of hearers, they can be of limited value. Presenting the word of the Lord effectively and convincingly is a challenge for all.

Telling God's stories is more than the responsibility of the church, but of all individuals belonging to the church. It's both/and. Christians should not only hear the stories in church but be inspired to share the stories in their homes and with their neighbors. Every Christ-follower's primary function in the church and in the world is to be a messenger telling people about things Jesus said and did.

Christians should not only hear the stories in church but be inspired to share the stories in their homes and with their neighbors.

Can anything be clearer in Scripture than God's speaking? And his commissioning others to speak on his behalf? And Jesus' speaking? And his commissioning his followers to speak on his behalf? Written Scripture was secondary. Yet for most churches today, the secondary has upstaged the primary. Isn't it time to consider ways to flip the script and put oral Scripture back in its rightful place?

RETRIEVING ORAL FEATURES
FROM WRITTEN SCRIPTURE

To the extent we can come closer to presenting Scripture as the original speakers did and hearing it as the original audiences did, then there's a greater chance of people understanding and being impacted by God's words as he intended. Woe if the words of the Lord fall on deaf ears.

But simply reading through a written passage of Scripture, we may not find much to guide us in determining how it would have been spoken or heard in its original setting. A written document is not a complete source of information about an event. Stated technically, "textual meaning deals with much that is not semantically or intentionally explicit—in particular with a text's presuppositions, implications, and entailments as well."[1]

Written accounts generally presuppose that an audience already has some background knowledge, such as about the culture, the people, and even circumstances pertaining to the event. Consequently, in order to retrieve more than what is stated in a text of Scripture, interpreters look for cues in the text that may lead to additional information that is helpful for understanding the account. This is essentially what commentators have been doing for centuries.

The cues we're particularly interested in, which are often overlooked, relate to helping today's hearers experience events as original audiences did. The dramatic elements of biblical accounts and the evocative language are often overlooked or underplayed in interpreting Scripture. Yet they're the precise elements that hearers find helpful in understanding the dynamics and poignancy of Scripture.

It may strike our intellectual sensibilities as odd, but one of the most important aspects of biblical stories is emotions. Recent studies in the field of emotional intelligence underscore the key role that emotions play in decision-making, speaking, and acting.[2] Rationality and emotionality go hand-in-hand; people do not function solely on the basis of one or the other. But giving more attention to emotional intelligence

---

[1]Daniel J. Treier, "Speech Acts, Hearing Hearts, and Other Senses: The Doctrine of Scripture Practiced in Hebrews," in *The Epistle to the Hebrews and Christian Theology*, ed. Richard Bauckham, Daniel R. Driver, Trevor A. Hart, and Nathan McDonald (Grand Rapids, MI: Eerdmans, 2009), 338.
[2]See, for example, Daniel Goleman, *Emotional Intelligence: Why It Can Matter More Than IQ* (New York: Bantam, 1995); Robert J. Emmerling, Vinod K. Shanwal, Manas K. Mandal, eds., *Emotional Intelligence: Theoretical and Cultural Perspectives* (Hauppauge, NY: Nova Science, 2008).

has the potential to enhance our appreciation for the transforming power of Scripture.

What this means for God's word is that emotional involvement in the stories of Scripture, both those telling the stories and those hearing them, can be essential for the effectiveness of the communication. Oral presentations are an opportunity to highlight the emotions that may be latent in written versions of stories. When the fixed words on a manuscript are performed, the words can be transformed into a dynamic event for both performers and hearers.[3]

Tom Steffen and William Bjoraker have advanced a helpful strategy for embracing the oral culture of Scripture.[4] Based on their personal experiences with modern oral cultures, they identify elements typical of orally focused interaction: entering into the experience of the characters in a story; appreciation of creative expression; sympathy with emotions; community participation rather than isolation as individuals; preference for wholes over smaller portions; use of imagination; and so forth.[5] They recommend giving special attention to the components of biblical stories: characters, circumstances, culture, conversations, chemistry, choices, chances, conflicts, confrontations, consequences.

Borrowing from and building on their work, reflecting on key questions can lead to comprehending a written passage more fully:

- What can we learn about the characters in the account?

- What was going through their minds?

- Was there a dilemma or tension evident?

- What words or ideas were repeated or emphasized?

- What occurred that was unexpected or particularly shocking?

---

[3]Holly E. Hearon, "The Implications of Orality for Studies of the Biblical Text," in *Performing the Gospel: Orality, Memory, and Mark*, eds. Richard A. Horsley, Jonathan A. Draper, John Miles Foley (Minneapolis: Fortress, 2006), 12.

[4]Tom Steffen and William Bjoraker, *The Return of Oral Hermeneutics: As Good Today as It Was for the Hebrew Bible and First-Century Christianity* (Eugene, OR: Wipf and Stock, 2020).

[5]Steffen and Bjoraker, *The Return of Oral Hermeneutics*, 68-72, 106-34.

- What in the account suggests emotional involvement?

- What can we infer about the story that was pertinent, though not explicitly stated?

- In what ways did the characters in the account act and/or speak justly or unjustly?

- In what ways are we sympathetic with the circumstances the characters were in?

- What were the long-term results of what happened?

- What do we learn about God and his ways, and ourselves and our ways?

In other words, rather than simply reading the words on a page, hearers seek to put themselves in the stories and in the lives of the characters.[6] It entails imagining what it was like for the initial followers of Jesus to tell others what they had experienced based on being present at events in Jesus' life. Hearing stories well is then the basis for the next step: telling them effectively.

PREPARING A PERFORMANCE OF SCRIPTURE

Imagine a bystander giving a personal account of what happened when Jesus came to Bethany, the home of Mary and Martha, after their brother Lazarus had died and been in a tomb for four days.

It was one of the most unexpected days of my life. It started out sad, but by the end it turned into one of the most amazing and exciting days ever! I will never forget how it changed my thinking.

---

[6]"By comparison with readers of modern literature, the hearers of performances or 'readers' of oral traditional 'texts' must participate far more actively in realizing the work, and far more actively than scholars interested only in analysis of an artifact"; Richard A. Horsley and Jonathan A. Draper, *Whoever Hears You Hears Me: Prophets, Performance, and Tradition in Q* (Harrisburg, PA: Trinity Press International, 1999), 162.

I had gone up from Jerusalem to Bethany to express my condolences to Mary and Martha in the untimely death of their brother Lazarus. He had already been in the tomb for four days, but the funerary events were continuing with constant wailing and weeping. Anguish and hopelessness were evident everywhere.

Jesus had arrived a little before I did and had already spoken with Martha. Just as I got there, I saw Mary fall at his feet in tears, saying, "Oh, my Lord, how my heart aches. If you had only gotten here sooner, Lazarus would not have died." Hearing Mary's despair was heartbreaking.

Sensing Mary's deep distress, Jesus was obviously moved. His compassion for the sisters was palpable. I held my breath. What would he say? Then with his head bowed low, he spoke ever so gently, "Where . . . is . . . the body?" With that, tears began flowing from his eyes.

Martha had now joined Jesus and Mary, and together the three of them walked dejectedly to the cave outside Bethany where Lazarus was entombed. Others followed along. Standing before the tomb, Jesus said, "Remove the stone."

Really? we wondered. Why?

Martha blurted out, "Oh no! You surely don't want to do that. The stench will be unbearable!"

Then Jesus said something very puzzling: "Hold it, Martha: Remember what I told you. If you believe in me, you will see the glory of God." And he motioned to the men to move the stone.

Looking up to heaven, Jesus prayed, "Thank you, Father, that you hear me. I know that you are always listening. But I am saying this now for the benefit of the people here, so that they will know that you sent me."

Finishing his prayer, Jesus paused and then abruptly called out in a loud voice, "Lazarus! Come out!" We all stepped back, stunned, not sure what was going to happen.

But shock of all shocks, here came a man crawling out of the tomb with the grave clothes still wrapped around him. And it was Lazarus! He had been dead but was suddenly alive!!

Wow! Impossible! I had heard about Jesus performing miracles, but to see this with my own eyes is amazing. I guess with Jesus anything is possible.

Is there any doubt he's the Messiah?! I am going to begin following him!

━━━━━

A performance of Scripture entails re-oralizing written words in order to approximate the consciousness of the original characters in the account. Live events of Gospel performances create opportunities for performers and audiences alike to enter into a text and experience it more dynamically and transformatively than a simple reading can.[7]

Two scholars in particular, David Rhoades and Thomas Boomershine, have widely promoted and demonstrated oral performances of books of the New Testament, designed to bridge the gap between ancient performances of Scripture and modern readings. They have memorized selected New Testament books (for example, the Gospel of Mark and even the entire book of Revelation) and have presented them in various institutions and churches.[8]

The recitations of the biblical text are valiant efforts to bring into the present the ancient practice of performing Scripture. Many have listened to the presentations and have gained a new appreciation for the power of the spoken word. Much depends on the skill and diligent work of the performers. Whether that procedure will catch on and become a movement remains to be seen.

---

[7]See Erika Fischer-Lichte, *The Transformative Power of Performance: A New Aesthetics*, trans. Saskya Iris Jain (London: Routledge, 2008); cited in Kelly R. Iverson, *Performing Early Christian Literature: Audience Experience and the Interpretation of the Gospels* (Cambridge: Cambridge University Press, 2021), 46.

[8]See, e.g., David Rhoads, *Reading Mark: Engaging the Gospel* (Minneapolis: Fortress, 2004); Thomas Boomershine, *The Messiah of Peace*, Biblical Performance Criticism Series 12 (Eugene, OR: Cascade, 2015); video recordings of the latter are available at www.messiahofpeace.com.

Larry Overstreet has proposed creating dramatic monologues in which the presenter takes on the persona of a biblical character.[9] It involves analyzing the personality of the biblical individual(s), reconstructing the circumstances, and inferring what people were likely thinking and feeling and how they were responding. Overstreet has presented dramatic monologues as sermons in multiple churches. More of the same would be appropriate.

On a smaller scale, Tom McComiskey and Jeff Arthurs have encouraged more interpretive readings of Scripture in worship services.[10] McComiskey introduces his book saying, "I am surprised at how frequently I hear the Scriptures read carelessly with little attention to the reader's responsibility to interpret the biblical author's thought or intention." This too is a move in the right direction.

All of these approaches hold potential for assemblies of believers to gain a fresh appreciation for hearing the word of the Lord, for understanding it more completely, and for being transformed by it. Any strategy for re-oralizing texts is worth undertaking.

The starting point is always the biblical text. But it is not necessarily limited to the wording in the text. As noted above, written accounts often do not include matters that ancient audiences would have already been familiar with. But for modern audiences to understand the stories as the original audiences would have, it's helpful to include supplementary information.

In preparing the example above, I noted first that when Lazarus died, many had gone from Jerusalem to Bethany to comfort Mary and Martha, and when Jesus unexpectedly raised Lazarus from the dead, they put their faith in him (Jn 11:18-19, 45). So I decided it might be helpful to tell the story from the perspective of one of the visitors.

---

[9]R. Larry Overstreet, *Biographical Preaching: Bringing Bible Characters to Life* (Grand Rapids, MI: Kregel, 2001), 142-57 and 175-83.

[10]Thomas Edward McComiskey, *Reading Scripture in Public: A Guide for Preachers and Lay Readers* (Grand Rapids, MI: Baker, 1991); more recently, see Jeffrey D. Arthurs, *Devote Yourself to the Public Reading of Scripture: The Transforming Power of the Well-Spoken Word* (Grand Rapids: Kregel, 2012).

Next, I looked for background information to supplement the biblical record, such as the extensive wailing and mourning that continued for at least a week, and what was entailed in burials in rock-hewn tombs.[11] The original audiences would have known about these matters even though they are not mentioned in the biblical account.

I then considered wording from different Bible translations and adapted them so that modern audiences can identify with the experiences and emotions of the characters in the story. Jesus going to Bethany and raising Lazarus was a day full of drama, shifting quickly from the despair of death to the delight of resurrection. And that had a profound effect on the people present, and hopefully can on audiences today as well.

CONCLUSION

Considering what we have learned about the oral culture of the Bible, the implications for how we understand and respond to Scripture are far-reaching. Of all the things we can do to interpret Scripture correctly, there's probably nothing that will improve our understanding more than learning to hear as if we were the original audiences. We at least need to read Scripture with our ears tuned to hear it.

We at least need to read Scripture with our ears tuned to hear it.

The corollary to that is learning to speak as if we were the original storytellers. Throughout the Bible, speaking for and about God, and speaking for and about Jesus, is emphasized repeatedly. Approximately half of the biblical record is narrative, and story after story reveals much about the Trinity and about humanity. The better we know the stories

---

[11] Andreas J. Köstenberger, "John," in *Zondervan Illustrated Bible Backgrounds Commentary*, ed. Clinton E. Arnold (Grand Rapids, MI: Zondervan, 2002), 109-10.

and the better we tell the stories, the better for God's purposes and for all concerned. It's our mission as his messengers.

The implications of biblical orality are not only far-reaching but wide-ranging. And that will be underscored by the next four propositions, which are various experiments in oral interpretation.

PART FOUR

EXPERIMENTS IN ORAL INTERPRETATION

PROPOSITION 15

HEARING IS MORE THAN READING

UNDERSTANDING SCRIPTURE HOLISTICALLY

The words that God has spoken are alive and effective,
sharper even than a two-edged sword.

HEBREWS 4:12

POSSIBLY THE MOST IMPORTANT TAKEAWAY from this study of biblical orality, and the easiest error to correct, is the faux pas of zeroing in on a word or verse in the Bible and failing to take into account the full counsel of God, the entire scope of divine revelation.

Understanding the Bible atomistically rather than holistically could be the most serious oversight from reading Scripture textually rather than orally. Unfortunately, it's a widespread practice of taking verses out of context, and it can lead to incorrect interpretation as well as to disruptions in the unity of the community of believers.

Many Christians are inclined to grab hold of select verses that soothe their souls or challenge their values, then exorcise them from their Bibles, hang them on the wall, memorize them, declare them to be their life verses, and if they're an athlete, write them on their shoes: "I can do all things through Christ." But is that a good thing? Maybe in some senses, but there's an inherent problem.

"Ask and you shall receive" can be big boost to Christians' morale, assuring them that God will give them what they want, regardless of what the true will of God may be for them. But is that consistent with the rest of Scripture?

"All things work together for our good" can be a wonderful encouragement to someone facing great hardship or loss. God is sovereign, so it's guaranteed that one way or another, everything will turn out well for anyone who loves God. But is that supported by the full counsel of God?

Taking such verses out of context and misapplying them can be as misleading as the prosperity gospel is for impoverished people. The claim is well-known: with enough faith and a generous financial donation, God will grant unimaginable material blessings.[1]

The problem is, single statements are not necessarily valid reflections of what a speaker or author actually intends to communicate. It's true for the Bible, especially since the world of the Bible was a culture of orality.

HEARING TAKES INTO ACCOUNT THE WIDER CONTEXT

As emphasized several times in this book (for example, Proposition 4), inherent to oral culture is high context. It's an elevated sense of the importance of the larger context both of communications and circumstances. The meaning of a statement cannot be properly understood without considering it in light of the overall meaning of the communication.

Those of us not situated in oral culture are inclined, unfortunately, in the opposite direction. For us, every statement is expected to be accurate in and of itself. We feel free to slice and dice communications, including Scripture, into bits and pieces, and then to quote a piece of the whole as gospel truth.

If we learn anything from how the original hearers understood Scripture, it is to take in larger swaths of divine revelation rather than to snitch snippets out of whatever context. Sentences, even paragraphs,

---

[1]A case in point is Joel Osteen; see Richard L. Schultz, *Out of Context: How to Avoid Misinterpreting the Bible* (Grand Rapids, MI: Baker Books, 2012), 99; also, a book by a nephew of the televangelist Benny Hinn: Costi W. Hinn, *God, Greed, and the (Prosperity) Gospel: How Truth Overwhelms a Life Built on Lies* (Grand Rapids, MI: Zondervan, 2019).

must not be interpreted as if they are complete statements of truth. Oral interpretation recognizes that the sum is greater than the individual parts.

> *Oral interpretation recognizes that the sum is greater than the individual parts.*

One of the negative impacts impressed on our consciousnesses by the Authorized Version was that each verse is a separate paragraph, and the surrounding context is secondary if necessary at all. But the Bible is not a dictionary with individual entries defining meaning. Nor is it an encyclopedia where you can turn to a page or two and find a full discussion of a particular topic. The truths of Scripture come to us whole cloth, not scraps, not nestled in a couple of threads.

This point has been emphasized for years: the meaning of a communication is easily misunderstood by analyzing words rather than focusing on clusters of sentences and paragraphs.[2] But bringing our thinking and practices in line with that conviction is challenging, partly because it's contrary to our scientific inclination (more on that below).

Words and sentences are vehicles of meaning, but not in and of themselves and definitely not isolated from the larger context. Meaning is more about thoughts and concepts, and words are signposts pointing in the direction of meaning.[3]

A case in point is word studies, which unfortunately have become an overused way to seek to understand Scripture. Using a biblical concordance to track down every occurrence of a word and seeking a common meaning of the word that will apply in all situations is a flawed

---

[2] "It is not words which provide the basic unit of meaning but the larger elements of discourse, sentences and paragraphs"; Peter Cotterell and Max Turner, *Linguistics and Biblical Interpretation* (Downers Grove, IL: IVP Academic, 1989), 28; similarly, as noted by James Barr, *The Semantics of Biblical Language* (Oxford: Oxford University Press, 1961), "It is the sentence (and of course the still larger literary complex such as the complete speech or poem) which is the linguistic bearer of the usual theological statement and not the word (the lexical unit) or the morphological and syntactical connection" (263).
[3] "The smallest potentially independent unit of meaning in a text or discourse is, arguably, the concept"; Cotterell and Turner, *Linguistics and Biblical Interpretation*, 193.

strategy. (The corresponding abuse of etymologies for determining the meanings of words has been addressed above in Proposition 9.)

Relying on "word chains—connecting verses through 'links' of word usage and treating key words like *stone* the same wherever they were found in the Bible . . . wouldn't have become popular without the development of concordances."[4] Those who want to read the Bible literally would be expected "to care more about how the first Christians received Scripture. But the tool they were using for their Bible reading pushed them in this other, 'scientific' direction instead."[5]

Almost every word in any language has ranges of meaning, and what a word denotes in one context may have little or nothing to do with what it denotes in another.[6] Better than dictionaries of words would be dictionaries of thoughts. The best available in that regard is a topical thesaurus of the Bible.[7]

In order to recapture meanings that texts had for ancient audiences, we need to replace close dissections of short passages with broad expositions of long texts. This points to several ideas, but one certainly is that our modernist, scientific tendencies to take something like a rose into a laboratory and dissect it, by which it loses its fragrance—and by comparison, a text loses its power—needs to be reconsidered.

We don't need microscopes when studying Scripture. Something closer to a macroscope would be better. "Microdosing of Scripture without a grasp of the whole can easily distort our interpretations."[8]

The goal for preaching and teaching should not be how many sermons or lessons can be extrapolated out of one verse but more like

---

[4]Daniel G. Hummel, "When Concordances Broke Context: A Look at the History of our Bible Study Tools Suggests Caution Is Called For," *Christianity Today* 66, no. 9 (December 2022): 46 (emphasis in original).

[5]Hummel, "When Concordances Broke Context," 48.

[6]See the criticism of the editors of the *Theological Dictionary of the New Testament*: "It never seems to have occurred to them that a lexicon, as a book organized under *words*, is not a good instrument for . . . theological thought as of the type found in the NT"; James Barr, *The Semantics of Biblical Language* (Oxford: Oxford University Press, 1961), 233 (emphasis in original).

[7]A. Colin Day, *Roget's Thesaurus of the Bible* (San Francisco: HarperSanFrancisco, 1992).

[8]Dru Johnson and Celina Durgin, "Wasting Quiet Time: If Daily Devotions Aren't Yielding True Bible Fluency, Is There a Better Way?" *Christianity Today* 67.3 (April 2023): 65.

how many paragraphs can be formed into one sermon. If linguists are correct that a paragraph is generally the smallest unit of meaning, then preachers and teachers, take note. If we miss the larger development of thought that hearing a complete text would bring to listeners' attention, then our interpretations will likely miss the mark.

The book *Out of Context* recounts a litany of verses misunderstood because their context is ignored. Examples abound, from the "Jabez prayer" to the children's jingle, "Every promise in the book is mine."[9] Want to understand Matthew 18:20 regarding where two or three are gathered together in its proper context? See page 45. Want to reconsider what Jesus meant regarding our future heavenly mansions (Jn 14:2)? See page 72. Want to correct the misunderstanding of Philippians 4:13 and what it truly means to be able to do all things? See page 44. These are just a few examples discussed in this important book.

A verse commonly taken out of context, which is not discussed in *Out of Context,* is Romans 8:28. The Greek construction can be translated in several ways, which contributes to the problem. Unfortunately, most English versions make it sound like all things work together for *our* good. There are even worship choruses that promote the idea. And with readers commonly failing to take in the wider context, misunderstanding is likely.

Here's a suggested translation of Romans 8:28-29a: *Now we know that for those who love God—for those who are called with his purpose in mind—all things work together for good; because those whom he foreknew, he also predestined to be conformed to the image of his son.*[10] That's a valid translation and may open the door to a clearer understanding of what the actual point of the verse is. There are several factors to consider.

---

[9] Richard L. Schultz, *Out of Context: How to Avoid Misinterpreting the Bible* (Grand Rapids, MI: Baker Books, 2012), 11-18, 81-82.

[10] Similarly, The Voice version translates Rom 8:28 as, "We are confident that God is able to orchestrate everything to work toward something good *and beautiful* when we love Him and accept His invitation to live according to His plan" (emphasis in original).

- The purpose of God working all things together is immediately evident in the next verse: *to be conformed to the likeness of his Son.*

- Jesus made it clear that being one of his disciples wouldn't be an easy road: "Whoever wants to be my disciple must deny themselves and take up their cross and follow me. For whoever wants to save their life will lose it, but whoever loses their life for me will find it" (Mt 16:24-25 NIV); he also said to expect persecution (Mt 5:10-12; 10:23).

- Paul bemoaned all the trials and tribulations that he experienced (2 Cor 11:23-29). (Consider also the laments in the book of Psalms; e.g., Ps 13).

- Paul declared, counterintuitively, "Whatever were gains to me I now consider loss for the sake of Christ. What is more, I consider everything a loss because of the surpassing worth of knowing Christ Jesus my Lord, for whose sake I have lost all things. I consider them garbage, that I may gain Christ" (Phil 3:7-8 NIV).

- Paul summarized his life of sacrifice, "I know what it is to be in need, and I know what it is to have plenty. I have learned the secret of being content in any and every situation, whether well fed or hungry, whether living in plenty or in want" (Phil 4:12 NIV).

- We're warned that *the whole world is controlled by the evil one* (1 Jn 5:19; cf. 2 Cor 4:4). The devil may be on a short leash, but God gives him a lot of room to roam and create havoc, as he did for Job (Job 1:8-12; cf. 1 Pet 5:8).

- Joseph noted near the end of his life: *You wanted to harm me, but God used it for a good purpose, to keep alive a great nation, as can be seen today* (Gen 50:20).

In light of the immediate context and the broader context, it's hard to imagine that Paul was assuring us that everything would turn out in ways we would want them to: goodness on our terms. Clearly, the grand story of Scripture is not about us and our good, but about God and his good. *Whether you eat, drink, or whatever you do, make sure you do everything for the glory of God* (1 Cor 10:31). *From him, through him, and for him are all things* (Rom 11:36).

It's almost certainly a misinterpretation of Romans 8:28, then, to ignore its immediate context and the context of Scripture as a whole and think that God is going to make everything happen for *our* good. Admittedly, to think that way is a temptation hard to resist, especially under the influence of the entitlement culture prominent today. We want things to work out for our good, and that gives us hope in the midst of trials.

But our hope should focus on God's good that can come out of our difficulties. We should take our eyes off ourselves and focus on his will and ways. We want his will to be done, not our own, and his kingdom to come, not ours.

There's a caution here for those who translate the Bible. The meaning of a verse may be more than the words alone seem to express. Context may be necessary to supplement and clarify what a statement in Scripture was intended to communicate. It's unfortunate that most English translations of Romans 8:28 allowed, even encouraged, readers to misunderstand the point. (A fuller discussion of contextual translation will have to wait for another time.)

Moving on, regarding what Jesus said about asking and receiving whatever one wants (Mt 7:7), the broader context is again essential to understand the statement correctly.

- Jesus was a prophet and often spoke as a prophet.[11] That included energizing language to get his point across, adding force to fact.[12]

[11]See David L. Turner, *Israel's Last Prophet: Jesus and the Jewish Leaders in Matthew 23* (Minneapolis: Fortress, 2015); Jeffrey A. Gibbs, "Jesus as Prophet in the Gospel Narratives," in *A Handbook on the Jewish Roots of the Gospels*, ed. Craig A. Evans and David Mishkin (Peabody, MA: Hendrickson, 2022), 162-71; for a sustained discussion of Jesus as prophet, see N. T. Wright, *Jesus and the Victory of God* (Minneapolis: Fortress, 1997), part 2.

[12]See Proposition 12 above regarding Quintilian's explanation; for additional insight into energizing language, see D. Brent Sandy, *Plowshares and Pruning Hooks: Rethinking the Language of Biblical Prophecy and Apocalyptic* (Downers Grove, IL: IVP Academic, 2002), 90-102; and most important, Walter Brueggemann, *The Prophetic Imagination*, 2nd ed. (Minneapolis: Fortress, 2001).

Actually, that's likely part of the explanation for various things he said, such as, *If you have faith as tiny as a mustard seed, you'll be able say to this mountain, "Move from here to there, and it will!" There isn't anything that will be impossible for you!* (Mt 17:20).

- What Jesus said is clarified in 1 John: *Beloved, if our hearts don't condemn us . . . and whatever we ask for, we receive, it's because we obey his commandments and do things that are pleasing to him* (1 Jn 3:21-22).

- James makes clear that making requests of God with wrong motives dooms the answer (Jas 4:3). Asking amiss gets us nowhere.

- Jesus could have been speaking proverbially, as we find, for example, in the book of Proverbs. His statements could have been maxims, rules of thumb as it were, rather than propositional declarations.

- We know that God's promises may depend on our obedience and are not blank checks. For example, note what God said to Abraham: *You must keep my covenant* (Gen 17:1-2, 9; cf. Ex 19:5); or what Joshua said to the Israelites, *Not a single promise has failed . . . but if you break the covenant . . .* (Josh 23:14-16); or what God said to Solomon and Ahab (1 Kings 9:4-7; 21:21, 29); or what God said to Jeremiah (Jer 18:2-10).[13]

We're now better prepared to understand Jesus' statement. He never intended a wide-open offer of satisfying our unlimited desires if we simply ask. Of course, we already knew that because many of us have probably tried the formula only to be disappointed. Teenagers praying for God to remove the acne from their faces overnight—mustering all the faith they possibly can that he could and would—is almost certainly going to leave them disappointed, and worse, questioning the promises of Scripture. Unfortunately, we probably don't do enough to

---

[13]For other examples, see Ex 32:9-10, 14; 1 Chron 28:7-9; Is 38:1, 3.

help people understand the importance of context for understanding what Scripture is truly communicating.

THE INTERPRETIVE FLAW AND DISUNITY IN THE CHURCH

Since 1782, the Latin phrase *e pluribus unum* (out of many, one) has appeared on the Great Seal of the United States and has become a common motto. It's a wonderful idea, if it could only be true. The present climate suggests we're going the wrong direction, seemingly irreversibly.

Unfortunately, the church seems to have been squeezed into the world's mold. The unity that's supposed to be the body of Christ's true nature isn't. We seem unable to escape the shadow of the failed motto of the US. It's a lack of obedience to God's intent for his body.

Concluding his three years of ministry, Jesus—while looking ahead to centuries of absence from the earth—summoned all his might on that foreboding night to pray one of the most important prayers ever. The prayer culminated in a stunning announcement: "I have given them the glory that you gave me, that they may be one as we are one—I in them and you in me—so that they may be brought to complete unity. Then the world will know that you sent me and have loved them even as you have loved me" (Jn 17:22-23 NIV).

The glory of the Trinity, which God shared with Jesus, he now shares with us. The manner and means by which God was in Jesus is the way he is in us. As God and Jesus are one, Jesus and we are one, and we and others in the body of Christ are one. It's an amazing amount of oneness: God, Jesus, his disciples, all of us. An essential feature of the gospel message is this amazing union: deity and humanity all bound together in oneness and likeness.

The glory that Jesus invests in us is the same divine incarnational glory that he manifested throughout his earthly ministry. *The Word became flesh and came to live among us; we saw his glory—the glory of the one and only one, full of grace and truth, who came from the Father* (Jn 1:14). The culmination of Jesus' incarnation was more than the cross, providing salvation for souls. It is all souls who become his followers being glorified and unified.

What could be more important? Our shared unity and glory have an end result: "Then the world will know that you sent me and have loved them even as you have loved me" (Jn 17:23 NIV). Unity, glory, ministry.

Unfortunately, the most flagrant failure of the church today is arguably divisiveness among Christ-followers. It's puzzling that it's gotten to this point.[14] Probably the biggest contributing factor is surprisingly right under our noses.

It's how Scripture is misinterpreted, constructing arguments on selected verses, without taking into account the larger context of Scripture and the larger context of the worldwide church. A few favorite verses can be the basis of isolated beliefs which are not shared with the community of faithful believers. It's moving beyond the historic defining doctrines of our faith, the rule of faith, and separating over ancillary matters.

But that's not what we were called to. "I appeal to you, brothers and sisters, in the name of our Lord Jesus Christ, that all of you agree with one another in what you say and that there be no divisions among you, but that you be perfectly united in mind and thought" (1 Cor 1:10 NIV). "There is one body and one Spirit, just as you were called to one hope when you were called; one Lord, one faith, one baptism; one God and Father of all, who is over all and through all and in all" (Eph 4:4-6 NIV). "Make my joy complete by being like-minded, having the same love, being one in spirit and of one mind" (Phil 2:2 NIV).

When we construct our views on a selection of verses interpreted a certain way, while others have their own set of verses interpreted their

---

[14]There are many books addressing this topic, but apparently there need to be more; see, e.g., Ephraim Radner, *A Brutal Unity: The Spiritual Politics of the Christian Church* (Waco, TX: Baylor University Press, 2012); and more recently Richard Lints, *Uncommon Unity: Wisdom for the Church in an Age of Division* (Bellingham, WA: Lexham, 2022). Cf. Richard Lints, "Christian Unity in a Divided Age," *Christianity Today* 67, no. 1 (January-February 2023): 48-50.

own way—and in both cases not having carefully interpreted Scripture in context—it's a head-on collision.

With interpreters coming to conclusions with little regard for other viewpoints and claiming to have a corner on the truth, unity becomes nearly impossible. The absence of collectivism and believers rarely joining together with faithful believers of other persuasions exacerbates the problem. "Bible professors have long noted that the natural habitat of Scripture is in the ears of gathered Christians, not in the eyes of individuals."[15]

The church has become captive to the ways of the world. It's a captivity of individualism, of microscopic reading, of one-upmanship, of exceptionalism, of arrogance—with church after church (and denominations) differing on many matters and claiming their view is the only valid one: sovereignty versus freewill, grace versus works, gifts of the Spirit, fulfillment of prophecy, Communion, modes of baptism, worship styles, personal convictions, political persuasions—the list never ends. Echoes of the call to "let my people go" could probably be heard if anyone is listening.

Our calling as Christians is to be a hallowed witness to the world, messengers sharing the good news, showing how true followers of Jesus are different, how we love and live in harmony with one another even as we do with Jesus. Jesus sought to create a community of unity that would stand tall in the world. But our individualism and taking verses out of context keep us small, if at all. Most important, our unity has the potential to give people all the more reason to recognize Jesus as Lord.

But regrettably, disunity characterizes us, and non-Christians don't know whom to believe. Consequently, more and more people find it increasingly difficult to believe. The demographic research showing the decline in the number of Americans who claim to be Christians over the past fifty years is stunning.[16]

---

[15]Johnson and Durgin, "Wasting Quiet Time," 69.
[16]See, e.g., the Pew Research Center: www.pewresearch.org.

The countercultural community of grace, acceptance, and healing is MIA (missing in action). Oh yes, there are exceptions, but overall, the unmistakable display of humility, cruciform living, the fruit of the Spirit, and unity across the spectrum of true believers simply isn't.

We're part of the *already* in preparation for the *not yet*.[17] More than an analogy of the future kingdom, we are the rehearsal for the new heaven and new earth, the prelude of the glory of the great multitude from every nation, tribe, people, and language, standing before the throne, wearing white robes, and waving palm branches (Rev 7:9).[18] We are the present manifestation of God's kingdom and the image of God's Son.

Compromise the church, and we risk compromising God and his kingdom. The bedrock issue beneath the ways the church is failing its mission of unity is arguably hermeneutical. We are not a community of faithful interpreters seeking to find common ground in understanding and applying Scripture. Maybe it is too much to ask. Except that Jesus prayed for it.

The importance of interpreting Scripture in context can hardly be overstated, both for understanding God's communication to us and our communication to the world for him. Hopefully we can make significant progress in becoming the messengers and models God desires us to be: unity, glory, ministry. "Do your best to present yourself to God as one approved . . . who correctly handles the word of truth" (2 Tim 2:15 NIV).

---

[17]I am not suggesting that the kingdom is reducible to the church or that the two are indistinguishable; see Thomas C. Oden, *Life in the Spirit: Systematic Theology, Volume 3* (San Francisco: HarperSanFrancisco, 1992), 287; Stanley J. Grenz, *Revisioning Evangelical Theology: A Fresh Agenda for the 21st Century* (Downers Grove, IL: IVP Academic, 1993) 182-83; Stanley J. Grenz, *Theology for the Community of God* (Grand Rapids, MI: Eerdmans, 1994), 472-85.

[18]Kevin J. Vanhoozer, *The Drama of Doctrine: A Canonical-Linguistic Approach to Christian Theology* (Louisville, KY: Westminster John Knox, 2005), 443.

PROPOSITION 16

HEARING IS MORE THAN READING

IMAGINING CREATION AND INCARNATION

Your word is a lamp for my feet and a light for my path.

PSALM 119:105

POETRY WAS A POPULAR MEDIUM in the biblical world, and there are ample examples in the Bible. Not only in the Old Testament—the books of Job, Psalms, Proverbs, Ecclesiastes, Song of Songs (as well as scattered throughout narrative portions), and most of the prophetic books (which escapes many people's notice)—but also in the New Testament: Mary expressing her anticipation of giving birth to the Son of God (Lk 1:46-55); Zechariah's excitement about the birth of John the Baptist (Lk 1:68-79); Simeon's thrill upon taking the baby Jesus into his arms (Lk 2:29-32).[1] In addition to those poetic verses, we should note "the poetic quality of much of the teaching of Jesus and the book of Revelation."[2]

I make no claim to be a poet, but in this proposition, I explore the place for imagination in the form of poetic verse for understanding the

---

[1]Other poetry in the Old Testament includes Gen 49; Ex 15; Deut 32–33; Judg 5; 2 Sam 2, 22–23; 1 Chron 16; for other poetry in the New Testament, see especially Phil 2:6-11.

[2]Tremper Longman III, "Biblical Poetry," in *A Complete Literary Guide to the Bible*, ed. Leland Ryken and Tremper Longman III (Grand Rapids, MI: Zondervan, 1993), 81; Jesus' "sermons and his discourses are essentially poetic in style" according to Leland Ryken, *Words of Life: A Literary Introduction to the New Testament* (Grand Rapids, MI: Baker, 1987), 102.

power of the spoken word.[3] Poetry is the creative use of words to enhance the presentation of ideas that might otherwise be overlooked in simple narrative.[4] Poetry speaks beyond what the words on the surface can reveal.

> *Poetry speaks beyond what the words*
> *on the surface can reveal.*

After all, the Bible "is an affective book that communicates much of its meaning by moving the feelings and the will of its readers."[5] We have good reason to explore using poetic style to enhance the meaning and power of divine truth revealed orally.

CREATION

Distant nebulas spawning galaxies
  black holes spinning round
Stars twinkling across light years of void
  Sunrays sparkling on drops of moisture
Earth settling into its course
  planets and moons taking up vast orbits
Breezes unbound starting unexplained journeys
  day and night sharing time and space
Land and seas measuring off boundaries
  islands gliding across oceans, seeking resting places

---

[3]I have been inspired by the poetry of Amanda Gorman; see Amanda Gorman, *The Hill We Climb: An Inaugural Poem for the Country* (New York: Viking, 2021); *Amanda Gorman Poems: Call Us What We Carry* (New York: Viking, 2021); see also Leland Ryken, *Sweeter than Honey, Richer than Gold: A Guided Study of Biblical Poetry* (Bellingham, WA: Weaver, 2015); Leland Ryken, *Poetry of Redemption: An Illustrated Treasury of Good Friday and Easter Poems* (Phillipsburg, NJ: P&R, 2023).
[4]Volumes in the Ashgate Studies in Theology, Imagination, and the Arts encourage imagination as a means for enhancing the understanding of Scripture and theology. For example, Malcolm Guite, *Faith, Hope and Poetry: Theology and the Poetic Imagination*, Ashgate Studies in Theology, Imagination, and the Arts (London: Routledge, 2016); see also Trevor Hart, "Imagination and Responsible Reading," and Nicholas Wolterstorff, "A Response to Trevor Hart," in *Renewing Biblical Interpretation*, ed. C. Bartholomew, C. Greene, and K. Möller, Scripture and Hermeneutics Series 1 (Grand Rapids, MI: Zondervan, 2000), 307-33 and 335-41.
[5]Longman, "Biblical Poetry," 69.

Mountains rumbling, lifting skyward
    valleys clicking into appointed spaces
Trees poking through sod, stretching leg-like trunks
    arm-like branches reaching skyward, green hands clapping
Flowers filling fields and prairies, opening emerald-like petals
    no room for weeds in the carpet of colors
DNAs forming sequences, creatures arching backs
    lifting heads, rising from beds
Man looking at himself, woman looking at herself
    looking at each other
Everything new—first time, first light, first life, first love.

CREATION AND INCARNATION IN PARALLEL

Where to begin pondering Jesus, the Son of God, in earthly façade? Maybe looking back across many centuries and revisiting the pedigree of his genealogy. Matthew did, noting especially that Gentile blood had seeped into the royal line (Mt 1:1-17). Maybe looking back several centuries and re-experiencing Isaiah's hope-filled promise to the captivity-trapped chosen people. Mark did: *The voice of one crying in the wilderness, "Prepare the way for the Lord"* (Mk 1:1-3). Maybe looking back and marveling at the unexpected arrival of the Son of God as an infant. Luke did: *she wrapped him in binding cloths and put him to bed in a feeding trough* (Lk 2:1-24).

But John began his Gospel looking back to the beginning of everything: *In the beginning was the word* (Jn 1:1).[6] God's original creation of a seemingly endless universe, from subatomic particles to massive stars, was and is a wonder to behold. It's far more than the wildest of imaginations can contemplate.

But divinity taking up residence in humanity was and is equally a wonder to behold, a creative act in its own right: *The word became flesh and came to live among us* (Jn 1:14). "In Genesis 'in the beginning' introduces the story of the 'old' creation; in John it introduces the story of the 'new

---

[6]"The vocabulary of John's preamble is decisively shaped by the opening verses of Genesis"; J. Ramsey Michaels, *The Gospel of John*, NICNT (Grand Rapids, MI: Eerdmans, 2010), 46.

creation.'"[7] Only God could make both happen: two miracles of creation. Who can imagine the full significance of either, especially in parallel?

"Poetry may be especially fitted as a medium for helping us apprehend something of the mystery embodied in the phrase, 'the Word was made flesh.'"[8] Thus, we envision the cosmic parallels of the drama of creation and incarnation happening something like this.[9] (An oral reading by two people is recommended, one reading the lines on the left and the other the lines on the right.)

A faint rumbling in the distance
    as if percussionists were practicing their timpanis
    wind whooshing back-and-forth, a voice preparing to speak
Stirring the still formless void—
    The Spirit of God moving over the face of the waters.

                    Suddenly a sound like the blowing
                    of a violent wind came from heaven!

Finishing its work, the holy tempest moves on
    yet a holy suspense lingers—waiting
Something is happening . . . someone is happening
    suddenly a sound shatters the emptiness, *Let there be!*

                    In the beginning was the Word.
                    And the Word was with God.
                    And the Word was God!

A light, first only a flicker
    candlelight piercing the nothingness
    beams of wave-particles splintering voids of darkness
    shafts of light penetrating the vastness—
The once-black darkness sent fleeing
    Let there be light. And there was.

---

[7] Edward W. Klink III, *John*, ZECNT (Grand Rapids, MI: Zondervan, 2016), 86; cf. F. F. Bruce, *The Gospel of John: Introduction, Exposition and Notes* (Grand Rapids, MI: Eerdmans, 1983), 29.

[8] Guite, *Faith, Hope and Poetry*, 2.

[9] "The solemn repetition—Word, Word, God, God, Word—captures the reader's attention from the outset by giving the language a poetic or hymnic quality"; J. Ramsey Michaels, *The Gospel of John*, NICNT (Grand Rapids, MI: Eerdmans, 2010), 47.

> *"I am the Light of the world!" The true light,*
> *which enlightens everyone, was coming into the world,*
> *the light of the glory of God in the face of Jesus Christ!*

A surrealistic permutation of molecules, elements, isotopes
  splendor of radiant energy—
Majestic matter escaping the clutches of eternity
  the Voice proclaims, *Let the ground appear . . . and water . . . and creatures;*
  and let us make someones.

> *The Word became flesh and made his residence among us!*
> *"This is my Son, the Beloved One: I delight in him!"*

The Artist-Architect, the Someone, steps back and reflects on the
  somethings—
  his creative acts defining him and us:
  Everything, it's very good.

> *Through him all things came into being!*

At once the sound becomes stately, symphonic—
  mountains, valleys, creatures clap their hands, lift their voices
  reverberating in a pinnacle of praise
It is a holy hallelujah.

> *A multitude of the heavenly host singing Yahweh's praises,*
> *"Glory to God in the highest!"*

How close to reality this attempt, using poetic imagery is for grasping the power and parallels between creation and incarnation, we can only imagine. Two sacrosanct, corresponding movements reveal where we came from and where he came from—never to be repeated, always to be celebrated. Mystery enshrouds the mirror images of the creative events, and the more imprecise our knowledge of something, the more appropriate poetry to portray such enigmas.[10]

---

[10] "Metaphor says what cannot be said otherwise, at least not so effectively, or so well, and possibly not at all"; James D. G. Dunn, *Jesus Remembered*, Christianity in the Making 1 (Grand Rapids, MI: Eerdmans, 2003), 486.

God creating matter was no minor matter; God becoming matter was the most major matter. We do well to intuit the holy significance of the twin events of creation, marveling at all its—and his—majesty.[11] Ponder the might of divinity overwhelming the muck of humanity; the miracle of grace overpowering the madness of evil; the new order of Jesus' kingdom overcoming the disorder of human attempts at kingdom-building; regal deity poured into an uneasy vessel.[12]

From heavenly majesty Jesus entered the mundane, from which he would not seek escape. In the words of Dietrich Bonhoeffer, "Wealth in poverty, light in darkness, succour in abandonment."[13] In the words of Paul, *Being in the form of God he humbled himself and took on the form of a human* (Phil 2:6-8). In any words, amazing. (For the poem that follows, an oral reading by two people is recommended, one reading what Nicodemus asked and the other what Jesus asked.)

QUESTIONS AND ANSWERS OF THE NIGHT

"Who are *you*, Jesus?
teacher? Okay, yes; but who are you, really?
miracles? Okay, yes; but who are you, truly?"

"What do *you* know, Nicodemus?
about the kingdom of God, certainly?
about being born again, justly?"

"What are *you* saying, Jesus?
an adult, becoming a fetus again, essentially?
passing through the birth canal, seriously?"

---

[11]John's prologue "doubtless represents one of the most beautiful and carefully crafted poetic portions in the entire NT"; Andreas J. Köstenberger, *John*, Baker Exegetical Commentary on the New Testament (Grand Rapids, MI: Baker Academic, 2004), 19-20; but see D. A. Carson, *The Gospel According to John*, Pillar New Testament Commentary (Grand Rapids, MI: Eerdmans, 1994), 112-13.

[12]According to Craig Evans, "The most important of Jesus' activities can be gathered into two major groupings: (1) the proclamation of the kingdom of God and the appointment of the twelve apostles; and (2) controversy with the ruling priests and a Roman execution"; Craig A. Evans, "What Did Jesus Do?" in *Jesus under Fire*, ed. Michael J. Wilkins and J. P. Moreland (Grand Rapids, MI: Zondervan, 1995), 103.

[13]Written from prison in a love letter to his fiancé Maria, December 1943; Dietrich Bonhoeffer, *Love Letters from Cell 92*, ed. Ruth-Alice von Bismarck and Ulrich Kabitz (New York: HarperCollins, 1995), 109.

"What do *you* know, Nicodemus?
  about entering the kingdom of God, worthily?
  about being born of water, strangely?"

"Also, what do *you* know, Nicodemus?
  does what I say surprise you, entirely?
  you don't understand new birth, fully?"

"Again, what *do* you know, Nicodemus?
  about the wind blowing where it wishes, mysteriously?
  about those born of the Spirit moving about, freely?"

"Have not I told you about things of this world, correctly?
  yet are you doubting things, earthly?
  how will you then believe things, heavenly?"

"How can these things be, Jesus?
  are you telling the truth, plainly?
  do I need to understand everything, clearly?"

"Aren't you a teacher yourself, Nicodemus?
  and you don't understand, minimally?
  who then will believe *you*, rightfully?"

"Have I told you anything unbelievable, falsely?
  will you not accept my testimony, surely?
  what else can I say, so you'll believe, finally?"

It's night, but I'm beginning to see the light, truly.

"God's grace on display, abundantly,
  giving his Son—me, willingly,
  those who believe—in me will not die, certainly."

"God's mission for me, redeemingly,
  yet ones who do not believe, judged, unfortunately,
  while ones who do believe, vindicated forever, completely."

   Yes, teacher I am,
   and miracles I do;
   I am the *light* of the world.

Presenting divine revelation in poetic verse heightens the effect, and an appreciation for that among Christians in the modern Western world is finally catching on. It used to be that most Christians were only interested in literal language. After all, that's what many blindingly assume Scripture consists of. But Malcolm Guite's sonnets, for example, are beginning to turn the tide, appealing especially to the younger generation, even though he is grandfather to that age group.[14] Certainly with the prominence of poetry in divine revelation and the place for imagination in the oral interpretation of Scripture, it will be appropriate for more and more Christians to read and write in poetic style with the goal of grasping the power of the spoken word more fully.

---

[14]See Kara Bettis, "The Subversive Bard," *Christianity Today* 67, no. 1 (January-February 2023): 52-57; see also Micah Mattix and Sally Thomas, eds., *Christian Poetry in America since 1940: An Anthology* (Brewster, MA: Paraclete, 2022).

HEARING IS MORE THAN READING

EXPERIENCING JESUS' RETURN TO NAZARETH

Over times past and in various ways God spoke to our ancestors
through the prophets, but in recent days near the end,
he has spoken through his Son.

HEBREWS 1:1-2

IT WAS A STRATEGIC MOMENT in the synagogue of Jesus'
hometown of Nazareth—at the beginning of his public ministry—
except that the people present weren't prepared for it to be the beginning of anything, whether for Jesus or themselves. Life didn't change
much in the rural villages of Galilee, and one wondered if it ever would.
Likewise for Jesus; he had apparently worked faithfully, day in and day
out, for years doing various kinds of woodworking, carpentry, masonry,
and construction—without much change.

But what transpired that day in Nazareth would reveal much about
who Jesus was, who he would seek to minister to, and how his message
would be received. And it would become singularly important for
Luke's Gospel and how he understood what Jesus came to do—and
what Jesus did.

Though Matthew and Mark's Gospels offer their own versions of the
day's events (Mt 13:54-58; Mk 6:1-6), both placing it later in Jesus'
public ministry and providing much less detail, we are exploring the

situation as Luke's Gospel presents it (Lk 4:14-30).[1] Immediately after Jesus' baptism and temptation, the scene in Nazareth was next.

Reliving the accounts in Scripture can enlighten our understanding.

In order to understand how this complex and conflicted story unfolds, we're seeking to put ourselves back into the lives of people as if we were there two thousand years ago. Reliving the accounts in Scripture can enlighten our understanding. We'd like to know what they knew, experience what they went through, appreciate their reactions and emotions. To do that we will include the oral elements emphasized above: evocative language, visual imagery, graphic descriptions, imagination, and so forth. We're seeking to understand the story better through the use of oral interpretation. The following reconstruction is presented as a first-person account as if some women are telling the story.[2]

O Little Town of Nazareth

You'd probably consider our tiny town an unpretentious village.[3] The population, though no one bothers to count—except, of course, the

---

[1]Reading Luke's account, it appears that Jesus was alone when he went back to Nazareth, whereas Mark records that Jesus was accompanied by his disciples. Following Luke's storyline, it was sometime later that Jesus called fishermen to follow him, but in Mark's account the disciples had already been following Jesus for days. These kinds of differences are common in the Gospels and apparently did not pose a problem to the compilers or hearers of the Gospels, nor should they for us; see John H. Walton and D. Brent Sandy, *The Lost World of Scripture: Ancient Literary Culture and Biblical Authority* (Downers Grove, IL: IVP Academic, 2013), 296, 307-8.

[2]As noted previously, written versions of events, or of what someone said, are often condensed; there's always more than meets the eye of the reader. So we'll need some additional insight and informed imagination to flesh out the story. But we'll stay true to the facts as preserved in the biblical account.

[3]"Nazareth was literally 'off the map' in the time of Jesus"; the village is not mentioned in any other sources of the day, such as in the works of the first-century Jewish historian Josephus. "All available evidence suggests that the population of first century AD Nazareth was at best a few hundred people and maybe as few as one hundred." Paul H. Wright, "The Size and Makeup of Nazareth at the Time of Jesus," *Lexham Geographic Commentary on the Gospels*, ed. Barry J. Beitzel and Kristopher A. Lyle (Bellingham, WA: Lexham, 2016), 37, 39; today Nazareth is divided into

tax collectors—could be one or two hundred. In contrast to the urban Jerusalem and all its residents, we are more of a rural outpost, surrounded by fields and farmlands, a humble hamlet to be sure.

Living in the heart of Galilee, it is a journey of several days going south and up into the mountains in order to make our way to Jerusalem, which many of us try to do each year for Passover.[4] The problem is, Jerusalem becomes overrun with so many people, all the children and crying babies, plus so many sheep being slaughtered; it is a huge commotion and conglomeration. One wonders sometimes if it's worth the trip, but we go anyway.

In Nazareth, we're never overcrowded, nor is there much to get excited about (unless it is the birth of the newest baby, which is especially a big deal for us women). We're basically satisfied to have a roof over our heads and wheat in the storage jar for making bread. Though in another sense, we are overcrowded—if you consider our large families in our tiny houses. But we make do, even if only having the barest of necessities.

Maybe it's our simple lifestyle that doesn't appear honorable or attractive. We sense condescension among people outside Galilee toward those of us inside. People can ask some jeering questions: "Is it possible for anything good to come out of Nazareth?" (see Jn 1:46); "the Messiah certainly couldn't come from Galilee, could he?" (see Jn 7:42). Too bad they feel that way; it's more their problem than ours.

Our region certainly has a checkered past. Across the centuries, numerous battles have been fought on our soil, foreign armies vying for control of the area. Warfare leads to many injuries and casualties among the warriors, but it also takes a toll on local inhabitants. Soldiers pillage villages and homes for supplies, often confiscating anything of value (see Lk 3:14). We have been beaten down time and time again, and recalling the stories of wars and atrocities is enough to keep anybody's

---

several parts: Nazareth proper, with a considerable Muslim population but also several Christian communities of various persuasions; and upper Nazareth to the east, which is a Jewish city.
[4]Craig Keener, *The IVP Bible Background Commentary*, 2nd ed. (Downers Grove, IL: IVP Academic, 2014), 186.

spirits low, with little positive to look back on or encouraging to look forward to. Injustices of all sorts have been commonplace. We women are especially vulnerable.[5]

Adding to the difficulties, about a hundred years before the birth of Jesus, Aristobulus, a king ruling in Jerusalem, ruthlessly forced the practices of Judaism on people in Galilee—even though many were Gentiles—demanding that all the males be circumcised.[6] It was an odd sort of affair: Gentiles suddenly supposed to be Jews. Did anyone really think that we Jews by birthright would accept such non-Jews without proper lineage?

The very idea of forcing Judaism on Gentiles only added to the ethnic animosity. Our Jewish laws prohibit us from associating with Gentiles (Acts 10:28), making the close proximity a constant issue of trying to avoid each other. Consequently, some Gentiles moved out of Galilee. Of course, there's a similar issue in Jerusalem and Judea, with the Roman government assigning various rulers and soldiers to make sure nothing gets out of hand, who, of course, are also Gentiles and are generally intolerant of our Jewish customs.

Making matters worse here in Galilee, it was soon after Jesus' birth that revolts broke out with the intent to put an end to the military occupation by the Romans.[7] The Jewish leaders of the insurrections mounted attacks from various villages near Nazareth, putting these towns at high risk.

Eventually, in order to quash the rebellion, the Roman army sacked Sepphoris, the capital and largest city in Galilee, killing thousands,

---

[5]"The history of these places that Jesus knew was blood-soaked"; Elaine A. Phillips, "On the Brow of the Hill at Nazareth: Luke 4:16-20," *Lexham Geographic Commentary on the Gospels*, ed. Barry J. Beitzel and Kristopher A. Lyle (Bellingham, WA: Lexham, 2016), 102.

[6]As reported by Josephus (*Antiquities* 13.319); see Sean Freyne, "Galilee," in *The Eerdmans Dictionary of Early Judaism*, ed. John J. Collins and Daniel C. Harlow (Grand Rapids, MI: Eerdmans, 2010), 655; cf. "Galilee of the Gentiles," according to Is 9:1.

[7]Judas the Galilean was one of the insurrectionists; "The first century AD was one of the most violent epochs of Jewish history, with the cauldron of unrest reaching its apex in the destruction of Jerusalem by the Romans in AD 70"; W. J. Heard and K. Yamazaki-Ransom, "Revolutionary Movements," in *Dictionary of Jesus and the Gospels*, 2nd ed., ed. Joel B. Green, Jeannine K. Brown, and Nicholas Perrin (Downers Grove, IL: IVP Academic, 2013), 789.

burning anything that would burn, and damaging everything else. Unfortunately, a considerable number of Jews had lived and worked there. It was especially bad when the Romans sent off all survivors to be sold as slaves; we dread the thought of it.[8] For us in Nazareth, this was too close for comfort. Sepphoris lay just three and a half miles away.[9]

No wonder many people consider Galilee an undesirable place to live. Frankly, from time to time we ask ourselves, "What bad thing is going to happen here next?" With Herod Antipas, son of Herod the Great, in power; with the hodge-podge of ethnicities—some being avowed Gentiles, who make no claim to be Jews; others of us being faithful Jews, such as Joseph and Mary; and yet others being nondescript half-breeds—just about anything can go wrong.

JESUS, THE CRAFTSMAN FROM NAZARETH

Now about Jesus. His hometown is Nazareth? Well, yes, but it's just a humble little town. We had known him personally as he was growing up, some of us even being his relatives. Though he wasn't born in Nazareth, from the time he was a tiny toddler all the way to his midthirties, he lived among us. He was part of a large family: four brothers and several sisters.

Early Christians wrote more than fifty accounts of Jesus' life, in addition to the four canonical Gospels, with some of the stories (known as the "Infancy Gospels") reporting fanciful miracles that Jesus performed as a child. For example, according to the Infancy Gospel of Thomas, Jesus fashioned clay sparrows and miraculously brought them to life. But none of these other "gospels" give evidence of being inspired.[10]

---

[8]"Sepphoris, in particular, had a strong Jewish influence. When residential houses were excavated . . . finds indicated that a substantial portion of the city's population was Jewish." Jens Schröter, "Jesus of Galilee: The Role of Location in Understanding Jesus," in *Jesus Research: An International Perspective*, ed. James H. Charlesworth and Petr Pokorný (Grand Rapids, MI: Eerdmans, 2009), 44.

[9]The apostle Paul would later be accused of being "the ringleader of the Nazarene rebellion" (Acts 24:5).

[10]See Timothy P. Henderson, "Gospels: Apocryphal," in Green et al., *Dictionary of Jesus and the Gospels*, 346-52; H.-J. Klauck, *Apocryphal Gospels: An Introduction* (London: T&T Clark, 2003); Kraus et al., *Gospel Fragments*, Oxford Early Christian Texts (Oxford: Oxford University Press, 2009);

In addition to hearing about some unusual events surrounding Jesus' birth in Bethlehem, just south of Jerusalem, we also heard about an unusual episode when he was just twelve years old (Lk 2:41-51). It was after Passover on the way back to Nazareth from Jerusalem that Jesus went missing from the rest of the caravan. Thankfully, Joseph and Mary, having returned to Jerusalem, found him in the temple courts conversing with some of the smartest people of the day, asking unexpectedly intelligent questions and answering theirs.

Upon return to Nazareth, the word of what happened got around. But we didn't know quite what to make of it. One thing for sure, we don't remember hearing Mary brag on how wonderful her son was. After all, she had other children to make sure were treated fairly. Knowing Mary, she probably thought about these things a lot but kept them to herself (see Lk 2:51). And since Jesus blended into our culture, lived according to our customs—and nothing else like it occurred for more than twenty years after that—we concluded it must have been a fluke. As far as we could tell, Jesus was one of the boys, though a very nice boy.[11]

One thing about Jesus was most unusual. In our culture for a man to be into his midthirties and to have never married would seem strange.[12] Surely, there had been many an eligible girl who tried to catch his eye, all the while hinting to her parents that they ought to talk to Joseph and Mary about arranging a marriage. We women wondered what kinds of conversations Joseph and Mary might have had with Jesus about such matters.

It was a very sad day when Joseph died, leaving Mary a widow. They were a peasant family, as indicated by the two turtledoves and young pigeons offered at the temple upon the birth of Jesus, which classified them

---

and W. Schneemelcher, ed., *New Testament Apocrypha*, trans. R. McL. Wilson, rev. ed., 2 vols. (Louisville, KY: Westminster John Knox, 1991-93).

[11] It's one thing for the people around Jesus to have no clue that he was more than human, but we have to wonder, What was going on in his mind?

[12] "Jesus himself chooses to remain single and celibate—a controversial choice, to be sure, but wholly consistent with his urgent eschatological hope. With the advent of God's kingdom at hand, there isn't time or energy for normal family entanglements." F. Scott Spencer, *What Did Jesus Do? Gospel Profiles of Jesus' Personal Conduct* (Harrisburg, PA: Trinity Press International, 2003), 105.

with the poor (Lk 2:24; cf. Lev 12:8). Fortunately, Jesus, being the eldest son, stepped up as the man of the house, continued the family business, and supported his mother while she cared for the rest of the children. It was a good thing he stayed here as long as he did. She needed him. Plus, with the rebuilding of the city of Sepphoris just a few miles away, there was no lack of work for wood workers and other types of construction.

> Regarding the dynamics of Jesus living out his childhood days, his teenage years, and into his thirties as a typical villager in the earthy culture of Galilee, the questions his village acquaintances asked are revealing: "Isn't this just Joseph's son?" (see Lk 4:22); "isn't his mother named Mary and his brothers—James, Joseph, Simon, and Judas—and aren't his sisters all with us?" (see Mt 13:55-56; Mk 6:3).[13] There seems to have been no premonition that Jesus was more than human, or at least they didn't want to admit it. All the years he lived there apparently seemed normal as he interacted with family and friends.

Jesus Returns Home

When Jesus unexpectedly walked back into Nazareth that day, we were delighted to have him back. He had been away for months, and there was hearsay from other areas of Galilee about his teaching in synagogues and even doing miraculous things (Mk 6:2). We wondered how that was possible for our homegrown carpenter's son. And if it was true, why there and not here?

So Jesus' coming back to his hometown was going to be interesting. Would he resume the family business and get back to a normal life? Or was he going to wow us by these new skills he reportedly had acquired? We weren't at all sure what to expect . . . or even hope for.

His first Sabbath in town, he went to the synagogue as we customarily do every Sabbath. After a reading from the books of Moses,

---

[13]The only suggestion in the Bible that Jesus' childhood was extraordinary was recorded by Luke (Lk 2:40-52), but there are reasons to think his childhood may not have been unique; especially Rom 8:3; Phil 2:7-8; Heb 2:17.

Jesus was handed the large Isaiah scroll by the synagogue official (cf. Acts 13:27). The scrolls in our synagogue, like most synagogues, are of the Pentateuch, the Psalms, and Isaiah. It's rare to have available any other of the Hebrew Scriptures.[14]

Unfortunately, only a few of us can read, let alone read Hebrew, since we speak Aramaic, but Jesus somehow had learned to read Hebrew. He commenced with reading aloud from the Isaiah scroll. We remember noticing that he seemed to unroll to a specific place; maybe it was assigned, maybe he carefully selected it. He read the following words and then stopped abruptly: "The Spirit of the Lord is on me, because he has anointed me to proclaim good news to the poor. He has sent me to proclaim freedom for the prisoners and recovery of sight for the blind, to set the oppressed free, to proclaim the year of the Lord's favor" (Lk 4:18-19 NIV; cf. Is 61:1-2).

Our first reaction was encouragement to hear again from the prophets that a new day would dawn in the future. Oh, if it could only be soon. If only the Messiah would come to our rescue. With all the troubles we'd been through in Galilee, we could certainly identify with the people in Isaiah's day and with their longing to be freed from exile. As for them, so for us. Any form of good news is welcome. Even in our day, there are so many hurting people, heartbroken, hopeless—for whom these words are especially meaningful.[15] Except that when you hear them over and over and nothing changes, you have to wonder if they'll ever come true.

Listening to Jesus, it didn't take long for it to begin to dawn on us that there could be more going on than just another reading from Isaiah. Jesus made no further comment and simply handed the scroll back and sat down. We waited. It was customary for someone to comment on

---

[14]In a synagogue, "the order of service following the recitation of the Shema (Deut 6:4-9) included liturgical prayers, followed by a reading from the Torah, followed by another reading, with commentary by a member of the congregation; this second reading was typically from the prophets. Then there would be a benediction"; David Lyle Jeffrey, *Luke*, Brazos Theological Commentary on the Bible (Grand Rapids, MI: Baker, 2012), 69-70.

[15]Regarding the people feeling like they were still living in exile, see N. T. Wright, *The New Testament and the People of God*, Christian Origins and the Question of God 1 (Minneapolis: Fortress, 1992), 268-70; *Jesus and the Victory of God*, Christian Origins and the Question of God 2 (Minneapolis: Fortress, 1996), 126-29.

what had just been read. But no one did. Was Jesus going to say something? It was a moment of suspense. We all turned and stared directly at him, wishing we could see inside to what he was thinking.

Who was going to break the silence? The synagogue official? Jesus? Jesus' family? It was Jesus who spoke up first, unexpectedly: "There's no more waiting; you heard it right: this Scripture is being fulfilled right in front of your eyes."[16]

> ## "You heard it right: this Scripture is being fulfilled right in front of your eyes."

Wow! You could have cut the air with a knife. No one dared breathe. As we remember it, Jesus didn't stand up and make the statement boldly; he remained seated and spoke softly, barely letting the words escape from his lips.

Our first reaction was disbelief. This couldn't be true; the good news Isaiah had prophesied so long ago was coming true in our time and in our insignificant village! Little by little, however, there was a stirring of hearts and minds. Maybe this was what we had longed for, for so long. "O LORD of hosts, how long will you have no mercy on Jerusalem and the cities of Judah?" (Zech 1:12 ESV).

Regardless of how Jesus knew all this, or what it meant, if he was correct, then this truly was exciting news. Everyone jumped up and started hugging one another and celebrating.

Jesus was an instant hero. We were thrilled by what he had read and said. Apparently, he knew things we didn't, and we were amazed and excited. Our lives were going to get a whole lot better, which hopefully would happen sooner rather than later.

---

[16]According to Craig L. Blomberg, *A New Testament Theology* (Waco, TX: Baylor University Press, 2018), 11 and 21-23, the integrating theme of the whole New Testament is the fulfillment of God's promises, as evident here at Nazareth, with the starting point for Jesus' public ministry being the fulfillment of Isaiah's prophecy.

But the celebration that had begun so quickly strangely began to scale back. Gradually a hush came over us again. We began to wonder, Was Jesus implying something about himself, not too innocently in fact, as if he himself was the fulfillment? After quietly living more than thirty years in Nazareth, was he somehow suggesting that he was more than ordinary, even anointed, actually the Messiah?

But, no—impossible! Preposterous! Isaiah's words couldn't apply to Jesus. What good news could he have to preach? How was a carpenter who had helped people with their building projects suddenly going to solve the problems of poor people, prisoners, and the blind? The Spirit of the Lord couldn't be on him. This bordered on blasphemy!

JESUS, A PROPHET?

We were in a quandary. Not being sure what was going on, some of us began to think one thing and some another. We were confused. Might Jesus have been a prophet in disguise all these years and it was just now coming to light? Truthfully, that seemed to be a far-fetched idea, but how else could we account for all this?

Others in the synagogue were not so optimistic: "He's no better than any of the rest of us, and for him to claim he is, makes no sense." These people began to look at Jesus in disgust.

On one hand, if prophets like Elijah and Elisha could do miracles, and if it's true that Jesus could, then maybe he was a prophet. Those of us thinking this way were amazed and excited that it could be true. If so, the future was suddenly a lot brighter.

The other possibility did not put Jesus in a favorable light. In our honor and shame culture, for Jesus—seemingly a commoner like everyone else—to claim such honor would be setting himself above the rest of us.[17] This didn't set well, and many began to take offense at what Jesus had said.

---

[17] For the implications of honor/shame culture for Jesus' first hearers, see Bruce J. Malina and Jerome H. Neyrey, "Honor and Shame in Luke–Acts: Pivotal Values in the Mediterranean World," in *The Social World of Luke–Acts: Models for Interpretation*, ed. Bruce J. Malina and Jerome H. Neyrey (Grand Rapids, MI: Baker Academic, 1999), 53-54.

To add to that, it's not uncommon to hear of supposed miracle-workers in our day, even claiming to be messiahs, impressing a few people, but never amounting to much.[18] So we really didn't know what to think about Jesus.

Some asked the question, "Isn't this just Joseph's son?" But exactly what the point was wasn't clear. Were they impressed that one of our own might somehow fulfill Isaiah's words? Or was it more of a sneer: "Who does he think he is anyway?!"[19]

What Jesus said next was a total shock. "Go ahead, you might as well quote your proverb: 'Physician, heal yourself!'" Those were explosive words and brought out an instant negative reaction. We'd heard the proverb before, but what right did Jesus have to make such a claim?

But he was right. The heart of the issue was, he'd have to prove that he was someone special by healing all the physical problems in Nazareth, otherwise we'd consider his claims bogus. If he had actually done miracles in other villages in Galilee and refused to do the same on his home turf for family and friends, how fair would that be?[20] Wasn't he obligated to us even more?

> "'Physician, heal yourself' was a common proverb, appearing in both Jewish and Greek writers. Here it may mean, 'Prove your worth as a physician.' Or, the emphasis may be on 'yourself,' with the idea, 'Heal your own people rather than outsiders from Capernaum.' Both ideas may be present."[21]

By this point, we were all beginning to fuss and fume about what Jesus was saying. He made it sound like it was our fault for feeling

---

[18]See, e.g., Richard A. Horsley and J. S. Hanson, *Bandits, Prophets, and Messiahs: Popular Movements in the Time of Jesus* (Harrisburg, PA: Trinity Press International, 1999).

[19]For detailed examination of possible explanations for why the people of Nazareth were irked, see Kenneth E. Bailey, *Jesus Through Middle Eastern Eyes: Cultural Studies in the Gospels* (Downers Grove, IL: IVP Academic, 2008), 147-69.

[20]See, e.g., Eric Eve, *The Healer from Nazareth: Jesus' Miracles in Historical Context* (London: SPCK, 2009).

[21]Mark Strauss, *Luke*, Zondervan Illustrated Bible Backgrounds Commentary, ed. Clinton E. Arnold (Grand Rapids, MI: Zondervan, 2002), 363.

entitled that he—if indeed he was a prophet—should do the amazing things here in Nazareth, which Isaiah said would happen. Was he really reneging on doing what would verify his professed identity?

It was a terrible feeling. We had felt Jesus' presence for years; looked into his face; chatted about this and that; trusted what he said; admired his work. But this was different.

Well, by his next comments, it became even clearer that Jesus was trying to make himself out to be a prophet. He really infuriated us when he said, "Of course, a prophet is not going to be accepted in his hometown."

Well, what did he expect? He hadn't used his powers to help people all those years living in Nazareth—if he truly had such power. And now he returns, reportedly having done miracles in other parts of Galilee, but he can't do much that's miraculous here (Mt 13:58; Mk 6:6). How can we trust him when the whole situation is so contradictory?

Unbelievably, it got worse. Jesus started talking about the days of the prophet Elijah, when there were many widows in Israel suffering because of the famine, and God had miraculously provided unlimited quantities of flour and oil for a widow. Even more striking, God raised her son back to life (1 Kings 17:7-24). But this didn't happen in Israel. It was a Gentile widow in Sidon of all things! How could Elijah ignore all the needy Jewish widows and cater to one who in our minds didn't deserve it?

Then Jesus switched to the prophet Elisha. Apparently he didn't think we caught his point about Elijah, so he added another example, in this case from the life of Elisha. At a time when there were many in Israel struggling with leprosy, God miraculously healed a leper so that his skin became as clean as a young boy's (2 Kings 5:1-27). But again, it was not in Israel. It was another Gentile, a Syrian! Similar to Elijah, Elisha had bypassed all the needy Jewish lepers and went to the aid of a Gentile.

By Jesus' bringing up two cases of the prophets ministering to Gentiles, was he possibly inferring that we Israelites were actually the guilty party? Because we often rejected the messages of the prophets calling us back to the covenant relationship, was the issue the prophets giving up on us and going elsewhere?[22] Because we were as bad off spiritually as the people were back then?! That implied accusation didn't sit well.

A PREMEDITATED ATTEMPT AT STONING

That did it. All of us in the synagogue had had enough. We felt betrayed by one of our own. We had considered him one of us, a close friend even. But it sounded like he cared more for Gentiles than his own people. Plus, he was clearly claiming to be a prophet, yet as far as we were concerned, he was proving the opposite.

For false prophets, the sentence is death (Deut 18:20). So we rushed at him, forcing him out of the synagogue and out of town, pushing and shoving him to the brow of a nearby cliff where we were going to throw him off and stone him. In our minds, he was deserving of execution.

Remarkably, not a single person spoke up in Jesus' defense or tried to come to his rescue—surprisingly, not even one of his own family. They were probably too frightened and couldn't believe what was happening.

When we got to the precipice, some already had stones in their hands. But suddenly, mysteriously, something like a trance came over us. Our bodies went limp, and we couldn't follow through with our plan to push him off. We were gob smacked, utterly astonished. It allowed Jesus to walk right through the middle of us and freely go on his way. Unbelievable.

After a while, thankfully, our strength returned, but by then it was too late. Jesus was long gone. We ambled back to our village, puzzled by the day's events. Our anger had subsided, and shame had taken over. We were dejected and felt pretty foolish. Apparently, life in our humble hamlet was going to stay the same after all.

It's strange. Jesus hasn't been back to Nazareth in the three years since, even with family and relatives still living here. It's probably just

---

[22]"Jesus is here reminding his hearers pointedly of the same thing John did in the previous chapter (Luke 3:8-9): if Israel thinks its special covenant relationship with God is all that matters, their disobedience notwithstanding, they have not been paying sufficient attention to either the Law or the Prophets." Jeffrey, *Luke*, 71.

as well. Unless he changed his tune, the outcome wouldn't be much different. Frankly though, we've wondered from time to time if we did the right thing in trying to kill him.

We've heard that Jesus is on his way up to Jerusalem for Passover. It will be interesting to see what happens. A lot will depend on what he does, and what the religious officials decide about him. Maybe he'll get off better than he did here; then again, maybe not.

CONCLUSION

In order to understand the Gospels fully, it's important to grasp events in Jesus' life from his perspective and from the perspective of the original audience. The ins and outs of the complex situation when Jesus returned to his hometown of Nazareth is a case in point.

Our objective in retelling this day in the life of Jesus is to experience as much as possible how the event would have been heard and processed at ground zero, in three ways: how the participants in the story felt; how a subsequent oral performance of the story would have likely impacted the initial hearers; and how it can impact us. The power of story, however, is often more than can be put into words.

In what ways are we sympathetic with the people of Nazareth? With the awkward situation that Jesus was in? Are we surprised with Jesus' boldness in drawing examples of prophets from the Old Testament who unexpectedly ministered to Gentiles? Are we prepared for "Jesus of Nazareth" to become a prominent part of his identity throughout his life, effectively saying, Jesus of the hinterland, the God of humility? By any measure, the title is the irony of all ironies (Phil 2:6-8).[23]

Everything that went through the minds of Jesus and of the villagers is beyond us. But the closer we can come to reconstructing what those

---

[23]See Karen R. Keen, *The Word of a Humble God: The Origins, Inspiration, and Interpretation of Scripture* (Grand Rapids, MI: Eerdmans, 2022).

thoughts and feelings may have been, and experiencing them alongside the characters in the story, the more we'll appreciate the significance of the event, even if things didn't turn out well for Jesus or for them.

By the very nature of human interaction and communication, the thoughts and emotions in play in a particular situation can only partly be perceived, even for people personally present. Thus, the retelling above is certainly not the last word on this day in the life of Jesus. Others will be able to improve on this attempt and should. Luke recorded the events for good reason, and we should give due diligence to understand what transpired from all angles.

There's another side of the coin. An intellectual study of this account would seek to interpret it in light of, for example, the developing thought of Luke's Gospel; various ways Jesus presented himself as the Messiah; themes that would develop more completely during Jesus' public ministry—portending future events in his life; and so forth. All of that is important and not to be replaced by the retelling above.[24] But to read only intellectually is to read inadequately if not incorrectly. We need both.

We will now move on to our last experiment in oral interpretation, this time from something Jesus said near the end of his time on earth.

---

[24]See especially these commentaries: I. Howard Marshall, *The Gospel of Luke*, New International Greek Testament Commentary (Grand Rapids, MI: Eerdmans, 1978); Joseph A. Fitzmyer, *The Gospel According to Luke: Introduction, Translation, and Notes*, 2 vols., Anchor Bible (New York: Doubleday, 1982); Darrell E. Bock, *Luke*, Baker Exegetical Commentary on the New Testament, 2 vols. (Grand Rapids, MI: Baker Academic, 1996); Joel B. Green, *The Gospel of Luke*, The New International Commentary on the New Testament (Grand Rapids, MI: Eerdmans, 1997); David E. Garland, *Luke*, Zondervan Exegetical Commentary on the New Testament (Grand Rapids, MI: Zondervan, 2011); Jeffrey, *Luke*; James R. Edwards, *The Gospel According to Luke*, Pillar New Testament Commentaries (Grand Rapids, MI: Eerdmans, 2015); Nicholas Perrin, *Luke: An Introduction and Commentary*, Tyndale New Testament Commentaries (Downers Grove, IL: IVP Academic, 2022).

PROPOSITION 18

HEARING IS MORE THAN READING

RETHINKING THE VINE AND THE BRANCHES

Let what Christ taught dwell in you in all its richness.

COLOSSIANS 3:16

ONE GOSPEL, INITIALLY ORAL; eventually written in four Gospels. Four compilers of the Gospels; each with different emphases and intended audience—yet one gospel. Two Gospels compiled by disciples of Jesus, privileged to have firsthand knowledge of things he said and did; the other two not—yet one gospel. Four unique perspectives on three years of his life—yet all Jesus' gospel.[1] It's the greatest story ever told; the best documented account from ancient history.[2]

The oral gospel consisted of an inexhaustible repository of divine truth, statements Jesus made and actions he performed.[3] Without a

---

[1]If we go deep enough, a couple of qualifiers are necessary for this paragraph. We cannot be completely sure who compiled the Gospels; N. T. Wright and Michael F. Bird, *The New Testament in Its World: An Introduction to the History, Literature, and Theology of the First Christians* (Grand Rapids, MI: Zondervan, 2019), 557, 581, 607-8, 652-60. Regarding a central message in the Gospels, see, e.g., Mark L. Strauss, *Four Portraits, One Jesus: A Survey of Jesus and the Gospels* (Grand Rapids, MI: Zondervan, 2007). Different emphases in the Gospels are widely recognized, though probably not intended for completely different audiences; see Richard Bauckham, ed., *The Gospel for All Christians: Rethinking the Gospel Audiences* (Grand Rapids, MI: Eerdmans, 1998).

[2]To have four contemporary accounts of the same time period in ancient history is unheard of. "Historians are hard-pressed to find another ancient figure who is the subject of four major works produced well within the same century in which he lived." David Mishkin, "Introduction," in *A Handbook on the Jewish Roots of the Gospels*, ed. Craig A. Evans and David Mishkin (Peabody, MA: Hendrickson, 2022), 1.

[3]"Even the four men who wrote the Gospels omitted much that would interest modern readers, skipping over nine-tenths of his life"; Philip Yancey, *The Jesus I Never Knew* (Grand Rapids, MI: Zondervan, 1995), 20; regarding the incomplete account, see Jn 20:30; 21:25.

basic understanding of his words and deeds, it's impossible to comprehend the significance of the divine presence among us, and just as important, to put our faith in him and become disciples. Jesus *is* the gospel. If we do not know the gospel, we cannot know him.[4]

Jesus' gospel had numerous unexpected elements and consequences. The truths were progressively revealed: Jesus came to preach the kingdom of God (Lk 4:43); to fulfill the law and the prophets (Mt 5:17); to call not the righteous but sinners (Mt 9:13); to proclaim justice to the nations (Mt 12:18); to seek and to save the lost (Mt 15:24); to give his life a ransom for many (Mt 20:28). Followers gradually come to recognize the cross as his destination. He said so himself.

What it means to be a disciple was progressively revealed as well. Jesus invited a few fishermen and others to follow him. They readily agreed. It wasn't unusual for teachers to have disciples that followed them.[5] But over the next three years he kept raising the bar, setting his discipleship apart from others and testing his followers' resolve.[6] It wasn't going to be an easy road. *If anyone wants to follow me, they must deny themselves and take up their crosses every day* (Lk 9:23; cf. Mt 10:38; Lk 14:27). *Those of you—who do not give up everything you have—cannot be my disciples* (Lk 14:33).

Some things Jesus said, however, were unexpected and leave us scratching our heads. *Don't suppose that I came to bring peace on earth. No! Not peace, but a sword!* (Mt 10:34). *Do you think I came to bring peace on earth? Definitely not, but rather division!* (Lk 12:51). *I have*

---

[4]To be clear, "it is not the message itself which saves men and women but the historical events of Jesus' life, death, and resurrection." Nigel Scotland, quoted in Sidney Greidanus, *The Modern Preacher and the Ancient Text: Interpreting and Preaching Biblical Literature* (Grand Rapids, MI: Eerdmans, 1988), 92.

[5]"Jesus took a commonly occurring phenomenon in the ancient world—the master-disciple relationship—and in the course of his ministry refashioned it to express his kind of discipleship"; Michael J. Wilkins, "Disciples and Discipleship," *DJG*[2] (Downers Grove, IL: IVP Academic, 2013), 211.

[6]"Not all those who came to Jesus in the early days came for the same reasons"; Michael J. Wilkins, *Following the Master: Discipleship in the Steps of Jesus* (Grand Rapids, MI: Zondervan, 1992), 103; see the discussion of five stages of discipleship at 100-119. The willingness to follow Jesus was only the first step in the process of turning toward true faith; throughout most of Jesus' public ministry "the turning was slow and incomplete." Richard V. Peace, *Conversion in the New Testament: Paul and the Twelve* (Grand Rapids, MI: Eerdmans, 1999), 280.

come to throw fire on the earth. And I'm wishing it were already ignited! (Lk 12:49). These are statements in a different league, especially when Jesus would say later, *Peace is what I leave with you. It's my peace I am giving you* (Jn 14:27; see also Lk 24:36; Jn 16:33).

The written Gospels, however, in contrast to the oral gospel, are not an inexhaustible repository of Jesus' words and actions. As John stated at the end of his Gospel, *There are so many other things that Jesus did, which if someone were to record them, I can't imagine that the whole world could contain all the scrolls that could be written!* (Jn 21:25). We should not suppose, though, that the Gospels are a Reader's Digest version of Jesus' life. But his words and deeds were simply too great and grand to record everything on papyri or parchment. He is God after all and cannot be fully contained or known.

We can be confident that the words in the Gospels point to the most important things to know about Jesus. Yet there's more to do to understand everything he said and did in their original context. Even Jesus left things he said unexplained—surprising his hearers and leaving it up to them to figure out the meaning of his poignant statements.

The Gospels, then, leave ample room for study, for research, for hypotheses, for debates, for tentative conclusions, even for imagination.[7] It's not a frivolous enterprise, definitely not willy-nilly make-believe. Oral interpretation, including historical imagination, must be true to the text, to the speaker(s) and hearers of the text, and to the circumstances. By reconstructing the orality of a biblical account, we want to understand Jesus and his kingdom as fully as possible, and the only recourse is to retrieve as much insight as possible from the available information and construct more complete scenarios. "NT texts are not self-sufficient verbal artifacts that contain within themselves all that is needed for their interpretation."[8]

---

[7]"Historical reconstruction is impossible without imagination"; James H. Charlesworth, "Introduction: Why Evaluate Twenty-Five Years of Jesus Research?" in *Jesus Research: An International Perspective*, ed. James H. Charlesworth and Petr Pokorný (Grand Rapids, MI: Eerdmans, 2009), 9, 14.

[8]Joel B. Green, "The Challenge of Hearing the New Testament," in *Hearing the New Testament: Strategies for Interpretation*, 2nd ed., ed. Joel B. Green (Grand Rapids, MI: Eerdmans, 2010), 12.

The Gospels, then, leave ample room for study,
for research, for hypotheses, for debates,
for tentative conclusions, even for imagination.

THE VINE

On the eve of his crucifixion, with the eleven disciples gathered around,[9] Jesus was giving what was in effect his last will and testament.[10] In the midst of the evening he gave an unexpected declaration. It was momentous in its own right and is suggestive for the purposes of this book. As we'll see, Jesus said things pertaining to his gospel that are, unfortunately, often incompletely understood and sometimes misapplied.

It would be helpful to know more about what it would have been like to have been a disciple of Jesus for three years. What the disciples were confident they understood. What they were possibly struggling to understand. And particularly on this auspicious evening, how the disciples likely heard and responded to Jesus' words.

Jesus' saying that he was the true vine (Jn 15:1) turned out to be a pinnacle statement of spiritual identity, both for him and his followers. He went on to say that unfruitful vines would be cut off. Both assertions had far-reaching implications. The following reconstruction is presented as a first-person account as if the disciples themselves are giving the report.

---

[9]Judas had already left the upper room bent on betraying Jesus (Jn 13:30). Subsequently, Jesus and the remaining disciples also left and walked toward the Garden of Gethsemane (Jn 14:31; 18:1).

[10]Farewell addresses were a common genre in the Greco-Roman world; in addition to the one by Jesus preserved in John's Gospel, see Lk 22:14-38; for summary, see L. Scott Kellum, "Farewell Discourse," *DJG*[2], 266-69.

Our few short years as Jesus' disciples were full of mindboggling events and unexpected statements. When Jesus said something about the temple being destroyed and then restored in only three days, we heard but didn't understand what he was getting at until much later (Jn 2:19-22; cf. 12:16). Also, he used a figure of speech about being a gate for the sheep, but we couldn't figure that out either (Jn 10:6). We were often puzzled and full of questions (Jn 4:33; 9:2; 13:36; 14:5, 8). It got to the point that some among us gave up following Jesus out of frustration (Jn 6:66).

Another quandary made us feel like we were between a rock and a hard place. Our Jewish leaders were overtly antagonistic to Jesus, even threatening to kill him (Jn 7:1, 13, 44; 8:40-44, 59; 9:22; 11:8, 57; 10:31).[11] It was partly understandable. Jesus seemed to be presenting a lot of new ideas, almost like he was nudging us away from considering ourselves children of Abraham.[12] But if so, then in what sense would he be the Messiah for Israel? The situation was very confusing.

When we heard Jesus repeat what he had said other times, "I am" (*egō eimi*), it didn't take much for us to realize that another profound declaration was forthcoming.[13] His other "I am" statements were all groundbreaking metaphors, especially "I am the bread of life," and "I am the way, the truth, and the life."

But this time, hearing Jesus say, "I am the true vine" was even more striking. Recalling several Hebrew Scriptures that we'd heard read in the synagogue, it was evident that vine and vineyard were common figures of speech representing Israel. But Jesus, the vine?

---

[11]"The plot of the Fourth Gospel is characterized by a strong Jewish opposition to Jesus"; Lidija Novakovic, "Israel," *DJG²* (Downers Grove, IL: IVP Academic, 2013), 405.

[12]Regarding the perceived obsolescence of Judaism, see David Mark Ball, *"I Am" in John's Gospel*, Journal for the Study of the New Testament Supplements 124 (Sheffield: Sheffield Academic Press, 1996), 273-74.

[13]See Catrin H. Williams, "'I Am' Sayings," in *Dictionary of Jesus and the Gospels*, 2nd ed., ed. Joel B. Green, Jeannine K. Brown, and Nicholas Perrin (Downers Grove, IL: IVP Academic, 2013), 396-99; Andreas J. Köstenberger, "'I Am' Statements," in *A Handbook on the Jewish Roots of the Christian Faith*, ed. Craig A. Evans and David Mishkin (Peabody, MA: Hendrickson, 2019), 159-64.

It was Hosea who said that Israel had the potential to be a fruitful vine (see Hos 10:1). In addition, the Holy of Holies in the Jerusalem temple is adorned with a supersized golden grapevine just above the linen curtain, and it is full of beautiful grape clusters, reminding us of the metaphorical connection between Israel and the vine.[14]

Most significant was a prophetic story told by Isaiah (Is 5:1-7). The choicest of grape vines were carefully planted, with a watchtower erected for protection and a winepress ready for harvest. Unfortunately, the vineyard produced only bitter grapes, which were totally worthless for making wine. With the winepress sitting empty, the vinedressers were frustrated that their work had gone for naught.[15]

> The book of Isaiah begins with a collage of imagery picturing Israel's idolatry, exaggerated pride, and impending humiliation. The faithful city had become a harlot; bejeweled and bedazzled women sought attention for themselves; the vineyard was only producing rotten fruit. The bottom line was, Israelites by birth were not acting like Israelites of faith. God announced he could no longer tolerate such despicable conduct. He didn't want empty prayers, pointless sacrifices, and meaningless worship. And he was going to clean up his vineyard. The rocks, rubbish, and overgrowth were unacceptable. Severe judgment was pending, not unlike what happened to Sodom and Gomorrah![16]

The prophet, speaking for God, then announced a verdict that was devastating. The vineyard would no longer be cultivated and pruned; its protection would be removed; rain would no longer fall; and the vineyard would be trampled and destroyed. Isaiah shockingly concluded

---

[14]Arnold C. Schultz, "Vine, vineyard," in *The Zondervan Encyclopedia of the Bible*, ed. Merrill C. Tenney and Moisés Silva (Grand Rapids, MI: Zondervan, 2009), 5:1024-25; Andreas J. Köstenberger, *John*, Zondervan Illustrated Bible Backgrounds Commentary (Grand Rapids, MI: Zondervan, 2002), 143-44.

[15]It is "possible to imagine [the Judean farmers'] outrage when they are told that for all their effort, the outcome is only bitter grapes"; John N. Oswalt, *Isaiah*, NIVAC (Grand Rapids, MI: Zondervan, 2003) 112-13.

[16]Thanks to my colleague Skip Forbes for his suggestion and assistance with this sidebar.

his parable with a finger-pointing pronouncement, "The vineyard of the Lord Almighty is the house of Israel!" (see Is 5:7).

It was a dagger piercing the heart of any of us who considered ourselves part of God's chosen people. But guilty of what? And did the consequences need to be so severe?

Actually, it was not only Isaiah who used the vine metaphor to picture the sinfulness of our people. Other prophets did as well. The passage in Hosea goes on to say, "that the peoples' hearts were full of deceit and they would suffer the consequences" (see Hos 10:2). In the words of Jeremiah, Israel is a "wild vine, not a true one" (see Jer 2:21; see also Jer 12:10-11; Ezek 17:5-12; 19:10-14).

With the vine/vineyard metaphor in the Scriptures consistently pointing to our failures as the chosen people, plus with the severe judgment pending, it made sense that something drastic needed to change. But how could the people of Israel be transformed into a vine to produce good fruit?

Here's where Jesus' adding "true" (*alēthēs*) as a qualifier set this vine apart. The opposing parallelism between Israel as the vine, which was marked by failure, and the new vine marked by truth was an exciting possibility to think about. Perhaps one was a foil for the other. Might this be the sense in which Jesus was the vine?

We had heard Jesus use the words *true*, *truth*, and *truly* numerous times,[17] like a drum beat—true, true, true—and it left an indelible impression.[18] Jesus was presenting himself as the whole truth and nothing but the truth. And in contrast to the decadent Israel pictured in the prophets, we could see how Jesus could be saying that he was the true Israelite, the real vine.

---

[17]Unique to the Gospel of John, Jesus is recorded using the words *true*, *truth*, and *truly* over fifty times. (In contrast, each of the other Gospels have fewer than ten references to *true*, *truth*, *truly*.) For hearers listening to large portions of John's Gospel rather than short portions, Jesus as the epitome of truth would have been striking.

[18]Repeated references "would have sounded a staccato beat of significance for the ancient listener"; Paul Borgman and Kelly James Clark, *Written to Be Heard: Recovering the Messages of the Gospels* (Grand Rapids, MI: Eerdmans, 2019), 117.

With Jesus having previously stated, "I was sent only to the lost sheep of Israel," the light began to dawn that part of his mission could be culminating in, and even be crowned by the very announcement, "I am the true vine." Amazing! That might be the most important statement ever made about the future of Israel. Our people could now continue to exist and flourish in the person of Jesus as the vine. That is, as long as our identity as Israelites was in alignment with Jesus.[19]

The failures that the vine had represented could now be left in the past. The new vine would be a reconstituted Israel, but not a different vine. Jesus remained in solidarity with that self-same Israel of the past.[20] We remember that he said, that he did not come to replace the Law or the Prophets but to raise them up to their rightful place (see Mt 5:17). But it did mean that the future of Israel would depend on being closely connected to this vine, the one and only vine.[21]

Jesus' saying, "I am the true vine!" was indeed thrilling to contemplate. Especially when earlier in his ministry he had emphasized Israel's failures and seemed to insure their horrific destiny. He even declared on one occasion—having not found anyone in Israel with faith like a Gentile centurion—that the children of Abraham were doomed: they will be thrown out into total darkness where they will weep and gnash their teeth forever! (see Mt 8:12; cf. Mt 3:9; Jn 8:39-41).

But now we could see that Jesus was not relegating all things Jewish to the dung heap. There is hope for us and for our kin. It's up to us to avoid the doom of the old vine by joining the new life in the true vine.

---

[19]Regarding Israel in John's Gospel, see Lidija Novakovic, "Israel" in Green et al., *Dictionary of Jesus and the Gospels*, 403-7.

[20]"Although Jesus takes on the role of Israel in his claim to be the 'true vine,' the emphasis of the episode is on what Jesus offers to the disciples and not on the ineffectiveness of what has gone before"; Ball, *"I Am" in John's Gospel*, 274.

[21]"The new concept is that God's vineyard holds *one vine*, and Israel must inquire if it is attached to him. No longer is Israel automatically seen as vines growing in God's vineyard. Men and women are now branches growing from one stock"; Gary M. Burge, *John*, NIVAC (Grand Rapids, MI: Zondervan, 2000) 417.

It's both his spiritual identity and ours, not tied to geography or gene-alogy. It's the true, new vine in place of the old, failed vineyard![22]

This was all very good news. If there was any doubt whether it was worth following Jesus, this settled it. As Jesus' followers, we could be the new Israel! And based on something else Jesus said that night, the covenant relationship was still in force, now updated in his very person.[23] This was a sweeping, life-changing message, a defining moment. Every Jew needed to hear about it.

Well, readers, to what extent this proposed account matches how the disciples heard and understood what Jesus said about the vine, there's no way to know for sure. But it could have been this way, and given Jesus' intentions and their circumstances, it almost certainly was this way. Unfortunately, checking a range of commentaries, all of which appear to operate with a text-only approach to interpretation, much of the impact of Jesus' saying he is the true vine is overlooked.

Several commentators do not even acknowledge the background of the vine imagery in Isaiah and elsewhere, failing to see that Jesus was presenting himself as the new Israel.[24] The commentators that agree on that point fail to grasp the extent of the ways the disciples would have been impacted by Jesus' declaration as noted above.[25]

---

[22]"The implication is not that the new community replaces Israel; rather, it is Jesus himself who stands in for Israel. And it is the relationship to Jesus that defines membership in Israel"; L. Scott Kellum, "Farewell Discourse," *DJG*[2] (Downers Grove, IL: IVP Academic, 2013), 268-69; "This does not mean that the church will replace Israel but rather that God's blessings to his people—in keeping with his promises to Abraham and David—will be mediated through Jesus, the true Israel." Andreas J. Köstenberger, "'I Am' Statements," in *A Handbook on the Jewish Roots of the Christian Faith*, ed. Craig A. Evans and David Mishkin (Peabody, MA: Hendrickson, 2019), 162.

[23]Noam Hendren, "The New Covenant," in Evans and Mishkin, *A Handbook on the Jewish Roots of the Christian Faith*, 28-33.

[24]Quoting Michaels, for example, "The point is not to differentiate him from other 'vines' (Israel, for example), but simply to claim him as the very embodiment of what every vine should be—above all, the source of life to its branches." J. Ramsey Michaels, *The Gospel of John*, NICNT (Grand Rapids, MI: Eerdmans, 2010), 801.

[25]See C. H. Dodd, *The Interpretation of the Fourth Gospel* (Cambridge: Cambridge University Press, 1953), 410-12; C. K. Barrett, *The Gospel According to St John: An Introduction with Commentary and*

THE BRANCHES

Jesus didn't stop with the momentous statement declaring that he was the vine. There was much more on his mind. He made a bold announcement that is often misapplied.

First, describing branches that are "in" him, Jesus noted that fruit-bearing branches will need to be pruned.[26] In the disciples' world, such pruning was common practice as vinedressers trimmed back branches so they could become even more productive. And when Jesus said, "Remain in me, and I will remain in you," it wasn't difficult to see that he was extending his analogy about being the vine to include the disciples as branches attached to the vine. "No branch can bear fruit by itself; it must remain in the vine." In other words, with Jesus as the vine and with healthy branches attached to him, the vineyard would produce good fruit, in sharp contrast to the vineyard described by Isaiah, which had yielded only bitter grapes.

That was all well and good. But the disciples were probably ill-prepared for what Jesus said next. His Father, the gardener, "cuts off every branch that bears no fruit." The privilege of remaining in the vine was good news; but this was bad news. It sounded categorically harsh. No fruit, no future. Of course, vinedressers were known to trim off lifeless branches, but Jesus was speaking of cutting off people.

In Isaiah's analogy of a fruitless vineyard, the verdict was also expressed in the harshest of terms. "Now I will tell you what I am going to do to my vineyard: I will take away its hedge, and it will be destroyed; I will break down its wall, and it will be trampled!" (Is 5:5 NIV). Typical of the prophets, "the worst-sounding judgment that can be

---

Notes on the Greek Text (London: MacMillan, 1955), 392-94; George R. Beasley-Murray, *John*, WBC 36 (Waco: Word, 1987), 271-72; Craig S. Keener, *The Gospel of John: A Commentary* (Peabody, MA: Hendrickson, 2003), 2:988-1002; the commentators that give the most attention to the implications for the disciples are Andreas J. Köstenberger, *Encountering John: The Gospel in Historical, Literary, and Theological Perspective*, 2nd ed. (Grand Rapids, MI: Baker Academic, 2013), 148-51; Edward W. Klink III, *John*, ZECNT (Grand Rapids, MI: Zondervan, 2016), 650-51; and Grant R. Osborne, *The Gospel of John*, Cornerstone Biblical Commentary (Wheaton: Tyndale, 2017), 224-25.
[26]The Greek preposition *en* has a wide semantic range and may denote "in alignment with, in union with," which fits the context here.

expressed in human language is inadequate to picture God's perfect wrath . . . it was a rhetoric of persuasion calling for repentance."[27]

The upshot was, all Israelites were put on notice. With the vineyard of the house of Israel now being relocated in the person of Jesus, there was no place in the new version for dead, useless branches. Whoever had been part of Israel, the original vine, would be lopped off, gathered up, and thrown into a burning fire if they continued in disbelief and unfruitfulness. Jesus was the only way. If not him, it was the highway.[28]

In contrast to Jesus' threatening language, he offered heartwarming news as well. As a prophet in the pattern of the Old Testament prophets, Jesus made both criticizing and energizing statements, often in extreme, even hyperbolic language.[29] "If you remain in me and I in you, you will bear much fruit . . . if you remain in me and my words remain in you, ask whatever you wish, and it will be done for you" (Jn 15:5, 7 NIV).[30] (Beware of assuming it's an unlimited promise that we can ask for anything we want and it's automatically ours. See Proposition 15 above.)

Branches attached to the vine yielding wonderful fruit and granted amazing privileges was beautiful to contemplate. The opposite—branches shriveling up and dying, incapable of producing fruit, condemned to destruction—was dreadful to behold. Everything now centered on Jesus and being attached to him. Neither genealogy nor any other "-ology" would make the grade. "Only belief in Jesus will prevent

---

[27] D. Brent Sandy, *Plowshares and Pruning Hooks: Rethinking the Language of Biblical Prophecy and Apocalyptic* (Downers Grove, IL: IVP Academic, 2002), 79-80.

[28] Some wonder if the picture of Jesus in the Gospel of John comes across as antisemitic. But Jesus was simply erecting a boundary between those who were Israelites by birthright, and those who could now be Israelites by new birthright; for discussion, see Craig A. Evans, "Jews and Judaism in the Gospel of John," in *A Handbook on the Jewish Roots of the Christian Faith*, ed. Craig A. Evans and David Mishkin (Peabody, MA: Hendrickson, 2019), 221-25; R. Alan Culpepper and Paul N. Anderson, *John and Judaism: A Contested Relationship in Context*, Resources for Biblical Study 87 (Atlanta: SBL Press, 2017).

[29] On criticizing and energizing, see Walter Brueggemann, *The Prophetic Imagination*, 2nd ed. (Minneapolis: Fortress, 2001).

[30] For discussion of the extreme energizing language typical of the prophets, such as "all the trees of the field will clap their hands" (Is 55:11), see D. Brent Sandy, *Plowshares and Pruning Hooks: Rethinking the Language of Biblical Prophecy and Apocalyptic* (Downers Grove, IL: IVP Academic, 2002), 23, 76, 79-102.

the Jews from dying in their sins."[31] The outcome was, as Paul would later write to the Romans, "Not all who are descended from Israel are Israel" (Rom 9:6 NIV).

"Very well," interpreters conclude, "true believers are branches attached to the vine and must remain so." The question is—as a former student put it—"If Jesus is the true vine, are we true grapes?" The metaphor is turned into a great sermon with a very practical application. Some go so far as to say, "Beware: You could be cut off!"

But wait. Who could be cut off? Now Christians need to be put on notice. Again, the original context determines meaning and application, and Jesus was specifically speaking about Israelites being cut off from the vine. From that point on, branches of the former vine (referring to Israel) needed to be attached to the vine, which was Jesus, or they would no longer be part of this new, true vine.

But is there other valid application? Can what Jesus said about the branches being attached to the vine rightly apply to believers in general, his body, the church? Here's where a fundamental question can help: How did the initial hearers understand to whom Jesus' statement applied?

Doug Moo suggests, regarding the debate over Paul's Greek phrase (in Rom 3:22)—whether it should be understood as "faith in Jesus Christ" or "the faith or faithfulness of Jesus Christ"—that we should consider what the original audience would have thought when they heard the phrase. Moo concludes that "faith in Jesus Christ" would have been the more natural way that Paul's letter, being read aloud to the congregation, would have been understood.[32]

Jesus was gathered with his disciples in the upper room, and they were all Israelites, so the immediate application in their minds certainly applied to their kin. Not aligning themselves with Jesus as the true vine

[31]Ball, *"I Am" in John's Gospel*, 273.
[32]Douglas J. Moo, *A Theology of Paul and His Letters: 25 Lessons on Major Theological Themes* (Grand Rapids, MI: Zondervan, 2022). Thanks to Randy Skinner for pointing me to Moo's comment.

and not bearing fruit was inviting judgment on themselves. Make the wrong choice, and suffer the consequences. That was what Jesus had in mind.

But beyond the first hearers present that special night, is there other legitimate application? Here's where we need to put the brakes on. What Jesus intended and what the original hearers understood is the clear meaning that we can be confident about. To take the words of Jesus elsewhere risks applying them wrongly.

As the apostles and others in the early church reflected on what Jesus said about being in him and he in us, they latched on to the concept of union with Christ. That's evident by the frequent mention of believers' being in Christ or Christ being in them throughout the epistles (for example, Rom 8:1, 9-11; 12:5; 16:7). On that basis, we can conclude that a recontextualization of what Jesus said can pertain to believers in general.[33]

But we must not go beyond this. Hearers generally did not cut up texts in pieces and try to make something out of every little piece. The question is, Was the concept of the branches being cut off also recontextualized to apply more broadly?

We look again to the apostles in the early church. Opposite to the evidence for their emphasis on union with Christ, the notion of being cut off does not appear in the epistles except possibly Romans 11:17-24, and in that case Paul's warning applies more to corporate Israel and the Gentiles as a whole rather than to individuals.[34] Thus, there does not appear to be a legitimate basis for seeking to apply the concept of being cut off beyond what Jesus intended. If correct, a problem is solved: the metaphor of severed branches does not apply to the church today.

---

[33] For discussion of contextualization, see Jeannine K. Brown, *Scripture as Communication: Introducing Biblical Hermeneutics* (Grand Rapids, MI: Baker Academic, 2007), 232-73; and additional bibliography in Proposition 2, note 14.

[34] Note that Peter spoke specifically to the Jews and warned them of being cut off (Acts 3:23); regarding Rom 11:22, not all commentators agree that Paul was speaking corporately about Gentiles, but most do; I think Wright is right: it's a warning to Gentiles as a whole. N. T. Wright, "The Letter to the Romans: Introduction, Commentary, and Reflections," in *The New Interpreter's Bible: A Commentary in Twelve Volumes*, vol. 10, ed. Leander E. Keck (Nashville: Abingdon, 2002), 686.

Unfortunately, it's common among commentators to attempt an application of the cut-off concept to Christians in general. Some commentators contend that Jesus intended the dead branches to refer to apostate Christians.[35] Others contend that the branches are professed Christians with three possible explanations for being cut off: they are taken up to heaven as an act of discipline; they perish without Christ; or they were merely professed believers in the first place.[36] But such attempts at application seem to be an example of inappropriate contextualization.

So Christians, commentators, preachers, teachers: beware of removing the metaphor of the branches being cut off from its original context and applying it incorrectly today. There's no need to find a way for the severed branches to apply to Christians at large.

Conclusion

The question raised by this proposition is similar to the question underlying the previous one. Can a Westernized, twenty-first-century reading of Scripture—even with the benefit of scholarly exegesis—provide sufficient understanding of what Jesus said and people associated with him heard two thousand years ago? Or can we think our way back into the life situation and the experiences of speaker and hearers and gain a better appreciation of the dynamics and intent of Jesus' poignant statements? Do not oral explanations of theological concepts communicate more effectively?

Do not oral explanations of theological concepts communicate more effectively?

---

[35]For example, D. A. Carson, *The Gospel According to John*, Pillar New Testament Commentary (Grand Rapids, MI: Eerdmans, 1994), 515.

[36]Homer A. Kent Jr., *Light in the Darkness: Studies in the Gospel of John*, 2nd ed. (Winona Lake, IN: BMH Books, 2005), 201-04.

Again, I make no claim that the reconstruction above is the final word on understanding Jesus' unique gospel. We haven't exhausted all there is to explore, and others will likely offer additional perspectives. Such is the nature of historical and theological reconstruction. It takes a village, and if a consensus will be reached, it requires openness to rethinking and humility.[37]

But we can at least agree that Jesus' analogy of the vine was laying important groundwork for the renewed people of God as part of the renewed kingdom of God in union with the true King of the kingdom. Ethnicity, genealogy, geography, and birthright would have nothing to do with it. Being in alignment with Jesus from henceforward would mean everything.

---

[37]Scholars offer additional reconstructions regarding the Gospels that are helpful. For example, there's a possibility that the Gospel of Matthew was presenting Jesus as the new Moses, though never explicitly stated: Dale C. Allison Jr., *The New Moses: A Matthean Typology* (Minneapolis: Fortress, 1993); Seth D. Postell, "Jesus [Not] as Moses in the Gospel of Matthew," in *A Handbook on the Jewish Roots of the Gospels,* ed. Craig A. Evans and David Mishkin (Peabody, MA: Hendrickson, 2021), 82-94; also, various insights into understanding passages in the Gospels are presented in this book: Paul Borgman and Kelly James Clark, *Written to Be Heard: Recovering the Messages of the Gospels* (Grand Rapids, MI: Eerdmans, 2019).

CONCLUSION

If you have to ask what jazz is, you'll never know.

Louis Armstrong

*If we have to ask what hearing the Bible is all about,
we'll never know.*

D. Brent Sandy

The church today stands at a crossroads. There's always been opposition from without and trouble from within. But through the years, each crossroads seems to become more critical. Fortunately, we're assured that Jesus will build his church, regardless of whoever or whatever opposes it (Mt 16:18). But we also know that a lot depends on us.

What does the church most need today? What will steady the ship on the stormy seas of change? Probably few would disagree that the highest priority for the church, the body of Christ, is understanding Scripture correctly. If the church doesn't get that right, it's at risk of not getting anything right.

Hidden in Plain View

Unfortunately, many Christians have little idea how the Bible came to be and how it came to us. For them it may as well have dropped out of the sky, showed up in our mailboxes or on our front steps, perfectly packaged with every word printed exactly on every page—over 700,000 words (in English)—precisely as God wrote it. As they have commonly heard, God is the author of Scripture.

Actually, the Bible has a lot to say about that. God didn't write; he spoke. He didn't dictate; he inspired. He didn't do all the communicating himself; he empowered others. Fundamental to this book is noticing something that often isn't. Speaking is the primary vehicle for communicating divine truth, and much of the speaking depends on God's representatives, including us.

Successful speaking depends on attentive hearing. People heard God speak and then spoke what they heard. That was repeated over and over again so that many could hear from God and speak for him. Otherwise, people around the world would never have heard what God said. It was all about hearing—and then speaking.

> *The long trail of orality, which for many of us has mostly been hidden from sight, is now difficult not to see.*

Recording divine speaking in written form would come later. Oral truth was perfectly fine on its own, for example, during the years of Jesus' sermons and teaching, and for decades afterward. Which means the eventual written word of God, which we're accustomed to focusing on, is derivative, not primitive ("primitive" in the sense of denoting the earliest stage of something). At its origin, divine revelation was a pre-literate oral text. God's speaking and his representatives' speaking truth for him were before everything else.

The long trail of orality, which for many of us has mostly been hidden from sight, is now difficult not to see. What effect might the orality of biblical revelation have on how we understand the nature of Scripture? Should we think of the Bible as primarily oral instead of written? And how can we best interpret the originally-oral-but-now-written word?

ORALLY WRITTEN SCRIPTURE

Examples of oxymorons abound in the English language: deafening silence, open secret, sweetly tart, heavenly distress, seriously funny, old news. For "orally written," the point is that even when an oral text was eventually recorded in written form, it could retain features of the original orality, giving it an oral register.

Most texts in the ancient world had an oral orientation, generally the product of previous oral accounts. In the case of the Gospels:

- Jesus spoke, people remembered, and they soon talked about it and told others.

- In the process of discussing the stories and recounting them in the presence of varied audiences, the accounts gradually reached a level of standardization as social memory came to agreement on the accuracy of the accounts.

- Recognizing the need for people everywhere to hear the stories and words of Jesus, individuals shared those accounts widely, often performed as dynamically as possible so that hearers could appreciate the significance of the original circumstances when Jesus was present.

- When it came time to put the resulting oral texts in written form, an oral text could be repeated aloud while a scribe wrote it down, or in some cases the scribe may have heard it so often that the oral text was recalled from memory as the scribe recorded it.

- In any case, the originator(s) of the oral text, the performer(s) of the text, and the scribe(s) of the text were fully aware that the written text would subsequently be read aloud as an oral account for an audience to hear. So it was natural for the written form to take on features of oral delivery.

- Finally, as written texts were repeatedly performed, the oral orientation of the texts benefited the performers so they could present them effectively and so the audience could hear and understand them as intended.

The result was orally shaped written accounts. It was a merger of oral and written, of orality and textuality. For us to correctly understand divine speech (oral), we must understand it via human words (written). And to understand the divine word (written), we must understand it as human speech (oral). The challenge for readers in the modern Western world is to grasp that reality and to respond accordingly.

DIVINE APPOINTMENT

Creation was God's initial act of incarnation. God is spirit, yet he spoke into existence physical objects spanning the universe, revealing aspects of his attributes (Ps 19:1). Stars, planets, people in their places: each a divine appointment.

God created humans and stamped his image on them, incarnating himself in human form. By nature, we are human, "carnate" creatures, yet remarkably we are designed to be like God: empowered to have dominion over what he created, commissioned to be his representatives. It's our divine appointment.

Yet another of God's remarkable acts of incarnation was his communication. He spoke profound eternal truths in human terms, thoughts, and manners of speaking. The standard protocol of God making himself known was speaking and ordaining others to speak for him. Again, divine appointment.

The supreme form of incarnation was God's Son, implanted in the dust of the earth, his divine appointment. Jesus spoke the truth and embodied the truth. He didn't compose a text; he didn't need to: he was (and is) the text. In the beginning was the Word.

People who could not read could read Jesus. He was and is the way, the truth, and the life. "Our understanding of the inspiration of Holy Scripture is signally illumined by the phenomenon of the speaking God taking flesh and, therefore, actual vocal cords. Here we find the key to the incarnational analogy of the Word made flesh and the word made Scripture."[1] He is the God of incarnation.

There is yet another form of incarnation: Jesus installed himself and his truth in his followers. He is the vine; we are the branches. Jesus never instructed us to compose a text. But he did summon us to speak the text, to embody the text, to be the text. It's our divine appointment. People should be able to read us too. This incarnation never stops.

Now if God spoke for people to hear and appointed others to speak on his behalf so that still others could hear, and if Scripture written retained much of its original orality, then Scripture can speak most effectively to hearers. That means our modern Western textual orientation can be a barrier between us and the ancient oral culture in which divine truth was revealed.

Unfortunately, the orality of Scripture has received less attention than any other form of guidance for interpreting Scripture.[2] Among the many manuals for general readers on how to interpret the Bible, it's difficult to find any discussion of the significance of orality or suggestions for how to interpret Scripture in light of orality.[3] It's puzzling. But can we actually reach back into the culture of the past to understand the Bible in the present?

UNLEASHING ORAL INTERPRETATION

Though we cannot turn back the hands of time and listen to Scripture as instinctively as the original hearers could, we can discern ways to understand the Bible more closely to how it was intended to be heard.

---

[1]Nigel M. de S. Cameron, "Revelation, Idea of," in *Evangelical Dictionary of Biblical Theology*, ed. Walter A. Elwell (Grand Rapids, MI: Baker Books, 1996), 681.
[2]Exceptions include Holly E. Hearon, "The Implications of Orality for Studies of the Biblical Text," in *Performing the Gospel: Orality, Meaning, and Mark*, ed. Richard A. Horsley, Jonathan A. Draper, John Miles Foley (Minneapolis: Fortress, 2006), 3-20; Joanna Dewey, *The Oral Ethos of the Early Church*, Biblical Performance Criticism 8 (Eugene, OR: Cascade, 2013); Rafael Rodríguez, *Oral Tradition and the New Testament: A Guide for the Perplexed* (London: Bloomsbury, 2014).
[3]For example, the "how to" book that has had the greatest impact over the past three decades is Gordon D. Fee and Douglas Stuart, *How to Read the Bible for All Its Worth*, 4th ed. (Grand Rapids, MI: Zondervan, 2014); it's especially helpful on genres, but has nothing about oral culture and interpretation.

The goal is to bring to life the actions and experiences recorded in the Bible and to hear God speaking to us through the words of Scripture.

We can read the Bible more macroscopically than microscopically. Rather than a well-drilling technique, we should take in larger vistas as drones can. To understand a passage or topic, the broader scope of the metanarrative, the genre, the themes, and the purposes is the starting point. The whole will be essential for correctly understanding the parts.

We can explore what can be known about the speakers/authors, audiences, and characters in the story/text. The social setting, life experiences, realities, and difficulties will be important to perceive. Not only being knowledgeable about such things but identifying with those issues and relating them to our situations will be helpful.

We can recognize that divine truth is relational and personal more than theoretical and propositional. Jesus as the divinely appointed representative didn't speak truth to hearers far away but to those nearby, generally in the context of relationship.

In contrast to a scientific precision of exact words for divine truth, in oral thinking the mind does not objectify matters as much as in textual culture.[4] We may need to modify what we expect Scripture to be and do.[5]

We can seek to experience Scripture in the way an oral performance would have impacted oral hearers. Reading the Scriptures in the church and academy should not be routine, but a dynamic presentation using the best techniques of drama possible. This will include taking advantage of evocative language, visual imagery, graphic descriptions, language expressing conflict, imagination, and using anything in the text that will help draw hearers into an experiential appreciation of the text.

---

[4]Walter J. Ong, *Language as Hermeneutic: A Primer on the Word and Digitization*, ed. Thomas D. Zlatic and Sara van den Berg (Ithaca, NY: Cornell University Press, 2017), 22.
[5]For discussion, see John H. Walton and D. Brent Sandy, *The Lost World of Scripture: Ancient Literary Culture and Biblical Authority* (Downers Grove, IL: IVP Academic, 2013).

We can take advantage of first-person dialogues in Scripture. Stories recounted in the voices of the characters themselves, rather than being summarized by a narrator, allow the story to be presented more effectively. Matthew and Luke's account of Jesus' temptation in the wilderness, for example, with six different first-person statements by the devil and Jesus (two for each temptation) allows hearers to experience the event realistically. (Mark's account, however, is condensed and includes none of the dialogue, and John's account doesn't even include the temptation account.)

We can use Bible versions that are translated with performances and hearing in mind. The best available at present is The Voice translation. "The goal of The Voice is to promote the public reading of longer sections of Scripture—followed by thoughtful engagement with the biblical narrative in its richness and fullness and dramatic flow."[6]

We can interpret Scripture collectively rather than individually. Groups and classes within individual churches can read, discuss, and come to conclusions about the meaning of passages. Even better, groups from churches across denominations can come together to read and discuss Scripture, seeking common understanding.

PRACTICAL APPLICATION

- Listen to the Bible on any one of various media platforms, noting how hearing Scripture can be different from reading it.

- Read the Bible in groups of two, three, or more, followed by discussion.

- Take advantage of the "Public Reading of Scripture" website; www.prsi.org.

- Be prepared to hear the God of the universe speak personally through Scripture, instead of simply reading the words of Scripture.

---

[6]*The Voice New Testament* (Nashville: Thomas Nelson, 2008), vii (emphasis in original).

- Remember that the term "word" (*logos*) almost always refers to a spoken word, not written; so, for example, instead of "Let the word of Christ dwell in you" (Col 3:16 KJV), the point is, "Let what Christ taught dwell in you" (see also Heb 4:12).

- Seek to understand Scripture in larger units, generally no smaller than paragraphs; refrain from taking verses out of context and thinking they can be correctly understood in isolation.

- For Bible translators, seek to convey the contextual meaning of verses, not limited to the specific words in a verse.

- Prepare performances of biblical passages for small group gatherings, Sunday school classes, worship services, special events, and so forth. Choose wording from various modern versions that will be most suitable for performance. Select participants who can be expressive verbally, facially, and bodily.

- Using Scripture as the foundation, create poetic lines that emphasize concepts in Scripture that may not be as evident in prose form.

- For musicians composing or selecting music for worship, choose songs with lyrics clearly based on Scripture.

- In children's and youth ministries, present the stories of Scripture in dramatic ways.

- For preachers, include more of what God says and less of human ideas; do less exegeting and more storying; instead of using personal stories to illustrate points, use stories from the Bible.

- For scholars writing commentaries on Scripture, give more attention to the orality of Scripture and the dynamic quality of how texts would have been heard.

- For Bible colleges and seminaries, offer courses in the oral performance of Scripture.[7]

---

[7]For an example at Dallas Theological Seminary, see https://voice.dts.edu/article/public-reading-of-scripture.

- For publishers interested in producing study Bibles, provide notes to help readers understand the oral dimensions of Scripture and to experience biblical stories as the original hearers did.

PARTING PLEAS

Interpreting Scripture orally is not only an adventure in hermeneutics but in transformation. Practicing the hearing of Scripture has the potential to place the words of God deeper and more personally into the consciousness of hearers. Intellectual engagement with Scripture is necessary, but the language of the heart and of emotional intelligence may be more effective in bringing about changed lives.

Interpreting Scripture orally has the potential of bridging some of the gap between academy and church. Much of what scholars do in their research is beyond the reach of people in the church. But if academy and church can join together in seeking to interpret Scripture orally, both will benefit. "The challenge for scholars in the twenty-first century is to effect a shift in the study of biblical texts away from the heavy, almost exclusive, emphasis on the literary nature of these texts to the study of the texts as sound maps intended to be heard in a rhetorical culture that emphasized the persuasive power of the word."[8]

Interpreting Scripture holistically and collectively—taking into account the full counsel of God and the command to maintain the unity of the body of Christ—will allow the church to more effectively accomplish its ultimate mission of being the presence of Christ in today's world.

"The [spoken] word of the Lord endureth forever." (1 Pet 1:25 KJV)

Soli Deo gloria!

---

[8]Holly E. Hearon, "The Implications of Orality for Studies of the Biblical Text," in *Performing the Gospel: Orality, Memory, and Mark*, ed. Richard A. Horsley, Jonathan A. Draper, and John Miles Foley (Minneapolis: Fortress, 2006), 3.

ACKNOWLEDGMENTS

As Woodrow Wilson wisely remarked, "I not only use all the brains that I have, but all that I can borrow." So it is for me. I would not think and write as I do apart from the influence of many people: family, friends, even foes. (Regarding the last, if I'm not shaking up a few people, then I'm probably not saying anything worthwhile.)

Thanks to colleagues, clergy, students for the camaraderie and collaboration as we've journeyed together. There are too many to name, but those who have been especially helpful as this book germinated and went through a long gestation include Kip Cone, Jesse Deloe, Skip Forbes, Luke Kelley, Andy Simkins, Randy Skinner, Darrel Taylor, and John Walton. Special merit goes to Scott Garber for his insights and wordsmithing; his seminal book, *White as Sin: A New Paradigm for Racial Healing*, is a model of his skills. (I take responsibility for times I failed to heed the advice freely offered me.)

And many thanks to Rachel Hastings, associate academic editor, and the IVP Academic team for seeing this book through the hoops of production.

To more than anyone else, thanks, Cheryl. Your unfailing love, companionship, patience, and counsel across fifty-two plus years—since we said "I do"—is an amazing gift. Maybe now I'll find time to do the "I dos" you've been waiting for, especially cleaning off my desk!

GENERAL INDEX

Abraham, 41, 47-48, 111, 140, 176
accommodation of divine truth, 12, 22, 31, 108
Achtemeier, Paul J., 100-101
Adam and Eve, 41
Alexander, Elizabeth Shanks, 57, 68
Alexandria, Egypt, 101
Allison, Dale C., Jr., 54, 182
Anderson, Paul N., 178
Ang, Soon, 32
apocrypha, other "gospels," 157-58
apostle(s)
    authority of, 21, 80, 82-83
    memories of Jesus, 88-89, 94, 180
application, 109-29, 133-44, 179-81, 187-91
appointment of agent(s) of revelation, divine, 53,
    46-54, 57-64, 66-67, 79-83
Aramaic, 20, 31, 160
Aristotle, 5
Arnold, Clinton E., 128, 163
Arthurs, Jeffrey D., 127
Augustine, 19
aural. *See* oral/aural intelligence
author(s), authorship, 8, 14, 22, 27, 52, 99-101,
    103, 188
    authors' assumption people would hear what
        they wrote, 8, 99-100
authority
    of apostles, 20, 21, 80, 82-83, 85
    of disciples, 83, 85, 93, 108, 116
    of Jesus, 20, 43, 66-67, 83, 85
    of Moses, 20, 47-57, 61, 67, 85
    of prophets, 20, 58, 60-61, 67, 85
    self-referential claims of limited value, 51, 67
    of what was spoken and heard, 21, 47, 63,
        102-3, 108
    of written Scripture, 12, 14, 17, 50-52, 63
    of written Scripture, based on the authority
        of oral revelation, 21, 52, 61-63
backgrounds, foregrounds, 32-33

Bacote, Vincent, 52
Bagnall, Roger S., 23
Bailey, Justin Ariel, 17
Bailey, Kenneth E., 163
Baker, Mark D., 33
Ball, David Mark, 172, 175, 179
Barr, James, 33, 75, 135
Barrett, C. K., 176
Barrett, Matthew, 13
Bartholomew, C., 146
Barton, Stephen C., 34
Bauckham, Richard J., 43, 91, 110, 122, 168
Beasley-Murray, George R., 177
Beck, David R., 74
Beitzel, Barry J., 154, 156
Berg, Sara van den, 28-29, 100, 188
Bernier, Jonathan, 73
Bettis, Kara, 152
Bible. *See* Scripture
big bang, 89
Bird, Michael F., 72-73, 89, 91, 167-68
Bismarck, Ruth-Alice von, 150
Bjoraker, William, 5, 10, 123
Black, David Alan, 74
Block, Daniel, 40, 63, 85
Blomberg, Craig L., 15, 161
Bochner, Stephen, 14
Bock, Darrell L., 32, 74, 76, 91, 167
Bond, Helen K., 70
Bonhoeffer, Dietrich, 150
Boomershine, Thomas, 34, 106, 109, 115, 126
Borgman, Paul, 174, 182
Bowley, James E., 48, 55-56, 169
Boyd, Gregory A., 19
brain, 6, 7, 10, 106
branch(es) attached to the vine, 144, 147, 175-87
    cut off, 171, 179-81
Briggs, Richard S., 4, 92-93
Brookins, Timothy A., 107

Brother Lawrence, 111
Brown, Jeannine K., 16, 27, 29, 33, 40, 54, 69, 100, 156, 172, 180
Brown, Walter E., 18
Bruce, F. F., 148
Brueggemann, Walter, 139, 178
Buchanan, Robert, 40
Burge, Gary M., 175
Calaway, Jared C., 49
Cameron, Nigel M. de S., 21, 187
Carson, D. A., 75, 150, 181
Charlesworth, James H., 157, 170
church, body of Christ, believers, 16, 69, 70-71, 78, 80-82, 94, 99, 120-21, 127, 133, 141-44, 179-81, 183, 188, 191
Clark, Kelly James., 174, 182
Collins, C. John, 40, 63, 85, 156
Collins, John J., 156
communication, oral compared to textual, 6-7, 13, 19, 22, 24, 27-30, 35, 43-44, 50-51, 53, 62-63, 67, 73, 80-81, 95, 99, 116-17, 134, 184, 186
context, importance of, 13-17, 26-30, 33, 104, 134-44, 179-81, 190
contextualization, 16-17, 29, 180-81
Cotterell, Peter, 75, 135
covenant, 18, 41, 47, 50, 57, 59, 61, 102, 140, 165, 176
Crisp, Oliver B., 16, 110-11
Culpepper, R. Alan, 178
culture, differences between, 7, 10-11, 14-15, 17, 23
collectivism, 6, 15, 89-91, 143, 189, 191
high context, low context, 26-28, 134
cultural intelligence, 11, 32
Danker, F. W., 20
David, 42, 44, 113, 176
Day, A. Colin, 136
Dead Sea Scrolls, 54-57
importance of the Law of Moses, 55-57
oral performance and oral texts, 56
scribal activity, 55-56
See also scribes
death by stoning, 165-66
Dehaene, Stanislas, 10
Deuel, David C., 40, 85
Deuteronomy, book of, 49
Dewey, Joanna, 34, 101, 103, 187
disciple(s), discipleship, 6, 17, 20, 65, 79-80, 83-84, 88, 92, 114, 116, 138, 141, 154, 168-69
disciples' quandaries, 171-77
memories of, 87-89, 91-95
responsibilities, progressively revealed, 119, 138, 169-70

Dockery, David S., 14, 51
Dodd, C. H., 176
Donne, Anthony Le, 90
drama, dramatic, dynamic(s), 10, 29, 102-6, 109-10, 115-16, 118-19, 122-23, 126-28, 148, 181, 185, 188-90
Draper, Jonathan A., 29, 123-24, 187, 191
Driver, Daniel R., 110
Dunn, James D. G., 6, 104, 149
Durgin, Celina, 136, 143
Dyer, Bryan R., 24, 74
Dyer, John, 7, 99, 109
Early, P. Christopher, 32
Eddy, Paul Rhodes, 19, 27, 100
Edwards, James R., 167
Eichenwald, Kurt, 15
Elder, Nicholas A., 25, 89-91, 101
Elisha, 42, 162, 164
Elwell, Walter A., 21
Emmerling, Robert J., 122
emotion(s), value for understanding and presenting biblical accounts, 103, 105-6, 116, 122-24, 128, 154, 167, 191
emotional intelligence, 122-23, 191
Enlightenment, 109
Enns, Peter, 18-19, 48
Epictetus, 4
Erickson, Millard J., 14
Ernest, James D., 81
Eusebius, 6
Evans, Craig A., 33, 139, 150, 168, 172, 176, 178, 182
Eve, Eric, 9, 17, 74, 90-92, 163
evocative language, 103, 122, 154, 188
Exodus, book of, 18, 49
eyewitness(es), 73-74, 76, 84, 91-93
Ezekiel, 58-59
faith, 16, 43, 82, 84, 92, 117, 127, 134, 140, 169, 175, 179
Falk, Daniel K., 56
farewell discourse, 171
Farmer, William R., 74
Fee, Gordon D., 187
Fields, Weston W., 54
figures of speech, 172
Fischer-Lichte, Erika, 126
Fitzmyer, Joseph A., 167
Fleming, Dean E., 17
Flint, Peter, 55
Foley, John Miles, 25, 123, 187, 191
Fonrobert, Charlotte Elisheva, 57, 68
Fowl, Stephen E., 110-11

Fredal, James, 107
Freyne, Sean, 156
fruit, fruitful, unfruitful, fruitless, 41, 118, 144, 173-74, 177-80
Furnham, Adrian, 14
Galilee, 20, 67, 153-59, 163
Ganssle, Gregory, 46
Garden of Gethsemane, 114
Garland, David E., 167
genealogy, 147, 176, 178, 182
Genesis, book of, 3, 18, 147
genres, 13, 171
Gentile(s), 20, 59, 83, 94, 107, 147, 156-57, 164-66, 175, 180
Georges, Jayson, 33
Gibbs, Jeffrey A., 139
Giese, Ronald L., Jr., 13
goal of this book, 7-8, 10, 17, 34-35
God
    blessings of, 133-34, 138-40, 164
    Creator, creation, 40-41, 45, 146-50, 186
    empowerment of representatives, 45-54, 61, 63, 80, 108, 184, 186
    God breathed, 22
    hearing him, 110-13
    Jesus speaking for and from God, 66
    not author, 22, 40, 44-45, 67, 184
    relationship with, 18, 50, 57, 59, 112, 165, 176
    revelation by speaking, 9, 12, 18-19, 22, 34, 40-54, 117, 121, 184
    wrath of, 59-60, 111, 173-74, 177-78, 180
Goldsworthy, Graeme, 33
Goleman, Daniel, 122
Gorman, Amanda, 146
gospel, oral, good news, 10, 20, 68-69, 71-72, 77, 80, 82, 84-87, 91-92, 94, 99, 134, 141, 168-71, 182
    fixity/fluidity of details, 26-28, 85, 153-54, 188
    storehouse, repository of truth, 8, 67, 69, 86, 95, 167, 170
    transition to written Gospels, 85-86, 91, 95
    transmission of, 6, 10, 20-21, 86, 91
Gospels, written, 15, 24, 26, 34, 43, 54, 67-77, 80-81, 85-86, 88, 91-92, 99, 103, 111, 126, 147, 153-54, 157, 166-68, 170, 185
    compiled, 69, 72-73, 76-77, 89, 91, 154, 168
    dates of composition, 70-73, 77
    differences between Gospels, 153-54
    importance of, 72, 168-70
    influence of orality on, 26, 69
    lack of evidence in Acts and the rest of the NT, 72

one gospel, yet four Gospels, 168
    research necessary, 170
Graupner, Axel, 52
great divide, 7
Greek/Roman literature performed, 101, 104-6
Green, Joel B., 23, 27-28, 34, 54, 74, 100, 156-57, 167, 170, 172, 175
Greene, C., 146
Greidanus, Sidney, 169
Guite, Malcolm, 146, 148, 152
Gutenberg Galaxy, 17
Gutenberg, Johannes, 17
Habets, Myk, 16, 110-11
Halbwachs, Maurice, 90
Hall, Edward T., 27
Hall, Mildred Reed, 27
Hanson, J. S., 163
Harlow, Daniel C., 156
Harmon, Matthew S., 15
Harris, William V., 23
Hart, Trevor A., 110, 122, 146
Harvey, John D., 74
Havelock, Eric, 5-6
Hawkins, Jeffrey L., 68
Heard, W. J., 156
hearing-dominant, hearing-prevalent, 9, 63, 68
Hearon, Holly E., 123, 187, 191
heart(s), written on, 69
Hebrews, book of, 43, 71, 110-11, 122
Henderson, Timothy P., 157
Hendren, Noam, 176
Henry, Patrick, 115
hermeneutic(s). *See* Scripture, interpretation of
Hesselgrave, David J., 16
high context, 26-28, 134
Hinn, Benny, 134
Hinn, Costi W., 134
historical reconstruction, 28, 127, 154, 166, 170-71, 182
Hodges, Louis Igou, 14, 51
Hoehner, Harold W., 69
Hofstede, Geert Jan, 32
Holmén, Tom, 91
Holy Spirit, 13, 16, 19, 44, 70, 80-81, 83, 88-89, 94, 107, 108, 120
holy, holiness, 112-13
    Holy of holies, 173
Horsley, Richard A., 29, 123-24, 163, 187, 191
Horst, Tina Stoltzfus, 32
Hubbard, Moyer V., 33
humility, divine, 155, 157, 165-66
Hummel, Daniel G., 136

Hurtado, Larry W., 23, 101
Iliad, 104-5
illocution, locution, perlocution, 4
imagination, 28, 103, 145-46, 152, 154
incarnation
    examples of, 43, 110, 186-87
    Jesus', 13, 19, 66, 116, 141, 147-50, 186
Inkson, Kerr, 32
individualism, 7, 15, 90, 102, 143
inspiration
    of spoken words, 4, 18-19, 21, 39-40, 44-45,
      52, 57, 83, 184, 186
    of written words, 12, 15, 18, 21, 39-40,
      51-52, 57
interpretation. *See* Scripture, interpretation of;
    misinterpretation of
Isaiah, 59, 147, 160-64, 173-74, 176-77
    scroll of, 160
Iverson, Kelly R., 17, 25, 101-2, 106, 127
Jaffee, Martin S., 57, 68
Jeffrey, David Lyle, 160, 165, 167
Jensen, Ryan, 33
Jeremiah, 58-64, 67, 83, 85, 140, 174
Jeremiah, book of, compilers, 59, 62
Jerusalem, temple, 172-73
Jesus
    absence of Apostles' reference to written
      records of Jesus, 71-72
    absence of writing, 19, 67-69, 71, 77, 99,
      184, 186
    actualization of truth, 66
    baptism, 67, 70
    birth, 67, 118, 145, 158
    craftmanship, 153, 159
    crucifixion, resurrection, ascension, 70,
      73, 79-80
    embodiment of the text, 77, 186
    family, 158-59
    healings, 78, 92, 163-64
    humility, 155, 157, 165-66
    "I am," 47-48, 172, 175-76, 179
    incarnation, 19, 147-50
    kingdom, 19, 71, 79, 107, 112, 139, 144,
      150-51, 169-70, 175, 182
    no instructions to write, 86, 99
    prayer for unity, 141
    prophet, 19
    spokesperson for God, 65-68, 81, 85-86, 186
    stories of/about, 67-69, 72, 81, 84-85, 93, 106,
      114, 116-17, 120-24, 128-29, 185
    transfiguration, 67
    twelve years old, 158
    unmarried, 158

Jew(s), Jewish, 83, 175-76, 178-80
    chosen people, 57, 59, 147, 174
    conflict with Gentiles, 156-57
    leaders antagonistic to Jesus, 172
John, Apostle, 71, 73, 94, 147-50, 170-81, 189
John the Baptist, 67, 70, 107, 115, 145
Johnson, Ben Campbell, 16
Johnson, Dru, 136, 143
Joseph and Mary, 118, 157-59, 163
    Mary widowed, 158-59
Josephus, 154, 156
Joshua, 49-50, 52, 102, 140
Jude, 71, 144
Kabitz, Ulrich, 150
Keck, Leander E., 180
Keen, Karen, 166
Keener, Craig S., 13, 76, 90-91, 155, 177
Kelber, Werner H., 7, 9, 25, 100
Kellum, L. Scott, 171, 176
Kennedy, George A., 107
Kent, Homer A., Jr., 181
King, Martin Luther, Jr., 115
Kingdom. See Jesus: kingdom
Kirk, Alan, 89-91
Klauck, Hans-Josef, 51, 157
Klink, Edward W. III, 148, 177
Köstenberger, Andreas J., 128, 150, 172, 176-77
Lawrence, Paul J. M., 40, 63, 85
Lazarus, 113, 124-25, 127-28
Leithart, Peter J., 41
libraries, 95, 101
Liefeld, Walter, 75
Lierman, John, 53
Lingenfelter, Sherwood, 32
linguist(s), linguistics, 28, 75, 135, 137
Lints, Richard, 142
literacy, 6-7, 9, 19, 101
    levels of, 23-25
literal sense of Scripture, 136, 152
logos, 72, 75-76
Longenecker, Bruce W., 24, 33
Longman, Tremper, III, 18-19, 145-46
Louw, Johannes, P., 20
Luke, 72-77, 80, 84, 92-93, 147, 153-54, 167, 189
    Gospel of, 72-77, 80
    prologue of, 73-77
Lyle, Kristopher A., 154, 156
Mackay, E. Anne, 105
Maier, Harry O., 33
Malina, Bruce J., 162
Mamo, Ermias G., 17
Mandal, Manas K., 122
manuscript(s), 24, 55-56, 60, 102, 123

Mark, Gospel of, 73-74, 103, 126, 147, 153, 189
Markley, Jennifer Foutz, 15
Marshall, I. Howard, 167
Mary Magdalene, 118
Matthew, Gospel of, 54, 70, 73, 80, 137, 147, 153, 182, 189
Mattix, Micah, 152
McComiskey, Thomas Edward, 127
McDonald, Lee Martin, 23, 28
McDonald, Nathan, 110, 122
McGilchrist, Iain, 10
McIver, Robert K., 90-91
McLuhan, Marshall, 8, 17
Mediterranean world, 15, 94
memory, memories, 20-21, 25-26, 46, 86-91, 93-94, 105, 116, 126, 133, 185
    of apostles, 88-89, 94, 180
    of eyewitnesses, 91-93
    of groups, 26, 89-91, 185
    reliability of, 87-95
    virtuous, 93-94
messenger(s), 79-87, 93-94, 116, 121, 129, 143-44
messengers, responsibilities, 128-29
Messiah, 162-63, 167, 172
metaphor(s), 149, 172-73, 174, 179-81
Michaels, J. Ramsay, 147-48, 176
Middle Eastern culture, 33, 163
Miglio, Adam E., 15
Miguelez, Laura C., 52
Millard, Alan R., 68
Miller, Shem, 24, 39, 56-57
Minchin, Elizabeth, 101, 105
Minkov, Michael, 32
miracles, 47, 66-67, 83, 89, 92, 126, 148, 150-51, 157, 162-64
Mishkin, David, 139, 168, 172, 176, 178, 182
misinterpretation, 8, 15, 71, 75-76, 134, 137, 139, 142
modern culture, contrast with ancient, 5-6, 8, 14, 17, 22, 26, 29, 31, 33, 35, 39, 50, 56, 68, 74, 106-7, 109, 123-24, 126-28, 152, 168, 186-87, 190
Moessner, David, 74
Möller, K., 146
Moo, Douglas J., 179
Moreau, A. Scott, 17
Moreland, J. P., 150
Moses, 18, 21, 41-42, 45-58, 61-64, 67, 71, 83, 85, 102, 117, 159, 182
    speaking, writing of, 50
    spokesperson for God, 21, 46-54, 57
Mulholland, M. Robert, 109, 111

Myers, Jason A., 107
Nazareth, 70, 87, 153-67
Neyrey, Jerome H., 162
Nichols, Bruce J., 17
Nicodemus, 118
Nida, Eugene A., 20
Nissinen, Martti, 56, 62
Noort, Ben van, 19
Novakovic, Lidija, 172, 175
O'Brien, Brandon J., 14-15
Odyssey, 104-5
Okholm, Dennis L., 52
Okpewho, Isadore, 5
Olson, David R., 6
Ong, Walter J., 6-7, 9, 28-30, 100, 188
oral/aural intelligence, 22, 32, 56
oral interpretation, 100-101, 129, 135, 152, 154, 167, 170, 187-89
    methods of, 8, 10, 14-15, 21-22, 33-35, 100-101, 109-29, 133-44, 152, 154, 166-67, 170, 181-82, 187-89
oral macrocosm, 17
oral text(s), 25, 34, 49, 56, 61, 63, 72, 85, 184-85
    authority of, 49, 61, 184
    definition of, 25, 72, 85
    oral literature, 104-5
    transition to written texts, 25-26, 85
    translation, 84
    transmission, 73
    See also written text(s)
orality, biblical, 11, 17, 21-22, 26-29, 31-34, 52, 69, 77, 99-101, 108, 117, 120, 129, 133-34, 170, 184-90
    characteristics of, 26-29, 31, 154
    influence of on written texts, 8, 10, 184-86
    preference for, 116-17
    related to textuality, 6-7, 10, 25, 30, 34, 52, 95
Osborne, Grant, 177
Oswalt, John N., 173
Overstreet, R. Larry, 118, 127
Papias, 6
parchment, 45, 52, 56-57
Paul, Apostle, 13, 21, 24, 53-54, 71-72, 82-85, 94, 99, 107, 118, 138, 150, 179-80
    in Rome, 71
Paul, Greg, 112
peace, 169-70
Pentateuch, 52, 55, 160
Pentecost, 20, 70, 83, 85
performance(s) of oral texts, 18, 30, 56, 106, 126, 166, 188, 190
    See also Scripture, performances of

Perrin, Nicholas, 27, 54, 100, 156, 167, 172
Peter, Apostle, 19, 44, 71, 83-84, 88-89, 94, 113
Peterson, Brooks, 32
Phillips, Elaine A., 156
physician, 163
Plato, 4-5
poets, poetry, 11, 18, 25, 40, 52, 101, 105,
    145-52, 190
    in Scripture, 145, 148, 150, 152, 190
Porter, Stanley E., 24, 33-34, 74, 91, 99
preacher, preaching, 59-62, 75, 83, 94, 107, 117,
    136-37, 162, 169, 181, 190
printing press, 39, 109
prophet(s), prophetic books, prophecy, 9, 18-19,
    21, 42, 44, 52-53, 56-64, 71, 110, 114, 117, 139,
    145, 153, 160-62, 164-66, 169, 173-75, 177-78
    criticizing and energizing language, 178
    false prophets, 165
    spokespersons for God, 21, 58-64
proverb(s), 63, 72, 140, 145, 163
Psalms, book of, 18, 38, 52-53, 138, 144, 160
Quintilian, 105-6, 119, 139
rabbi(s), rabbinic literature, 57, 68
Radner, Ephraim, 142
Rankin, Jeffrey J., 18
Rata, Tiberius, 18
rationalism, scientific reasoning, 106, 109, 122
Ray, Paul, 16
Reeder, Caryn A., 15
revelation
    divine, 4, 8-9, 13, 15, 18-19, 30, 35, 39-40, 45,
        48, 51, 58, 63, 134, 152
    oral, 18-19, 21, 57, 62, 69, 82, 95, 107, 109, 114,
        119, 184
Revelation, book of, 100, 118
Reynolds, Bennie H, III, 55
rhetoric, rhetorical strategy, 105, 107, 178, 191
Rhoades, David, 126
Richards, E. Randolph, 14-15, 23
Rodríguez, Rafael, 7, 17, 20, 24, 85, 187
Rommen, Edward, 16
Ryken, Leland, 145-46
Sanders, Fred, 16, 110-11
Sandy, D. Brent, 4, 7, 9, 12-13, 17-18, 21, 28, 52, 62,
    72, 75, 83, 85, 101, 105, 139, 154, 178, 188
Sanhedrin, 71, 94
Schaeffer, Francis, 63
Schiffman, Lawrence H., 56
Schneemelcher, W., 158
Schröter, Jens, 157
Schultz, Arnold C., 173
Schultz, Richard L., 75, 134, 137

Schwartz, Barry, 91
Scotland, Nigel, 169
scribes, 19, 24, 52, 55-57, 60, 62, 85, 102, 185
    accuracy of copying, 55
    oral transmission, 56
    textual transmission, 55
Scripture
    culture of, 10, 13-15, 21-22
    composition of, 10, 17, 73, 85, 91, 183-84
    God-breathed, 22
    high view of, 16, 112-13, 184
    impact of oral culture, 8, 10, 95
    interpretation of, 7-8, 10, 14, 16, 30, 109, 119,
        128, 133, 141, 144, 152, 183, 186-87, 189-91
    manuscripts of, 24-25
    meaning for original hearers, 8-9, 13, 16,
        27-30, 34-35, 63, 68
    misinterpretation of, 14-15, 33, 71, 75-76,
        100-101, 134-35, 139, 142-44
    oral culture's influence on, 8, 22-23, 26,
        34, 107
    oral version equal in authority to written,
        63, 95
    performances of, 30, 116-19, 124-29
    reading to various audiences, 102-4, 120-23
    speakers of, 116-17
    taken out of context, 133-41
    translations by author of this book, 10
    transmission from oral to written, 185-86
    word studies, 135-36
    written to be heard not read, 8, 10, 20, 30,
        99-103, 121-23, 126-27
scroll(s). *See* Dead Sea Scrolls: scribes
Sermon on the Mount, 44, 54, 113
Shanwal, Vinod K., 122
Shead, Andrew G., 58
Silva, Moisés, 173
Simpson, Benjamin I., 76, 91
Socrates, 4
Sparks, Kenton L., 10, 40, 50
Spencer, F. Scott., 158
Spicq, Ceslas, 81
Stallter, Thomas M., 7
Steffen, Tom, 5, 10, 123
Stein, Robert H., 74
Stephen, 71
stone tablets, 40, 52
stories. *See* Jesus: stories
Stovell, Beth, 34
Strauss, Mark L., 112, 163, 168
Stuart, Douglas, 187
symposium(s), 5, 105

synagogue(s), 14, 67, 107, 153, 159-62, 165, 172
telephone game, 91
temple, 59-60, 67, 158, 172-73
Ten Commandments, Ten Words, 18, 40-41, 51, 56
Tenney, Merrill C., 74, 173
textuality, 6, 10, 17, 19, 25, 30, 52, 68, 95, 100, 109, 186
    See also orality
Thatcher, Tom, 90-91
theology, 12, 43, 181-82
Thomas, David C., 32
Thomas, Sally, 152
Thompson, J. A., 62
Timothy, 72
Torah, 49, 63
Torrance, Nancy, 6
Tov, Emanuel, 55, 62
tradent(s), 84
transformation, spiritual, 16
translation, translators, 20, 31, 60, 62, 84, 137, 139
Treier, Daniel J., 110, 122
Trinity, 13, 45, 66, 128, 141
Trojan War, 105
true, truth, 84, 92, 134, 141, 143-44, 149, 170-82
    accommodation of, 31
    mystery/complexity of, 27, 148-49
    revealed in creation, 45
    revealed in incarnation, 45, 186-87
    revealed orally, 18, 22, 32, 35, 40, 43-44, 46, 57, 63-64, 66-69, 77, 80, 85, 93, 99, 108-9, 117, 146, 168-69, 184, 186-88
    understanding of, 13-16
Turner, David L., 139
Turner, Max, 75, 135

Tyler, Stephen A., 28
Ulrich, Eugene, 150
unity, disunity, 133, 141-44
Vanderkam, James C., 56
Vanhoozer, Kevin, 112
Vansina, Jan, 5
vine, vineyard, 171-79, 182, 187
Waltke, Bruce K., 55
Walton, John H., 4, 7, 9, 12, 15-18, 21, 28, 40, 52, 62-63, 72, 75, 83, 85, 101, 105, 113, 154, 188
Walton, Joshua T., 15
Ward, Colleen, 14
Way, Kenneth C., 15
Western civilization, culture, 6-7, 14-15, 17, 33, 68, 109, 152, 186-87
Whitman, Walt, 15
Wilkins, Michael J., 150, 169
Williams, Catrin H., 172
Wilson, R. McL., 158
Witherington, Ben III, 23, 99, 107
witness(es), 71, 81, 92, 143.
    See also messenger(s)
Wolf, Maryanne, 6-7
Wolff, Virginia, 115
Wolter, Michael, 52
Wolterstorff, Nicholas, 16, 40, 146
Woodruff, David M., 46
worship, 57, 112, 120-21, 127, 137, 143, 173, 190
Worthington, Ian, 105
Wright, N. T., 72-73, 160, 168, 180
Wright, Paul H., 154
Wu, Jackson, 17, 33
Yamazaki-Ransom, K., 156
Yancey, Philip, 114, 168
Zlatic, Thomas D., 28-29, 100, 188

SCRIPTURE INDEX

OLD TESTAMENT

Genesis
1, 3
1:2, 3
1:9, 42
1:28, 41
2:17, 41
3:6, 41
3:14-19, 41
6:7, 41
17:1-2, 41, 140
17:9, 140
50:20, 138

Exodus
1:11-14, 47
2:23-25, 47
3:7-10, 47
3:10, 41
3:14-15, 48
4:1, 47
4:5, 47
4:15, 48
4:16, 48
7:1, 48
11:4, 49
15:26, 42
17:14, 50
19:3, 46, 49
19:4-5, 41
19:5, 140
19:7, 49
19:9, 42
20:1, 18, 42
20:22, 18, 42
24:3, 50
24:7, 102
32:11-14, 49
33:14, 52

34:27, 50
34:28, 40

Leviticus
12:8, 159
27:34, 49

Numbers
17:1-11, 50
36:13, 49

Deuteronomy
1:1, 49
1:3, 49
4:12-13, 18
4:13, 40
5:1, 42
5:22, 18, 42
6:1, 49
6:4, 57
6:4-9, 160
10:4, 40
10:4-5, 51
18:20, 165
27:8, 50
28:15-68, 61
29:1, 49
29:20-21, 51
29:27, 51
31:6, 110
31:9, 51
31:19-22, 50
31:24, 51
32–33, 145
34:5-12, 52
34:10, 53

Joshua
1:13, 52

8:34-35, 102
23:14-16, 140

Judges
5, 145

2 Samuel
2, 145
2:22-23, 145
23:2, 44

1 Kings
9:4-7, 140
17:7-24, 164
21:21, 140
21:29, 140

2 Kings
5:1-27, 164
21:8-9, 52
23:1-3, 102

1 Chronicles
16, 145
28:7-9, 140

2 Chronicles
33:8, 52
34:29-32, 102

Nehemiah
8:1-18, 102
8:2-12, 50
8:9, 102
8:12, 102
9:13, 42
9:13-14, 52
13:1, 102

Job
1:8-12, 138

Psalms
13, 138
19:1, 186
19:1-2, 41
19:1-4, 45
29:4-9, 41
68:33, 39
95:7-8, 110
104:7, 42
119, 52
119:105, 145

Isaiah
5:1-7, 173
5:5, 177
5:7, 174
6:9-10, 10
6:10, 43
42:18-20, 42
55:9, 12
55:11, 42
61:1-2, 160

Jeremiah
1:6-10, 19
1:7, 58
1:9, 58
1:10, 58
1:18, 58
2:21, 174
5:20-21, 58
6:10, 42
7:1-11, 60
11:8, 61
12:10-11, 174
18:2-10, 140

25:1-3, *59*
26:1-24, *60*
31:33, *69*
36–37, *61*
36:1-2, *59*
36:3, *59*
36:4, *60*
36:6-7, *60*
36:21, *102*
36:22-26, *60*
36:23, *60*
36:32, *61*
51:64, *62*

Ezekiel
17:5-12, *174*
19:10-14, *174*

Hosea
10:1, *173*
10:2, *174*

Jonah
3:8-9, *59*
4:9, *59*

Zechariah
1:12, *161*

New Testament

Matthew
1:1-17, *147*
2:1-16, *70*
3:9, *175*
3:17, *43, 47, 115*
4:24, *20, 78*
4:24-25, *89*
5:10-12, *138*
5:13, *46*
5:17, *169, 175*
5:21, *54*
5:37, *4*
5:48, *113*
7:7, *139*
7:28-29, *89*
8:4, *53*
8:12, *175*
8:26, *42*
9:8, *89*
9:13, *169*
9:26, *78*

9:33, *89*
10:7, *20, 79*
10:10, *72*
10:20, *79*
10:23, *138*
10:34, *169*
10:38, *169*
12:18, *169*
13:15, *43*
13:34, *99*
13:54-58, *153*
13:55-56, *159*
13:58, *164*
15:24, *169*
15:26, *27*
15:31, *89*
16:9, *88*
16:18, *183*
16:24-25, *138*
17:5, *43, 47, 67*
17:20, *140*
18:20, *137*
19:7-8, *53*
20:28, *169*
22:31-32, *111*
22:43, *44*
23, *139*
23:9, *27*
23:15, *118*
23:24, *118*
23:27, *118*
24:14, *79, 120*
26:13, *88*
26:75, *88*
27:46, *115*
28:20, *80*

Mark
1:1-3, *147*
1:22, *89*
1:27-28, *89*
1:28, *20, 78*
1:44, *53*
1:45, *78*
2:12, *89*
4:39, *42, 115*
6:1-6, *153*
6:2, *159*
6:3, *159*
6:6, *164*
7:8-10, *53*
7:10, *53*

7:37, *89*
8:18, *88*
10:3-4, *53*
10:5, *111*
10:24, *89*
10:32, *89*
10:52, *92*
11:23, *106*
12:26, *53*
13:11, *79*
14:9, *88*
14:36, *114*
14:72, *88*
15:26, *24*
15:34, *115*

Luke
1–2, *74*
1:1, *76*
1:1-4, *73, 74*
1:1–9:50, *76*
1:2, *92*
1:46-55, *145*
1:68-79, *145*
2:1-24, *147*
2:22, *54*
2:24, *159*
2:29-32, *145*
2:40-52, *159*
2:41-51, *158*
2:51, *158*
3:1-2, *70*
3:8-9, *165*
3:14, *155*
4:14, *67, 78*
4:14-30, *154*
4:16-20, *156*
4:17-18, *67*
4:18-19, *160*
4:22, *159*
4:32, *89*
4:37, *78*
4:43, *169*
5:1, *75*
5:9, *89*
5:14, *53*
5:15, *78*
5:26, *89*
7:17, *79*
8:1-3, *92*
8:8, *65, 108*
8:24, *42*

9:23, *169*
9:44, *88*
9:59, *76*
9:60, *107*
10:1, *83, 92*
10:7, *72*
10:26, *111*
12:49, *170*
12:51, *169*
14:26, *27*
14:27, *169*
14:33, *169*
16:29, *54*
16:31, *54*
17:11-18, *92*
17:19, *92*
22:14-38, *171*
22:19, *88*
22:19-20, *72*
22:61, *88*
24:6, *88*
24:8, *88*
24:27, *54*
24:36, *170*
24:44, *53, 54, 111, 117*
24:47, *80*
24:48, *79*

John
1:1, *3, 147*
1:14, *141, 147*
1:29, *115*
1:41, *84*
1:45, *53*
1:46, *155*
2:19-22, *172*
2:22, *88*
2:23, *89*
3:16, *27*
3:34, *67, 111*
4:33, *172*
5:46, *53*
5:46-47, *111*
6:2, *89*
6:14, *89*
6:63, *67*
6:66, *172*
7:1, *172*
7:13, *172*
7:16, *67*
7:22, *53*
7:23, *54*

7:42, *155*
7:44, *172*
8:6-8, *44*
8:26, *67*
8:28, *4, 66*
8:39-41, *175*
8:40-44, *172*
8:59, *172*
9:2, *172*
9:22, *172*
9:29, *53*
10:6, *172*
10:31, *172*
11:8, *172*
11:18-19, *127*
11:45, *127*
11:57, *172*
12:16, *88*
12:27-29, *43*
12:49-50, *66*
12:50, *4, 19*
13:30, *171*
13:36, *172*
14:2, *137*
14:5, *172*
14:6, *65*
14:8, *65, 172*
14:8-10, *65*
14:10, *65*
14:12, *80, 82*
14:16-17, *80*
14:24, *65*
14:26, *80, 88, 94*
14:27, *170*
14:31, *171*
15:1, *171*
15:5, *178*
15:7, *178*
15:15, *82*
15:20, *88*
15:26-27, *81*
16:4, *88*
16:8-14, *13*
16:13, *44, 81*
16:15, *80*
16:33, *170*
17:8, *65, 78, 79, 116*
17:18, *79, 116*
17:20, *80*
17:22-23, *141*
17:23, *142*
18:1, *171*

18:20-21, *88*
18:21, *93*
18:22-24, *93*
20:21, *82*
20:30, *168*
21:25, *168, 170*

Acts
1:8, *79, 81*
1:16, *44*
2:1-41, *81*
2:5-13, *83*
2:6-12, *20, 85*
2:11, *83*
2:23-24, *103*
2:36-37, *103*
4:8, *44*
4:11, *103*
4:13-17, *102*
4:13-21, *94*
4:20, *88*
4:31, *44*
5:17-41, *94*
5:39, *103*
5:42, *87, 89, 94*
6:9-10, *45*
9:3-7, *83*
10:25-33, *102*
10:28, *156*
11:16, *89*
13:16, *107*
13:16-44, *107*
13:27, *160*
15:21, *54*
19:10, *89*
20:7-12, *84*
21:21, *54*
22:6-9, *83*
26:12-16, *83*
26:22, *53*
28:23, *71*
28:25, *44*

Romans
1:20, *45*
3:22, *179*
8:1, *180*
8:9-11, *180*
8:28, *137, 139*
8:28-29, *137*
9:6, *179*
10:14, *95, 117*

10:17, *117*
11:17-24, *180*
11:36, *139*
12:2, *16*
12:5, *180*
16:7, *180*

1 Corinthians
1:10, *142*
2:1, *82*
2:1-14, *103*
2:4, *82*
2:13, *44, 82*
9:1, *84*
9:9, *53, 54*
10:31, *139*
11:5-26, *28*
11:23-26, *72*
15:8, *84*

2 Corinthians
3:15, *54*
4:4, *138*
11:23-29, *138*

Galatians
1:11-12, *82*
3:1-3, *118*
4:4, *33*

Ephesians
4:4-6, *142*
4:11, *81*

Philippians
2:2, *142*
2:6-8, *150, 166*
2:6-11, *145*
2:7-8, *159*
3:7-8, *138*
4:12, *138*
4:13, *137*

Colossians
2:9, *66*
3:16, *168, 190*
4:16, *99*

1 Thessalonians
2:13, *21, 82*
4:2, *83*
5:27, *99*

1 Timothy
5:18, *72*

2 Timothy
2:15, *16, 72, 144*
3:16, *22*

Hebrews
1:1, *110*
1:1-2, *43, 153*
1:3, *43*
1:5-7, *43*
1:13, *43*
2:1, *43*
2:1-2, *110*
3:15, *110*
4:12, *133, 190*
10:31, *111*
12:9-11, *111*
12:25, *110*
12:29, *111*
13:5, *110*

James
1:22, *116*
4:3, *140*

1 Peter
1:15-16, *113*
1:25, *191*
5:8, *138*

2 Peter
1:21, *19, 44*
3:15-16, *71*

1 John
1:1-3, *88*
3:21-22, *140*
5:19, *138*

Revelation
1:3, *100*
1:7, *45*
7:9, *144*
21:5, *43*
22:17, *100*
22:17-18, *100*

ALSO BY D. BRENT SANDY

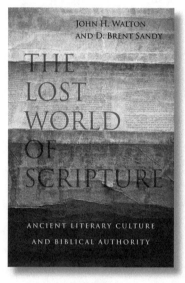

The Lost World of Scripture
978-0-8308-4032-8

Plowshares and Pruning Hooks
978-0-8308-2653-7